Ever wonder why:

- all the cubs in the family den are so different?
- you always butt heads with a certain family member?
- kid #1 pairs up with kid #3 when there's a family stand-off?
- kids #2 and #4 are always united against kid #3?
- everybody guesses you're the oldest child in your family, and you're a middleborn?
- the firstborn and secondborn in your family are night and day different?
- the baby of the family always gets away with every-thing?
- your perfectionistic firstborn sibling gets along so well with her fun-loving, practical joker, baby-of-the-family spouse?
- you pick the friends you do?
- you picked someone so different from you to marry?
- the slightest error you make ruins your day?
- you butt heads with the child most like you, rather than the child most different from you?
- your coworker is the way he/she is (and how you can get along with him/her)?

Then read on. This book will change your life.
I guarantee it.

The
**Birth
Order
Book**

The Birth Order Book

Why You Are the Way You Are

—— Revised and Updated ——

Dr. Kevin Leman

Revell

a division of Baker Publishing Group
Grand Rapids, Michigan

© 1985, 1998, 2009 by Kevin Leman

Published by Revell
a division of Baker Publishing Group
P.O. Box 6287, Grand Rapids, MI 49516-6287
www.revellbooks.com

Printed in the United States of America

Library of Congress Cataloging-in-Publication Data
Leman, Kevin.
    The birth order book : why you are the way you are / Kevin Leman.
        p.   cm.
    Rev. ed. of: The new birth order book : why you are the way you are. 2nd ed.
1998.
    Includes bibliographical references.
    ISBN 978-0-8007-3406-0 (pbk.)
    1. Birth order. I. Leman, Kevin. New birth order book. II. Title.
BF723.B5L46 2009
155.9′24—dc22   2009020404

To protect the privacy of those who have shared their stories with the author, some details and names have been changed.

13   14   15   8   7   6

To my firstborn, lovable, perfectionist Holly.
Your sense of fair play, creativity, love for God, and sensitivity to others make me proud to be your dad. I love you very much.

With special recognition to:

My firstborn sister, Sally,
with apologies for awakening you on at least one occasion by dangling a juicy night crawler under your nose. You are a very special sister.

Dr. John E. Leman Jr. (Jack),
my secondborn older brother and hero, whom I faithfully followed on more than one propitious childhood occasion when you tried to lose me in the woods. Thanks, Jack, for threatening to beat the tar out of the neighborhood bully for me.

May and John Leman,
my sweet mom and dad, who can now rest in peace, knowing they did a great job of raising three pretty good kids who loved them deeply.

Contents

Guess the Birth Order

Firstborn or only child, middle child, or lastborn/baby of the family? Venture a guess, then check page 327 to see if your answers match.

1. My sister was a charming show-off—make that a con artist who got away with everything—when we were growing up. Now she's the top salesperson in her company and highly successful.
2. I'd rather read people than books. I like solving problems and am comfortable being surrounded by people.
3. My brother Al was nicknamed "Albert Einstein" because he was so good in math and science. He's an engineer now and a conscientious perfectionist.
4. I don't know how my husband does it. His workshop is an absolute mess, but whenever he wants to find something, he knows exactly which pile it's in.
5. My friend is a bit of a maverick. She has a lot of friends but values her independence. She's a good mediator in arguments. She's about as opposite from her sister as you can get.
6. I get along better with older people than I do my peers. Some people think I'm stuck-up or self-centered. But in actuality, I'm not.

Introduction

Maybe Abel Did Have It Coming

Have you ever wondered why your sister or your brother is so different from you? After all, you grew up in the same family, yet you act so differently and see things so differently. You often view the same childhood experiences through completely different lenses and have opposite responses. How can that be?

Do you wonder why you continue to butt heads with a certain son or daughter of yours—but with the other children it's smooth sailing? Or why you can't quite see eye to eye with your boss or a certain co-worker?

Do you wonder why you feel compelled to act a certain way—like you've been programmed? Why you pick the friends you do? Why you're attracted to a certain type of person to marry (and who's really best for you)? Why you always find yourself being the one to mediate between two warring parties at work? Why you struggle day to day with never being good enough?

All of the answers to these questions have everything to do with birth order. Think of your family as a tree. Your mom and dad (or mom or dad, if you're from a single-parent family) form the trunk of the tree. The children in the family are the branches. Have you ever seen a tree where all the branches are growing in the exact same direction? The same is true with children. One of the best predictions in life is that whatever the firstborn in a family is, the secondborn in the family will go in a different (and oftentimes opposite) direction.

> Do you wonder why you feel compelled to act a certain way—like you've been programmed?

Think of the story of good ol' Cain and Abel, way back in time—the firstborn and secondborn brothers who got sibling rivalry off to a vicious start. If any brothers could be different, those two were. One was a gardener, work-with-the-earth type. The other was a shepherd, animal-lover type. To say there was jealousy when one was treated "better" than the other is a vast understatement. And you know where all that led. . . . That's why, when I first presented the idea of this book to my publisher, I wanted to call it *Abel Had It Coming*. But the editors and the movers and shakers (all firstborns or only children, by the way) shook their heads and won out against this lastborn of the family. So now, voilà! We have the descriptive and exciting title *The Birth Order Book*.

For over thirty-five years as a psychologist, I've studied birth order and the role it plays in making you the person you were growing up—and the person you are today.

Many psychologists believe that birth order has to do with only the ordinal position (the order in which you and your siblings were born) in the family. But if it were that simple, why would you need a book on it? After all, if you can do any math at all, it would be easy to figure out if you were a firstborn, middleborn, or lastborn.

Here's the rub. What if you're a middleborn but you act like a firstborn? Or what if you're a firstborn but you act more like a middleborn? Or what about if you are fourth in a group of seven siblings, spread thirteen years apart? Or what if you are the only boy in a family of three girls? The only girl in a family of four boys? What if the firstborn has mental or physical challenges? What is your birth order then?

With more than three decades of seeing the truth played out in the lives of the families I counsel, I am convinced that birth order isn't as simple as most "experts" try to make it. To my knowledge, I'm the only psychologist who takes into consideration all the variables, including the functional position (which I'll explain in this book).

> *Once you figure out your birth order, as well as the birth orders of those you love, you'll be way ahead of everyone else in the game of life.*

So no, birth order isn't simple, but it is easy to figure out with the information you'll read in this book. And once you figure out your birth order, as well as the birth orders of those you love, you'll be way ahead of everyone else in the game of life. By the time you've finished reading *The Birth Order Book*, you'll understand yourself better, your loved ones better, your friends better, and your co-workers and boss better, and you'll be able to navigate relationships in all arenas of life much more easily.

If you're a parent, I'll reveal the secrets of how you can best parent your firstborn, middleborn, and lastborn, and why treating everyone "equally" isn't the best *modus operandi*.

If you're married (or thinking about walking that flower-strewn aisle), I'll give you some tips about which birth order combinations make for the smoothest-flowing marriages (and why), and what you can do to make your relationship thrive— no matter your birth order—if you're already married.

If you're in the business world (part-time, full-time, at home, away from home) or you do volunteer work, community service, etc., you'll learn how to use your natural birth order to the best of your abilities, while also getting along with and encouraging your co-workers.

If you're a firstborn or an only child, you'll learn why you're so driven to do everything (and do it well), and what you can do about it before you drive yourself crazy or exhaust yourself. You'll also learn why books are some of your best friends.

If you're a middleborn, you'll find out why you always find yourself in the role of mediator, why you're on a different path than your firstborn sibling, and how you can keep yourself from being squeezed in the middle. We also might shed some light on that rebellious streak you know is hidden deep in your heart.

If you're a lastborn like me, you'll learn why you need some firstborns in your life (like my wife, Sande, and my assistant, Debbie, who help keep everything straight for this fun-loving baby of the family). And you'll also find out why sometimes you need to walk just a bit more softly around the older ones in the family, cut them a little more slack, and ease up on the pressure they're feeling to be the perfect role model.

> *Want to get inside the thoughts and feelings of the ones you love? Figure out why you do what you do?*

Hmm, I wonder what would have happened if Abel had taken that quieter, backseat approach and not irritated big brother Cain by outdoing his efforts. Ever think that maybe, in Cain's mind, Abel did have it coming?

Want to get inside the thoughts and feelings of the ones you love? Figure out why you do what you do? This fun, entertaining, informative book will show you how. I can't count the times I've heard readers say, "Dr. Leman, this book has changed my life. And it has changed how I see life too."

So what are you waiting for?

1

Birth Order

Does It Really Make Sense?

I can't count the times I've been asked that very question as I've counseled individuals and families and crisscrossed the talk-show circuit over the past thirty-five years. My first response usually runs along the lines of "Does a bear go potty in the woods?"

Yes, birth order makes sense. After all, how else can three or four or even eight little cubs be so different, yet come from the very same den? Birth order is simple, but it's not simplistic. There are standard birth order rules, and there are also exceptions to the standard birth order rules (both of which we'll also talk about in this book). However, the exceptions are explainable when you understand how birth order works. Even the exceptions develop because of when you were born into your family. I call it your "branch on the family tree," and that branch has had a great deal to do with why you are the way you are today.

Why should you care about birth order? Birth order can give you some important clues about your personality; your relationship with friends, co-workers, and loved ones; the kind of job you have; and how you handle problem solving.

Birth order is really the science of understanding your place in the family line. Were you born first? Second? Third? Or even farther down that line? Wherever you landed, it has affected your life in countless ways.

Which Traits Fit You Best?

Which of the following sets of personality traits fits you the best? You don't have to meet all the criteria in a certain list of traits. Just pick the list that has the most items that seem to describe you and your way of operating in life.

A. perfectionist, reliable, conscientious, a list maker, well organized, hard driving, a natural leader, critical, serious, scholarly, logical, doesn't like surprises, a techie

B. mediator, compromising, diplomatic, avoids conflict, independent, loyal to peers, has many friends, a maverick, secretive, used to not having attention

C. manipulative, charming, blames others, attention seeker, tenacious, people person, natural salesperson, precocious, engaging, affectionate, loves surprises

D. little adult by age seven, very thorough, deliberate, high achiever, self-motivated, fearful, cautious, voracious reader, black-and-white thinker, talks in extremes, can't bear to fail, has very high expectations for self, more comfortable with people who are older or younger

If you noted that this test seemed rather easy because A, B, and C listed traits of the oldest right on down to the youngest in the family, you're right.

If you picked A, it's a very good bet you're a firstborn in your family.

If you chose B, chances are you are a middleborn child (secondborn of three children, or possibly thirdborn of four).

If C seemed to relate best to who you are, it's likely you are the baby in the family and are not at all happy that this book has no pictures. (Just kidding—I like to have a little extra fun with lastborns because I'm one myself. More on that later.)

But what about D? It describes the only child, and I threw it in because in recent years I have been getting more and more questions from only children because families in general are having fewer children. These only children (also known as "lonely onlies") know they are firstborns but want to know how they are different from people who have siblings. Well, one way they are different is that the only child is a super or extreme version of a firstborn. They have many of the same characteristics of firstborns, but in many ways they're in a class by themselves. More on that in chapter 7.

> *Not all characteristics fit every person in that birth order.*

Notice that regarding each major birth order, I always qualify the characteristics by saying "good bet" or "chances are." Not all characteristics fit every person in that birth order. In fact, a firstborn may have baby characteristics, a lastborn can sometimes act like a firstborn in certain areas, and middle children may seem to be firstborns. I've seen onlies who you would swear were youngest children. There are reasons for these inconsistencies, which I'll explain as we go along.

Who's Who?

Birth order continues to be revealing when you look at who is in what occupation. For example, statistics show that firstborns often fill positions of high authority or achievement. *Who's Who in America* or *American Men and Women in Science* both contain a high percentage of firstborns. You will also find them well represented among Rhodes scholars and university professors.

Although we'll get more fully into this in the following chapters, I define a firstborn as:

1. The first child born in a family. (However, a firstborn child may not always play a firstborn role, due to the variables we'll discuss.)
2. The first child of that gender born in the family (the first son or the first daughter, even if there are other children before him or her).
3. A child whose next closest same-sex sibling is five or more years older than him or her.

As for presidents and pastors, you guessed it: a great number of them are firstborns. The way I define a firstborn, 28 out of 44 US presidents (64 percent) have been firstborns or functional (play the role of) firstborns. In fact, 8 of the 11 who ran for president in the 2008 election were firstborn sons or a firstborn daughter in their families.

A number of our presidents were born later in their families. In some cases they were born last, but in all cases they were the firstborn *males* in the family. That tells me they had excellent chances of developing firstborn traits and *functioning* as firstborns, which undoubtedly helped them be effective in their role of president and leader. (For a complete list, see "US Presidents and Their Birth Order," page 329.)

Of course, some US presidents have been middle children, and a few have been lastborns, including

---

Firstborns and Only Children

Reliable and conscientious, they tend to be list makers and black-and-white thinkers. They have a keen sense of right and wrong and believe there is a right way to do things. They are natural leaders and achievement oriented.

Only children take those characteristics a step further. Books are their best friends. They act mature beyond their years—they are little adults by age 7 or 8. They work independently. And they can't understand why kids in other families fight.

Ronald Reagan, the actor who made good in Washington. The big three of birth order—firstborn, middle child, and baby—was vividly represented during the 1992 presidential campaign when incumbent George Bush, Bill Clinton, and Ross Perot squared off in a televised debate. Clinton, the firstborn, was suave, confident, and loaded with answers, and projected strong leadership abilities. Bush, the middle child, used a mediatory negotiating style, even while in debate. Perot, the lastborn, was an outrageous baby and then some—hard-hitting, outspoken, asking lots of embarrassing questions of his opponents, and often having the audience in stitches.

In the 2008 US presidential election, the final four contenders for the biggest job in the world were an only child (Barack Obama—see page 331 for why he's considered an only child), a firstborn daughter (Hillary Clinton), and two firstborn sons (Mike Huckabee and John McCain). There truly is something unique about firstborns, the leaders of the pack.

And politicians aren't the only ones. Once when I was speaking to a group of fifty pastors, I commented in passing, "Pastors, you know, are predominantly firstborns." When they looked skeptical, I decided to poll the entire group to see if I was right. Forty-three out of the fifty were firstborn sons or only children.

Research bears out that firstborns are more highly motivated to achieve than laterborns. A much greater proportion

Middleborns

They're the hardest to pin down of all the birth orders, but they'll be the opposite of the child above them in the family. If the firstborn is very conventional, the second will be unconventional. Middle children walk to the beat of a different drummer. They are competitive, loyal, and big on friendships.

Being the middle child means living in a sort of anonymous haziness. But that's not all bad. If a middle child is anonymous, he can get away with occasional laziness and indifference. He's not pushed as hard or expected to accomplish quite as much as the one who came before him. The drawback is that without being pushed, he may never fulfill his potential. The middle child of the family is often the negotiator who tries to keep the peace.

of firstborns wind up in professions such as science, medicine, or law. You also find them in greater numbers among accountants, bookkeepers, executive secretaries, engineers, and computer specialists. And, oh yes, of the first twenty-three American astronauts sent into outer space, twenty-one were firstborns and the other two were only children. All seven astronauts in the original Mercury program were firstborns.[1] Even Christa McAuliffe, the teacher who died in the ill-fated *Challenger* space shuttle crash in 1986, was a firstborn who had four siblings.

In addition, a recent study announced on CNN that "Firstborns' IQs tend to be higher than those of their younger siblings."[2] Why? No one was quite sure, but speculations were that the firstborns benefited from receiving more of their parents' undivided attention for a while before siblings came along; the older child is given more responsibility and thus becomes more responsible, which builds brainpower; and the older child carries the parents' dreams, so he seeks to do more and go farther than his siblings.

The point is, more often than not you'll find firstborns in professions that take precision, strong powers of concentration, and dogged mental discipline.[3] When I served as assistant dean of students at the University of Arizona while also earning a doctorate, I always enjoyed testing the birth order theories I was learning. Once I asked a faculty member of the College of Architecture if he had ever noticed where the college's faculty members came from as far

---

Lastborns

These social, outgoing creatures have never met a stranger. They are uncomplicated, spontaneous, humorous, and high on people skills. To them, life's a party. They're most likely to get away with murder and least likely to be punished. They often retain their pet name.

But there's also a flip side to being the youngest. Although they're the little star in the family constellation, it's no fun being the smallest, because it means they spend a lot of their time wearing hand-me-downs that are ragged, incredibly out of style, or too big. Being the youngest also means that they get picked on from time to time and maybe get called an unflattering nickname.

as birth order was concerned. He gave me a blank stare and muttered, "Kevin, I really have to run."

Half a year later he stopped me on campus and said, "Do you remember that crazy question you asked me about the birth order of our architectural faculty? Well, I finally decided to take an informal poll. It turns out almost every one of our faculty is either a firstborn or the only child in the family." My friend was quite impressed.

> *Research bears out that firstborns are more highly motivated to achieve than laterborns.*

I was gratified to know that a basic birth order principle had proven out again. People who like structure and order tend to enter professions that are exacting. Architecture is one of those professions.

How Birth Order Plays Out in Hollywood

At the other end of the birth order scale, you'll find a lot of laterborns who are comedians. Babies of the family who are known and loved by millions of movie and TV fans include Eddie Murphy, Martin Short, Ellen DeGeneres, Whoopi Goldberg, Jay Leno, Stephen Colbert, Steve Carell, Jon Stewart, Billy Crystal, Danny DeVito, Drew Carey, Jim Carrey, Steve Martin, and Chevy Chase. Other babies of the family who kept us in stitches include the late comics John Candy and Charlie Chaplin.

It should be noted, however, that not all comics are pure lastborns. While Steve Martin is the baby of his family, he has an older sister, which makes him the firstborn son. Bill Cosby, one of the great comedians of all time, is a firstborn. He holds a doctorate degree and is a perfectionist. He gave all of his children names beginning with "E"—to remind them to always seek excellence.

Other firstborn entertainers and actors include Harrison Ford, Matthew Perry, Jennifer Aniston, Angelina Jolie, Brad

Pitt, Chuck Norris, Sylvester Stallone, Reese Witherspoon, and Ben Affleck.

Only children who are well known for their dramatic, and sometimes comedic, roles include Robert DeNiro, Laurence Fishburne, Anthony Hopkins, James Earl Jones, Tommy Lee Jones, William Shatner, and Robin Williams.

Newscasters and talk-show hosts on television are often firstborns and only children. While on a tour of thirty-one cities, I did a little survey and learned that out of ninety-two talk-show hosts, only five were not firstborns or onlies. Just a few of the more well-known firstborn talk-show personalities are Oprah Winfrey (who was also nominated for an Academy Award in her first movie, *The Color Purple*); Bill O'Reilly; Charles Gibson (the youngest in his family, but trust me, he functions more as a firstborn—more about that later); Geraldo Rivera; and the spokesman for excellence in broadcasting himself, Rush Limbaugh.

The Leman Tribe

In many families the three birth order positions—firstborn, middleborn, and lastborn—are played out in more or less classic style. The family I grew up in is a good example. Let me introduce you to them. My parents, John and May Leman, had three children:

Sally—firstborn
John Jr. (Jack)—middle child (firstborn son), born three years later
Kevin (Cub)—baby of the family, born five years after Jack

Sally, eight years my senior, is a classic firstborn who lives in a small town in western New York. Because we have our own summer place on a lake nearby, we all get to drop in at her immaculate home from time to time every summer vacation. The first thing we notice when we come through Sally's front door is the clear vinyl runner leading to every room in the house. We get the message: *thou shalt not walk on the blue carpet except when absolutely necessary.*

To say Sally is neat as a pin doesn't quite begin to tell the story. I suspect that from time to time she irons her welcome mat! Perhaps you use those garbage bags that have drawstrings? Sally does too, and she ties bows on hers. I've even caught her straightening up the brochures in a bank lobby while she awaited her turn. (No kidding.)

In short, whatever Sally does, she does it classy and she does it right. All her life she has been confident, creative, artistic, scholarly, and well liked. She was a cheerleader in high school and a National Honor Society type. She became a home economics teacher and a preschool director, and she's even written two books.[4]

No one in the Leman clan can forget the time we all went camping high in the Sierra Nevadas. After a terrific day in the great out-of-doors, we were all ready to hop into our sleeping bags. Because at eight or nine thousand feet it gets rather nippy at night, even in the summer, most of us planned to sleep in our clothes. Not Sally. When she came out of her tent to say good night, she was attired in her usual classy nightie. She couldn't figure out why that was so funny to the rest of us. That's Sally. Why not add a little class to the campsite too?

But being perfect at what you do can have its drawbacks as well. Sally has butterflies at least two days before giving a small dinner party. Bigger dinner parties cause butterflies for a week or ten days. Naturally everything must be color coordinated: the napkins match the napkin holders, which match the decor of the formal dining room, which match . . . well, you get the idea. I'm convinced that if my sister had the opportunity, she'd put newspaper under the cuckoo clock—just in case.

Once when I was the keynote speaker at a conference and Sally was doing a workshop at the same conference, we had breakfast together at 9:05.

"So, Kevin," she said, "what are you speaking about?"

I sipped my coffee casually. "I haven't decided yet."

She gasped. "What do you mean? You must know what you're speaking about. You're going to be speaking in 55 minutes!"

> I'm convinced that if my sister had the opportunity, she'd put newspaper under the cuckoo clock.

"Well, I'll look at the people and then I'll decide."

She winced. "You're making my stomach turn."

If you're a firstborn, you can identify with my big sister right now, because there's not a firstborn on earth who gets up and wings it. Firstborns are prepared, organized, and ready to get things done. But if you're a baby? You're saying, "Way to go, Dr. Leman. Just roll with the punches."

So first in our family was Sally, the perfectionist.

Born second in our family was my brother, Jack. Typical of a lot of middle children, his precise personality traits are a bit more difficult to pin down. But secondborn children are known for going in exactly the opposite direction from the firstborn in the family. Typically the middle child is a mediator and a negotiator who avoids conflict. He can be a real paradox—independent but extremely loyal to his peer group. He can be a maverick with many friends. He is usually the one to leave home first; he finds his real companionship outside the family circle because he often feels left out of things at home.

In Jack's case, he didn't go in a completely opposite direction from Sally. He also turned out to be extremely conscientious, serious, and scholarly. But since all of these traits are ones belonging to firstborns, what happened to Jack? Well, he was a functional firstborn—the firstborn *male* in the Leman family. (More about this in chapter 8.)

26

One classic middle child trait that Jack possessed was to be a trailblazer who was willing to move far away from family roots in upper New York State. Sally followed the classic firstborn trait of staying with tradition and still lives just a few miles from where we all grew up. But if Jack hadn't made the major independent breakthrough of traveling all the way to Tucson to do his graduate work at the University of Arizona, neither my parents nor I would have ended up living there. As it was, my parents followed Jack to Tucson. I came along as well and have lived in Tucson ever since, for more than forty-five years.

> *Secondborn children are known for going in exactly the opposite direction from the firstborn in the family.*

And then there was little Kevin, who came along five years after Jack. My birth order rule of thumb says that when there is a five- to six-year gap between children, the next child starts a "new family," and you can make an educated guess that he or she will be a firstborn personality type in some ways. When there is a gap of seven to ten years (or more), the next child falls into the "quasi–only child" category because there are so many years between him or her and the sibling above.[5]

Keep in mind, however, that these rules of thumb are subject to how the child is parented plus other influences that occur within the family constellation. In my case, for example, the rule of thumb went out the window for one good reason. My brother took all the heat, because my parents expected a lot more from him than from his baby brother. Jack's given name was John E. Leman Junior. He was to be the medical doctor my father had always wanted to be but couldn't because he was very poor and only finished eighth grade. Dad projected onto Jack

> *When there is a five- to six-year gap between children, the next child starts a "new family."*

his own dreams of a fine profession and his own fears of not being somebody. With that kind of pressure on him, you can see why Jack took on many firstborn traits. While he didn't end up a surgeon or an anesthesiologist, he did become an extremely conscientious PhD in clinical psychology with his own private practice.

As for me, I was nicknamed "Little Cub," and the handle stuck. But instead of being ignored and left to myself, as many lastborns are, I became the family mascot who was always getting into something.

> *Babies of the family are very perceptive, and I learned very early that I had two superstars ahead of me.*

Babies of the family are very perceptive, and I learned very early that I had two superstars ahead of me. I quickly decided there wasn't a whole lot I could do by way of achievement to gain attention. My only real accomplishment from preschool up through high school was playing on the baseball team—that is, when I was eligible, usually the first six weeks of the spring semester before grades came out. (That tells you right off the bat a bit about my academic records in school.) Jack, a star quarterback, never bothered with baseball. In western New York, high school football was the major sport, while baseball was for hardy types willing to put up with freezing to death before small crowds in spring weather that often included late snowstorms.

But Little Cub wasn't going to be left out. What I lacked in achievement I made up for in mischievousness. I became a manipulative, charming, engaging, and sometimes devilish little show-off. At age eight, while trying to lead a cheer for my sister's high school team, I found my true calling in life. I learned that entertainers get attention. So entertain I did, especially for my classmates all through grade school and high school. I gained incredible skill at driving teachers a little crazy. I know they heaved a sigh of relief when Kevin Leman graduated at last.

It All Comes Back to That Family Tree

As you look back on your growing-up years, you too can probably come up with a cast of characters similar to the Leman kids: the good students, the athletes, the performers, the attention getters, and the ones who are hard to pigeonhole. After all my years of researching, studying, and helping families like yours, I am sure of only a few things:

1. *There is no greater influence during your growing-up years than your family.* Yes, I know about all the time you spend in school, Little League, Brownies, and music lessons. But all those things are just a drop in the bucket compared to what goes on at home. During those early years, your parents and siblings (if any) make an indelible psychological imprint, affecting your personality. And that family influence tends to persist through the years and across the miles as you grow up and move away.[6]

2. *The most intimate relationships in life are with your family*—the one you grew up in and the one you make for yourself through marriage. But the family you grew up in has the inside track. If you're married, think about how long you've been married. Now think about how long you've known your siblings. Some of you have known your siblings all your lives. Like it or not, you are tied to your siblings with bonds stronger than even the marriage bonds that tie you to your mate. And you have known your parent(s) all your life as well.

   Living in a family, then, is a unique and distinctive experience. The intimate relationships that develop in the family can be found nowhere else on earth.[7] And these relationships are created in great part by your order of birth.

3. *The relationship between you and your parents is fluid, dynamic, and all-important.* Every time a child is born, the entire family environment changes. How parents in-

teract with each child as he or she enters the family circle determines in great part that child's final destiny.

I mentioned earlier that my father, a very hardworking man, never had the opportunity to go beyond eighth grade. That lack of schooling was something he always regretted. He wanted very much for at least one of his sons to be a medical doctor. I don't think he was partial to doctors because of any visions of saving the world from disease and death. He just knew that doctors were well educated and well paid, and he wanted his children to have a better, easier life than he had. So the importance of education became a major value that my father communicated to all of his children—even to bear cub Kevin, who didn't show as much promise (or interest) as the older children.

> *Every time a child is born, the entire family environment changes. How parents interact with each child as he or she enters the family circle determines in great part that child's final destiny.*

Did my dad's values and speeches about education sink in? Well, the results tell their own story. Sister Sally got As all her life, right up through a master's program. Brother Jack is a clinical psychologist, and somehow bear cub Kevin wound up a psychologist too. Sally and Jack were no great surprise. They had it right from the start. But how did Kevin, the clown prince, get a doctor's degree? One answer is, "With a great deal of difficulty!" For now, let's leave it in the minor-miracle category. My high school teachers might even label it a *major* miracle. In fact, I know they would.

Use Birth Order to Your Advantage

As you read this book and learn more about why you are the way you are, you'll find practical ways to use your particular birth order to your advantage in personal relationships and even in the business world.

How does your branch fit on your family's tree? All of us sprout in our own unique direction and make our own unique contributions. But as you begin to understand birth order and how it influences you, you can improve your relationships in every arena of life. You'll even get some clues about the kind of jobs you enjoy (and the ones you don't), and why. You'll also discover how to get along better with bosses and co-workers—whether in business or community service.

> *How does your branch fit on your family's tree? All of us sprout in our own unique direction and make our own unique contributions.*

When you think about it, isn't everything in life about relationships? If you walked onto a car lot and no salesman greeted you with a smile, how would you buy a car, and how would he make a sale? Business is all about relationships.

And what about relationships with friends or acquaintances? Isn't it interesting that, in making friends, birds of a feather do flock together? You identify with friends of the same birth order. If you don't believe me, just do a poll of your friends and see what their birth orders are. For example, every summer we spend time in western New York State, where I grew up. My wife, my sister, and the wife of my lifelong friend Moonhead—all firstborns—love to go together to yard sales, antique shops, and arts and crafts shows. They enjoy passionately pursuing the same kinds of treasures. (I call them "expensive junk"—out of their hearing, of course.)

Is it true that people who are very much alike get along best in marriage? No, most often marriage partners who are too alike don't get along well because they're always treading on each other's territory. (It's why you don't often see two tax accountants married to each other.) Couples who are different from each other and work to understand and appreciate those differences are the ones who get along best. Good ol' variety is the spice of life.

As the people I've counseled better understand birth order, they've been able to turn their lives around. For example, Jan finally understood why her husband, John, was always so picky. And John gained insight into Jan's "little girl" ways that were driving him more bonkers by the day. Birth order also helps Mom and Dad get a handle on why 10-year-old Fletcher can go through life oblivious to his open fly and C+ average while his 13-year-old sister has straight As—and a good start on an ulcer.

> *Good ol' variety is the spice of life.*

Guessing Who's Firstborn

Wherever I go, I make it a fun hobby to guess the birth order of waitresses, cab drivers, or the people who attend the marriage and parenting seminars I conduct around the country.

For example, during a seminar I take a quick look around and spot ten people I believe are firstborn or only children. For this first spot-check, I go just by physical appearance. The folks I pick look like they've stepped off the cover of *Glamour* magazine or out of an ad for Brooks Brothers suits. They're easy to spot because every hair is in place and they are color coordinated from head to toe. Right there in front of everyone I go out on a limb and guess that each person I select is a firstborn or only child. I usually hit nine out of ten—and often ten out of ten.

This "prediction" starts a nervous rustling in the crowd, who begins to think I'm doing some sort of parlor trick (or that I'm a fugitive from a psychic hotline). Then I begin to explain.

The typical firstborn is usually easy to recognize. They're almost always neatly dressed and well groomed. The last-borns? They're the ones still hanging around talking by the punch bowl at the back of the room, and they haven't even realized I've started to speak yet. The middle children are the hardest of all to identify, because they've learned to negotiate that middle ground so successfully that the lines of who they are can become blurred, depending on which other birth orders they're spending time with.

When I finish explaining, I can see the "aha" on the seminar attendees' faces, because they've recognized themselves—and the truth about birth order—in my statements.

Sometimes I also do a birth order demonstration at my seminars. While in Phoenix recently, I picked a man out of the audience. In eight minutes I easily identified his birth order as well as that of his wife by asking only a few questions. When I asked him to describe himself, he said he was a loner and a reader and he appreciated order in his life. (Are you getting any clues yet?) Then I asked him to describe his mother. When

> *When he said she was very loving, very concerned about him, very intuitive, and a very good mom, I knew I had a firstborn on my hands.*

he said she was *very* loving, *very* concerned about him, *very* intuitive, and a *very* good mom, I knew I had a firstborn on my hands.

My next question was whether or not he had married his opposite birth order (which supposedly guarantees more happiness) or whether he had possibly "married his mother." Oh yes, I had his mother pegged as a perfectionist, because she had been *very* loving and concerned about him. It was my guess that his wife was also very loving but had a critical eye a mile wide and was as powerful as they come. So I went out on a limb a bit and speculated that his wife was quite protective and a perfectionist, that there was a right way to approach her, and that she probably liked to handle things herself. "My guess is, when you're driving, she's quick to criticize you," I said.

"Worse than that," he said. "She doesn't let me drive."

"Oh, *you're* the guy!" I said. "I saw you go by the other day. You were in the back, buckled into your car seat."

Just then his wife, who was sitting back in the audience, clapped her hand over her mouth and said very loudly, "Oh my gosh, I'm just like my mother!" No doubt she is. With birth order in families, what goes around comes around. Can you see it in your family too?

I Batted .500 on *The Today Show*

What about spotting babies of the family? They are often easy to identify. For example, while being interviewed by Katie Couric, former cohost of *The Today Show*, I told her that she was a baby in her family, probably with two older brothers and two older sisters.

It turned out I was one brother off, but Katie's mouth still dropped open and she sort of stuttered, "Well, yes. But how did you know?"

I quickly explained that while she was beautifully dressed and perfectly groomed, her perky, affectionate nature gave her away. As she worked with Bryant Gumbel, she often touched him or grabbed his arm—her very engaging nature came across loud and clear. Off camera Katie let me know she didn't like being called "perky" very much, but she had to admit I was right. The whole birth order concept still struck her as rather mysterious. I could tell that the staff who had been filming the interview enjoyed it too—they were chuckling.

When Roles Are Reversed

Sometimes extenuating circumstances tweak the natural birth order sequence. The result is that a laterborn child may act like a firstborn, or a firstborn can seem to have characteristics that are inconsistent with the way firstborns are "supposed" to act.

Everyone was certain that Alan—a capable, bright firstborn—would fly high in the broadcasting world. Just three years below him was a younger brother, Luke. Interestingly, both ended up in broadcasting, but Luke was the one who stole the limelight.

Now why was that? You see, sometimes a lastborn inherits the firstborn role by default due to . . .

But wait, I'm getting ahead of myself. All that is coming up next.

> *Sometimes extenuating circumstances tweak the natural birth order sequence. The result is that a laterborn child may act like a firstborn, or a firstborn can seem to have characteristics that are inconsistent with the way firstborns are "supposed" to act.*

2

But Doc, I Don't Fit the Mold!

Birth Order Variables—Part 1

I was just getting ready to speak at a conference about birth order when a guy stalked up to me. He was red faced and angry. "Wait just a minute, Leman," he said. "I've read all the stuff on birth order. Those descriptions don't fit my family at all. I'm the baby of my family, and I'm the most responsible one of the bunch. Not only that, but I'm the only one who reads. The rest just stare at the boob tube. How do you explain that?" He crossed his arms and glared at me, waiting for my answer.

Explain that I can, and a lot more. The so-called inconsistencies that occur when someone doesn't seem to fit into the typical birth order mold are only signposts pointing to what really is the most entertaining (and informative) part of birth order theory. To understand these signposts, you need to know the psychological term *family constellation—*

or, as I prefer to call it, the *family zoo*. Over the years I've counseled a lot of desperate mothers who have three or four little ankle-biters driving them up the wall. When I talk about the family zoo, these moms know *exactly* what I mean.

How any parent can have two, three, or more little critters in their particular family zoo who are so distinctly different is a question that birth order can help to answer. But you have to be aware of the variables—the different factors or forces that have an impact on each person, no matter what his or her birth order may be.

The variables for birth order include:

spacing—the number of years between children

the sex of each child—and in what sequence males and females are born

physical, mental, or emotional differences—yes, genes are important

sibling deaths—which, if occurring early, cause the child below to be "bumped up" to the next birth order

adoptions—which may or may not have an effect on birth order, depending on how old the child is when adopted

the birth order position of each parent—because, for example, firstborn parents usually run a much different and tighter ship than laterborns

the relationship between the parents—and the parenting style they use as they pass on their personal values to their children

the critical eye of a parent—because constant criticism takes its toll

the blending of two families due to death or divorce—because, for example, in a stepfamily certain birth orders often get stepped on

37

Birth Order: Not as Simple as 1-2-3

The reason birth order looks inconsistent to some folks is because they think (like the majority of "experts") that it's some kind of simple ordinal system based on birth rank. First-born children in a family are supposed to be this, secondborns are always like that, and thirdborn siblings are always another way.

> *Some children act and appear very different from their ordinal birth order.*

But some children act and appear very different from their ordinal birth order. And even when children seem to fit the typical descriptions of their ordinal birth order (#1, #2, etc.), they can exhibit characteristics of other birth orders. That's where the variables come in. They can cause a child born in one birth position to function, at least in part, with characteristics of another birth position.

For example, my son, Kevin II, was born right in the middle of the Leman family. He has two older sisters and two younger sisters. That gives him an overall ordinal position of "middle" in the family. However, he was also the baby—he was at the tail end of his two older sisters for five and a half years before his younger sister Hannah came along. And as the only son in the family, he is also a functional firstborn. So Kevin has the best of all worlds!

> *The key to understanding birth order is identifying and examining the dynamic, fluid relationships existing between members of the family.*

All birth orders have certain tendencies and general characteristics, but the key to understanding birth order is identifying and examining the dynamic, fluid relationships existing between members of the family. And that's where the variables can cause functional birth order characteristics—when a child born in one birth order functions like a child who is born in another.

The rest of this chapter will focus on the most obvious variables that can be seen in children—spacing; sex; and mental, physical, or emotional differences. We'll also consider less discussed variables, such as multiple births, the death of a sibling, and adopted siblings.

Spacing Can Create More Than One "Family"

An obvious and crucial birth order variable in any family is spacing—when each child arrives. Whenever you think of spacing, you should include the phenomenon called *dethronement* of the firstborn, which happens the minute a little brother or sister comes into the world. Until that moment, the firstborn has been number one and the apple of everyone's eye. Suddenly there is another little apple on the branch (and it's smaller, cuter, and new to the family tree). The firstborn is no longer the only one who's special, and he may suffer some serious self-esteem problems if his parents don't make sure they let him know that he's still loved very much.

Many parents try to have their children two years apart (actually three is "ideal"), but these best-laid plans often go awry. Gaps of five to six years or more in the spacing of the children can create another "family." I say *can* since the other variables may come into play. For example, with the five-year gap between me and my older brother, I could have started a second family and become a functional firstborn, but other things intervened. To show you how a second family can actually occur, let's look at the example below:

Family A

Male—14
Female—13
– – – – – – –
Male—7
Female—5

The dotted line depicts the obvious split in this kind of birth order ranking. The gap of six years between the second- and thirdborn child could easily cause the thirdborn boy to develop firstborn tendencies. This doesn't mean he would have no characteristics of a middle child (in a family of four children, #2 and #3 are middle children). He could still become a negotiator; he could still have a lot of friends. But he also might be quite "adult"— conscientious, exacting—because he had so many older role models. Not only would his parents model adult characteristics for him but so would his much bigger (and more capable) brother and sister. And that's where he could learn to function in a number of ways as a firstborn.

> *Gaps of five to six years or more in the spacing of the children can create another "family."*

For another example, what do you think would happen if I removed the 7-year-old male and the 5-year-old female from the family, and then inserted a 3-year-old male?

Family B

Male—14
Female—13

- - - - - - -

Male—3

Now what do we have? When the gap between the last child and the one above becomes more than seven years, you have a very good chance of developing what we call a quasi–only child. The little 3-year-old is the baby of the family, ordinally speaking, and he may take on baby characteristics if his parents and those two older siblings dote on him. But if he's left to himself and doesn't get much "cute little cub" treatment, he can easily become much like an only child, because he will be working extra hard trying to emulate all those big role models above him who are so much more capable.

Meet the First Leman Family

Here's a real-life example of how spacing in children can affect birth order. My wife, Sande, and I first had our daughter, Holly. A year and a half later, Krissy joined the family. Four years later Kevey (Kevin II) was born.

Our first children followed the typical birth order patterns practically to a T. From day one, Holly was meticulous, perfectionistic, structured, hard driving, and very bright. She was also a stickler for the rules and being precise. If she wanted to know what time we were going to leave for an event, I couldn't get away with saying, "Around noon." I had to be clearer and make it, "We will depart the driveway by 11:55 a.m."

It was no surprise when Holly latched onto Judge Wapner's *People's Court* as one of her favorite TV shows. (And later she became a real fan of Judge Judy.) After graduating from college, Holly returned to Tucson to teach and joined the faculty of a local public high school, where she taught English and creative writing to seniors. During her first year, we would run across parents of students in her class who would tell us two things. They were essentially happy with Holly's teaching of their child, but the next word out of their mouths was "detention."

"Oh," I would reply, "your child doesn't always come to class prepared?"

"No, but he's learning!" would be the typical response.

Clearly firstborn Holly was a stickler for procedure, proper behavior, and coming to class prepared. Since then Holly has worn various hats at a variety of schools: as English teacher, administrator, the head of the English department, and curriculum developer.

Krissy, our secondborn, also wound up as a teacher of second graders. She was later appointed as director of curriculum. After her first year of work, her principal told her that she was the first teacher to serve on his staff in twenty-five years to whom he had no suggestions on how to improve. Then Krissy made the tough choice to bail out of the school system and become the best teacher we could ask for to our two grandchildren.

So was Krissy the same kind of hard-driving, precise, stick-to-the-rules-and-get-your-work-in-on-time personality as her sister? Not really. But on the other hand, Krissy was in full control of her class because she's very *relational* with kids, a sure sign of a secondborn who has learned to negotiate, mediate, and go outside the family to make friends. From early on, this was Krissy's pattern. We still talk about her first day at kindergarten when she frightened her mother out of her wits by going to her best friend's house after school instead of coming straight home on the bus.

It's important to know, however, that Krissy was our baby girl for at least four years before Kevin came along. So she was the baby of the family for much of her early life when her lifestyle (the way she sees herself and the world) was being formed. Maybe that explains why she can't seem to shake the "Krissy" handle. I've suggested that sometime before she gets her AARP card, she should switch to Kris or her given name, Kristin!

Then there's Kevin, our thirdborn, the baby of the first Leman family. He's a classic lastborn—playful, great sense of humor, very creative—but he also has tremendous writing skills At present Kevin is a comedy writer for one of the funniest shows on television. He has won two Emmys and written two movies to boot. He's a perfect example of a person whose personality encompasses a couple of birth orders: the baby who's always looking for fun (and notice that he earns his living writing comedy), and the creative, gifted writer—a quality of many firstborns.

Kevin had the best of both worlds. He was the baby of the family whose two older sisters used to dress him up for fun. Once we were on a trip in a big van that had a bed in the back where the kids could sleep. While Kevin was asleep, his older sisters completely colored his body with magic markers. Kevin didn't even wake up!

However, for all of his lastborn charms, Kevin is still the firstborn male in the family and has the resulting firstborn traits. Here's what I mean. When he attended art school, he was very well liked. One day a classmate who was struggling to get her life together asked him, "Kevin, why are you always so happy?"

"Do you really want to know?" Kevin said.

"Yeah, I do!"

"Well, I love God and I come from a really neat family."

When Kevin told me that story, I was so pleased I nearly popped my buttons. But I was even more impressed when he added the sequel: "Dad, that girl still smokes pot, but not as much. And she still rips things off sometimes. We went to Disney World together, and when we came out of this gift shop she had that look on her face. I stopped her and said, 'Okay, let's have it.' She took it out of her pocket and handed it to me. I marched her right back into the store and she gave it back."

You see, Kevin has a firstborn's strong sense of responsibility along with his fun-loving nature. As a man who's now 30, solidly entrenched in his career, and beloved by his family and co-workers, Kevin is far ahead of where I, his father, was at that point in life and then some!

How We Got Our "Second Family"

When the first edition of *The Birth Order Book* came out, our children were all young:

Family Leman (mid-1980s)

Holly—12
Krissy—10
Kevin—6

Sande and I thought our family was complete with our trio. Little did we know that a second family was on the way.

43

In 1987, more than nine years after Kevin was born—and Sande and I were both in our early forties—a little "surprise" package arrived, and we named her Hannah.

With such a large gap between Hannah and Kevey, Hannah definitely started a second round of birth order for the Lemans. She has been a joy to raise. Her firstbornness has always been on the compliant side. For example, at age 2 she'd organize us as parents, but always in a gentle fashion. When she needed a nap, she'd come up to us, take our hands, and say, "Tired now." At age 11 she was already a budding artist. Hannah is now 22 and a recent college graduate.

But our second family was still not complete with the birth of Hannah. Almost five and a half years later came our little "shocker," a little princess we named Lauren. Learning we were expecting for a fifth time—in our *late* forties—was a shock for both me and my usually implacable firstborn wife. After getting Hannah into preschool, Sande was just beginning to see some daylight and looking forward to having a little time for herself.

But by the time little Lauren arrived, everyone—including Sande, me, and the other kids—had adjusted to her arrival, and she was as welcome and as loved as her siblings had been. Today Lauren is 16, the baby of our second family and the true baby of our total family, though she, like Kevin, has all the responsible traits of a firstborn because there is a gap of five and a half years between her and her sister Hannah. Now we look like this:

Family Leman (2009)

Holly—36, classic firstborn, teaches English

Krissy—34, classic middle child, educator, mommy of two

Kevin—30, functional firstborn, Emmy-award-winning comedy writer

Hannah—22, exhibits many tender baby characteristics; teacher

Lauren—16, baby of the entire family but also a functional firstborn, very precise, cautious

For the first five years of her life, Hannah was the baby princess. Because of the huge gap between her and her older brother and sisters, Hannah actually had five "parents" who doted on her. At least, there were five very big and capable people she was trying to learn from and imitate. Then Lauren arrived and took the baby spot. And again, because of a rather large gap between her and Hannah (over five years), Lauren was not only the true baby princess of the family but also a candidate for functional firstborn traits. We like to say that Hannah had five parents and Lauren had six!

And the firstborn probabilities did develop. At age 2½ Lauren would set up her tape recorder on the floor and line up all her tapes next to it in perfect order. To a baby of the family like me, who could hardly line up to go to the bathroom, this was almost scary.

But Lauren topped that at 5 years old when all of us gathered in the kitchen to discuss how our normal scheduling had been totally sabotaged for the next evening. Sande had a doctor's appointment, so Krissy would have to pick up Hannah after school. Holly had a teacher's meeting she had to attend, and I also had a meeting. We were all due to meet for dinner at 5:30 at a certain restaurant for a family celebration. As we chewed on all the details together, 5-year-old Lauren interjected, "My, my, my, this is very complicated." Everyone sort of froze and just looked at her.

> *Don't sell short the powerful imprint you and all of those older siblings are making on that lastborn.*

I'm not sure where Lauren had learned the word *complicated* at that young age, but obviously she knew what it meant. (I can assure you I didn't when I was 5.) I doubt that's a typical observation for a 5-year-old, particularly for a baby of the family. But that's where that variable of spacing comes in with Lauren. Whenever there's enough of a spread between your lastborn and the one above to create the functional firstborn, don't sell short the powerful imprint you and all of those older siblings are making on that lastborn. Granted, your little lastborn isn't an ordinal firstborn, but he or she may carry some of the firstborn burdens. (More about that in chapter 4.)

Why Southwest Is Such a Fun Airline

One other good example of how spacing can create a firstborn personality in a lastborn child is Herb Kelleher, former president and CEO of Southwest Airlines. As I was reading with interest a business column in our local paper one day, I learned that Kelleher and his staff had built Southwest into one of the most profitable operations anywhere. One of the reasons he gave was, "We defined a personality as well as a market niche. [We seek to] amuse, surprise, and entertain."[1]

I jotted a note next to that quote that said, "Herbie must be a baby." Later, when I telephoned him for an interview, he told me that, indeed, he is the baby of the family (fourthborn of four), but that there is a nine-year gap between him and his next older brother. And the other brothers are thirteen and fourteen years older. With all that coaching and all those capable people to model after, it's no mystery that Herb Kelleher, baby of his family, made it to the top and became CEO of a prominent airline.

That's why Kelleher is a mixed bag. As a CEO he was in typically firstborn company. At the same time, he loves to enjoy himself, and that's his baby side. You may have seen past Southwest TV commercials where Kelleher was cast as a referee who called unnecessary roughness penalties on luggage handlers who were a bit too careless with the baggage. While he didn't force his employees to be amusing and entertaining, they often followed suit. If you've ever been on a Southwest Airline flight and have listened to the flight attendants singing their zany songs to the passengers, you know what I mean. Kelleher's legacy lives on.

While still CEO, Kelleher said, "We don't force attendants to be entertainers. We just tell them if they feel comfortable doing things like that, great! And if they feel uncomfortable, don't bother. They actually come up with many of these things themselves."[2]

The Gender Variable

Almost hand in hand with the spacing variable is the obvious variable of sex. We've already seen that a laterborn child can become the firstborn girl or the firstborn boy. And I've mentioned how a number of US presidents are functional firstborns because of being the first male in the family. I always find it fascinating how often birth order plays a role in developing political leaders.

Once I was speaking to a Young Presidents group at a resort in Tucson. Just as I reached the part of my talk where I stated how birth order impacts our lives, I spotted Fife Symington, who was then the governor of Arizona, in a far corner of the room. When I asked for a show of hands on who was a firstborn, a middle child, or a lastborn, the governor put his hand up to identify himself as a baby of his family.

I caught the governor's eye across the room and said: "Governor Symington, excuse me, but you are not a baby of the family."

He looked at me as if to say, *What? I ought to know where I was born in my own family—I am the baby.*

"I can see that you doubt me a bit," I said. "Would you tell me a bit about your family?"

"Well," replied the governor, "I've got three older sisters—"

"And you are the only son?" I interrupted.

"Yes, that's true."

"Bingo! I rest my case. Governor, you are a firstborn child—the firstborn *male* in the Symington family."

Interestingly, Symington went on to a tumultuous career as governor, which demonstrated that while he was a functional firstborn, he also had weaknesses typical of some lastborns.[3]

For one more illustration of how the sex variable affects birth order, let's consider a reverse of the Symington family and look at three boys followed by a girl. You don't have to be a certified psychologist to figure out that there will be something very special about one member of this family:

Family C

Male—16

Male—14

Male—12

Female—11

The fourthborn girl will definitely be a special baby princess. And in this kind of mix, which child is in the *least* preferable position? The thirdborn male—the 12-year-old—has to be sweating a bit. When his younger sister was born, Mom had already been down to the hospital three times and brought home a boy every time. She and Dad were pulling for a girl each time, and then that baby arrived, only fifteen to eighteen months behind the thirdborn male. He was bound to hear her footsteps even before she could walk!

> Any time the secondborn is of the same sex as the firstborn, there is bound to be more friction.

48

Who else in this family is in a favorable spot? A good bet is that firstborn male, who will likely excel at school. Of course, he will probably engage in plenty of rivalry with his younger brother, because any time the secondborn is of the same sex as the firstborn, there is bound to be more friction. If older brother is a scholar, secondborn is likely to be an athlete, or he may prefer the school band (maybe he'll form his own rock group) and leave athletics to the thirdborn boy. If the thirdborn does become an athlete, it could be fortunate because it will help him work out frustrations caused by having to compete with his princess baby sister.

> *When sex differences create someone "special," it can put pressure on the child immediately above or below that special person.*

Family C is just one example of how the sex of each child can affect the family. The rule of thumb is when sex differences create someone "special," it can put pressure on the child immediately above or below that special person.

In This Corner, Burly the Bigger

Another variable that can turn the birth order factor upside down, or at least tilt it a bit, is a marked difference in physical looks, size, or ability. Little Chester, age 10, is the firstborn, but he's still called "little" because his brother, one year younger, is nicknamed "Burly" and is four inches taller and twenty-five pounds heavier. Because it's a two-child family, the two males are natural rivals, so Chester better be extra quick or extra smart or he's in for a lot of difficult days—and quite possibly a role reversal in which Burly will take all the firstborn privileges and prerogatives by default while Chester slips back to second place. A role reversal is when two children do something of a flip-flop.

Another all-too-frequent example of this kind of variable is the two-girl family where one is extremely pretty and the other is extremely plain. If the plain one is the firstborn, her pretty little sister may drive her into a shell from which she will never escape. If the firstborn is the pretty one, the plain baby of the family better figure out some kind of secret weapon—athletics or being the family scholar—or she's in for a long and dreary career as the "homely little sister."

> *A role reversal is when two children do something of a flip-flop.*

In the examples of Burly and the pretty secondborn, marked physical differences cause a secondborn to function like a firstborn, and vice versa. Another physical difference that can flip-flop things in a hurry is when one member of the family suffers from serious disease or disability. For example, let's create a family where the firstborn has cerebral palsy:

Family D

Female—14, physically challenged with cerebral palsy
Female—12
Male—10

Here we have another case of a role reversal. The special person is born at the top, but her secondborn sister is almost certain to take the role of the firstborn in the family because of her older sister's extreme disability.

And what about little lastborn brother? He is, of course, the firstborn male in the family, and chances are that his cerebral-palsied sister will ace him out of the baby status. This lastborn son may have a few baby characteristics but may act more like a firstborn than anything else.

One other difference that counselors see a lot more of in recent years is a combination of physical/mental problems that have come to be called ADD (attention deficit disorder) or ADHD (attention deficit hyperactivity disorder). Whatever you call it, such a disorder can seriously affect the birth order factor. For example, suppose a family has a firstborn boy with ADHD and a secondborn girl who seems to be perfectly "normal." The almost classic response to this situation by the parents is that they will soon see the firstborn son as something of the family black sheep—always a problem—while their secondborn daughter takes over as far as gaining firstborn privileges and rewards.

Multiple Births

Another important variable in birth order is multiple births, which have been happening more often in recent years. The usual multiple birth that we've seen down through the years is, of course, twins. And twins are always special. Twins are usually very aware of who is the firstborn. One of them will let you know that he is older, even if it's by as little as one minute!

No matter where twins may land in a family birth order, they wind up as something of a firstborn/secondborn combination and are usually competitor and companion. The firstborn often becomes the assertive leader, and the secondborn follows along. This happens often, but not always. Some twinships can turn into real rivalries, particularly if the children are the same sex.[4] This is also a very common place to find a role reversal.

> *Twins are usually very aware of who is the firstborn. One of them will let you know that he is older, even if it's by as little as one minute!*

When it comes to the family zoo, a multiple birth is bound to cause pressure on anyone born above as well as anyone born below. Let's take a look at how this can work when twins arrive later, which is often the case because women in their forties are much more likely to have twins than women in their twenties.[5]

Family E

> Female—12
> Male—10
> Twin Males—7
> Female—3

Here we have twins with a firstborn female and a firstborn male of the family above them. Those firstborns can probably handle the special attention the twins are bound to attract, but that little sister at the bottom of the pack is going to have problems, even though she is supposedly the baby princess. At least she has a better chance than if she were a lastborn boy. A lastborn boy living under that 7-year-old "dynamic duo" would be even less special, and he could become very discouraged while trying to compete for attention. Unless the parents became aware of what was happening, the twins could blow out their little brother's candle.

> *If you have kids in higher positions in the family who do very well, that next-in-line child might think, Hey, what's the use of even trying? I can't measure up to what they've accomplished.*

It's a little like the experience I once had on *The View*. After I'd completed my six-minute spot, I knew from the enthusiastic response of the audience that I'd done a good job. I walked back into the green room, and everyone started clapping. Jon Stewart, the comedian who was supposed to go on next, looked up at me and said, "Thanks a lot." That's about as good of an endorsement as you can get from Jon Stewart. In other words, he was saying, "Hey, you're a hard act to follow."

The same is true with kids in families. If you have kids in higher positions in the family who do very well, that next-in-line child might think, *Hey, what's the use of even trying? I can't measure up to what they've accomplished.*

But pressure can come at the top of the family when a multiple birth occurs below. A graphic example of this occurred in November 1997 when septuplets were born to Bobbi and Kenny McCaughey of Carlisle, Iowa. The news reports revealed that the four girls and three boys had an older sister, Mikayla, who was 21 months old when the septuplets arrived and really didn't quite understand that all *seven* of them were coming home to stay. Talk about dethronement! You can bet your boots that little Mikayla soon started hearing the thundering hoofbeats of a stampede as all those little McCaugheys below her started claiming their share of the turf and then some.

Shortly after the birth of the McCaughey septuplets, I had the pleasure of speaking to one set of grandparents (Bobbi's mother and father) during a talk show. Later during the show, we discussed how these septuplets were bound to dethrone their big sister. I suggested that when Bobbi and Kenny brought the "Magnificent Seven" home from the hospital, they needed to constantly remind Mikayla that "You're a *big girl*. You take only one nap a day, but the babies have to take *this many* naps a day." One of the parents could hold up both hands—all ten fingers—to indicate for Mikayla that all her little brothers and sisters had to take ten naps a day—that's a total of seventy naps to her one!

Another obvious suggestion was that Mikayla be told that because she is a big girl, she can be a helper and get diapers, powder, and other things for Mommy as she cares for all the babies.

I'm also intrigued to follow the oldest of the McCaughey septuplets. While all of them were in the womb, little Kenneth Jr., the one nearest the cervical entrance, was literally holding up all his brothers and sisters because he was at the base of an inverted triangle that all of the babies formed inside the womb. Doctors nicknamed Kenneth "Hercules," not only because he had done a Herculean job in the womb but because he was the largest of the septuplets at three pounds, four ounces, and he was also the firstborn. With all that going for little Kenneth before he ever appeared in this world, you can imagine the kind of expectations that may have been placed on him and what he might accomplish in the future.

Deaths

Here are two examples of how death can affect birth order in a profound way. First, suppose a family has two sons and a daughter. At age 4, the older boy dies of spinal meningitis, leaving behind his 2-year-old brother and 6-month-old sister. The 2-year-old takes over the firstborn role and grows up that way, while his little sister, who actually was born a baby of the family, grows up more as a firstborn girl.

Second, suppose the oldest child in the family dies at age 12 in an automobile accident. His 10-year-old brother assumes the firstborn role and is suddenly given firstborn assignments and responsibilities. But is he really a firstborn? No, for ten years he grew up as a secondborn, content not to challenge his older brother for supremacy in the family. Now he is getting a lot of pressure that he really doesn't want and has no idea how to cope with because he has no experience in that area.

Before the accident he had been in a fairly easy position because his older brother had been the ice cutter on the lake of life. All of a sudden older brother is gone, and while the trauma of losing him is bad enough, on top of that the secondborn suddenly feels as if the world is on his shoulders. He becomes the family standard-bearer; he has to live his life as well as his older brother's.

A classic illustration of this very scenario happened when Joseph Kennedy Jr. died at the controls of his bomber in World War II, and his younger brother John had to become the family standard-bearer at the age of 19. For the rest of his life, even while in the White House, John Kennedy had to cope with the ghost of his older brother, who was the apple of their father's eye.

Adoptions

And what about adoption? How does it affect birth order? Actually, it doesn't, if the adoption occurs when the child is an infant. Today, however, many more people are adopting children who are a bit older—around 3, 4, 5, and so on. Newly adoptive parents must keep in mind that a child adopted at age 4 has operated at a certain birth order level in whatever "family" (birth family, foster family, or welfare institution) he was part of before the adoption. Just because he may wind up to be the oldest or youngest in his new family doesn't necessarily make him a firstborn or a lastborn. The birth order characteristics from the child's previous life follow the child into his new family.

All the children in your family must be accepted and loved equally. No child wants—or deserves—to feel like she is second fiddle her whole life.

There is another thing adoptive parents need to watch out for, particularly if they are adding an adopted child to other children already in the family. The obvious danger is to unconsciously favor a child connected to you by blood—a child you have birthed—over an adopted child. However, all the children in your family must be accepted and loved equally. This is an issue that parents who are considering adoption must carefully weigh in their own hearts before bringing an adopted child into their home. No child wants—or deserves—to feel like she is second fiddle her whole life.

I also advise parents not to adopt a child who is older than any biological children they already have. The adopted "intruder" may have a negative effect on the child directly beneath him or her. For example, suppose a couple has a 3-year-old

> *We are affected and influenced the most by whoever is directly above us in the family.*

child and decide to adopt a child who is 5. What happens? Their 3-year-old has just been knocked off his only-child mountaintop and now has to contend with someone bigger and smarter. Always remember the principle, which applies in this case: generally speaking, we are affected and influenced the most by whoever is directly above us in the family. When an older adopted child comes into a family, he or she is bound to collide with the biological child directly below in age.

So the typical birth order descriptions for onlies, firstborns, middleborns, and lastborns can be modified or even flip-flopped by certain variables over which the children, and usually the parents, have no control. But there are some things over which parents have great control. That's the subject of the next chapter.

3

What's Parenting Got to Do with It?

Birth Order Variables—Part 2

What's parenting got to do with altering birth order descriptions? A great deal. So far, we've talked about birth order variables that have to do with the children—spacing, sex, physical or mental differences, multiple births, deaths, and adoptions. But the *parents* are also a major variable. In this chapter we'll take a closer look at the birth order of the parents, the parent with the critical eye, parental values in general, and what happens in blended families. Parental factors are powerful variables that affect each child in the family, but particularly the firstborn or the only child.

What's Your Birth Order?

Just how does Mom's or Dad's order of birth affect the children? One typical force at work is the tendency for a parent to overidentify with the child in the same birth order position. This can lead to putting too much pressure on the child or spoiling or favoring the child.

When I was an adjunct professor at the University of Arizona and was teaching a graduate class in child psychology, I decided to do a "family zoo demonstration" in front of two hundred students, most of whom were employed as teachers or counselors. I brought in a mother, a father, and three children and had an interesting time interacting with all of them in front of the class.

Afterward, when the family had gone, I asked the group for some feedback. Because the majority of those in the class were not neophytes but practicing professionals, I was curious about their reactions. Each had different observations, but most agreed on one thing: "It seems as if you paid an awful lot of attention to the baby of the family—the 4-year-old girl."

For Parents

Good questions to ask yourself:

1. What's your birth order?
2. Which child shares the same birth order?
3. In what ways do you tend to overidentify with and favor that child?
4. How will keeping this tendency in mind help you balance your actions and responses to all your children?

Without thinking too much about it, I said, "Yeah, wasn't she cute?" But then it hit me. Of course I thought the baby was cute—I had been the baby in my family too! I had made a career of being cute and funny all through school and beyond.

When I interacted with our first three children while they were growing up, whose antics did I enjoy the most? Kevin II—our baby, of course. For example, when Holly was 13 and Krissy was 11 and they would complain to me about 7-year-old Kevey and his pestering ways, I would say, "Well, girls, let's remember he's the baby of the family. Little baby brothers do that kind of thing to sisters." I identified with Kevin. Do you think Holly and Krissy picked up on that? You bet they did.

The Critical Eye Is Hard to Live Under

In my case, I was overidentifying with my lastborn in an indulging way, because, as a baby of the family myself, I loved to pester my older sister and brother when I was small. But let me be clear that overidentification can also be done in a nonindulgent, hard-line way, particularly when both parents are firstborns. This almost guarantees that the parents will have what I call "the critical eye." Instead of overindulging their firstborn child, they'll probably be extra hard on him or her as they exert their own exacting standards and learn how to parent at the same time. To show you what I mean, let's look at the following example:

Family F

Husband—firstborn perfectionist dentist
Wife—firstborn PTA president, known for getting people organized
Female—16
Female—14
Female—12

Who has the best spot in this family? Obviously it isn't the firstborn girl for at least two reasons: first, she's the one Mom and Dad are going to have to practice on as far as parenting is concerned, and second, she will have to perform under their critical perfectionistic eye.

The best position in the family could be the secondborn girl because big sister has run interference for her to some extent and absorbed a lot of the perfectionistic energy that two firstborn parents are likely to pour into their first child. But what about the baby of the family, the thirdborn girl? Will she be able to charm and manipulate her folks? Doubtful, because parents tend to identify with the child nearest them in birth order. Chances are the firstborn dentist and his firstborn PTA president/wife won't be too enamored with any baby-of-the-family precociousness or manipulation.

What I hope is becoming very obvious to you is that in any family, a lot depends on the personality and parenting style of Mom and Dad. If the parents are authoritarians who come down too hard and too unreasonably on their firstborn, they can turn her into a rebel who, instead of excelling in school as most firstborns would, messes up just to foil the plans of her "perfect" parents.

Remember the two brothers who were in broadcasting who "reversed" roles (see chapter 1)? In the case of these brothers, that variable was a perfectionistic, critical parent who caused Alan to take a step into the background so that Luke thrived and jumped ahead. Luke surpassed his brother and became the functional firstborn.

When people call in to radio shows I appear on, they often tell me, "Doc, I have a firstborn who isn't doing well at all in school. What can I do to get him motivated?" Often I can pinpoint the problem around mistakes the parents are making with that child. For just one more look at how parenting style can make a real difference, let's consider another family:

Does a Critical Parent Live at Your House?

Here are some signs to watch for.

1. Your child procrastinates at everything she does.
2. Your child draws a picture, then tears it up, telling you it's no good.
3. Your child redoes his homework several times.
4. A simple half-hour homework assignment takes four hours.
5. Nothing is ever good enough.
6. You redo projects your child does (for example, you make the bed he already made).

Family G

Female—10
Male—8

The key here is how Dad treats the 10-year-old daughter and how Mom treats the 8-year-old son. Why is that? Because the cross-gender relationships in the family are the most important—mom to son and dad to daughter. If Mom pours too much into the 10-year-old daughter and doesn't have as much time for the 8-year-old boy, it will ensure that he'll be very different from big sister. It's also likely he'll take the role of firstborn boy and be more aggressive, always ready to protect his turf.

But if Mom pays lots of attention to her younger son, he'll become more a baby of the family, fun loving, affectionate, and probably more understanding of women. If he has a healthy relationship with Mom—meaning that she is loving, kind, and gentle but still doesn't take any guff from him—he will appreciate and respect women and be comfortable around them. As a rule, he will have an excellent chance to build a successful marriage.

> *In any family, a lot depends on the personality and parenting style of Mom and Dad.*

But suppose the father has a critical eye and is very demanding and exacting. There is a good chance he could "destroy" his firstborn daughter, and his son will become the true firstborn in the family. Firstborn girls who grow up under a very perfectionistic, critical father are often hard on themselves and put themselves in situations that aren't healthy as they look for the love, affirmation, and acceptance they didn't get from their own father. When such a firstborn daughter grows up and marries, her husband will pay the price for the sins of her father.

What Made Lee Iacocca Run?

Parental values are one of the variables that can override almost everything else in birth order. Lee Iacocca, former CEO of Ford and Chrysler fame, is a good example. Lee, a secondborn, has a sister, Delma, two years older. To understand him, however, you have to become acquainted with the values of the Iacocca parents—Italian immigrants who loved their children dearly but were always pushing them to "be the best you can be."

Lee was the baby of the family but also the firstborn male. As a result, he received all kinds of pressure and prodding to perform, particularly from Dad. For example, in high school Iacocca graduated twelfth in his class of more than nine hundred, yet what did Dad say? "Why weren't you *first?*" In his biography, Iacocca recalls, "To hear him describe it, you'd think I flunked!"[1]

This little anecdote sounds like a father who could ruin his son by always raising the bar too high, but fortunately, Iacocca and his dad were very close. Iacocca recalls, "I loved pleasing him, and he was always terrifically proud of my accomplishments. If I won a spelling contest at school, he was on top of the world. Later in life, whenever I got a promotion, I'd call my father right away and he'd rush right out to tell all his friends. . . . In 1970, when I was named president of the Ford Motor Company, I don't know which of us was more excited."[2]

Later Iacocca was fired by Ford but went on to mastermind a comeback from the dead for Chrysler. The values taught by his parents, particularly his father, gave him incredible resilience and steely resolve. Iacocca had style and all the tools to be a master CEO—aggressive, decisive, straightforward, compassionate, volatile, funny, and always someone who could tell it like it is. All of those traits could be traced right back to how a firstborn son grew up in a loving Italian home in Allentown, Pennsylvania.

Lee Iacocca is only one example of the power of family values. The influence your family has on you as you grow up can reach across time and distance to touch you in profound, and sometimes disturbing, ways years after you think you've "grown beyond all that."

Another good example of how parental values had much to say about making a leader is coach Lute Olson. When Lute came to the University of Arizona, I noticed immediately that he was a sharp dresser with a beautiful head of wavy white hair that was never out of place. The telltale signs of a firstborn perfectionist were there.

So imagine my surprise when I found out that while Lute may look and act like a firstborn or only child, he's really the baby of his family with three older brothers!

Because I am a fervent Wildcat fan and have even served as counselor to some U of A teams, I got to know Lute. And I couldn't help myself. I was determined to figure out why he didn't fit the pattern for his birth order, so I asked him. It turned out he got his meticulous keep-things-organized and everything-in-its-place approach to life from his Scandinavian parents. Lute grew up on a farm where no excuses were accepted if you didn't do your job. As Lute recalls, "You were expected to give it your best shot."[3]

> *The influence your family has on you as you grow up can reach across time and distance to touch you in profound, and sometimes disturbing, ways years after you think you've "grown beyond all that."*

So that's what Lute did. No wonder he's one of the most capable and successful college basketball coaches of all time and that he finally won it all when his Arizona Wildcats took the NCAA crown. Basketball fans may remember the moments just after Lute's team won the NCAA title and his Wildcat players mussed his hair on national television. For all I know, it was the first time anyone, including his wife, had ever seen Lute with messy hair. It was a moment to remember for many reasons.

Blended Families

What happens when parents become stepparents? Another way to ask this question is, what happens when two families blend because divorced or widowed parents remarry? The answer is, *plenty!* The blended family variable can throw birth order (and the family) into chaos.

With the divorce rate hovering around 50 percent today, the survival of any marriage is in jeopardy. But when you put a divorced mom and her kids together with a divorced dad and his brood, the odds get much larger. Sixty percent of second marriages fail. Simply said, love is seldom lovelier the second time around. That's not cynicism; that's real-life statistics.

Yet 1,300 new blended families form every day—and that's just in the United States. According to the Stepfamily Association of America, 40 percent of all marriages represent a remarriage of one or both parties. If remarriages continue at these rates, 35 percent of all children born will live in a stepfamily by the time they reach 18. And 1 out of 6 children under the age of 18 is a stepchild.[4]

When I speak about marriage, I often quote this equation: $E - R = D$ (Expectations minus Reality equals Disillusionment). That little equation can apply to a lot of things in family living, but another equation fits blended families much more aptly: $N \times R = C$ (Naïveté times Reality equals Chaos). Going through premarital counseling is a great help, but until you are all together under the same roof, you don't really know how it's all going to work.

> Going through premarital counseling is a great help, but until you are all together under the same roof, you don't really know how it's all going to work.

Handling firstborns, middleborns, and lastborns in one family is challenging enough. But bring two families together into a *Brady Bunch* or *Eight Is Enough* setting, and things get complicated in a hurry. Those classic shows, which still appear as reruns, create a plastic package where crises and problems are always solved neatly and easily as everyone blends into the "happily ever after." But in truth, it takes a lot of work, planning, talking, and give-and-take in a blended family.

So for those who are considering remarriage or are already in a blended family, what are the dos and don'ts?

1. Don't assume there will be "instant love" among all members of the new family. Sibling rivalry goes back to Cain and Abel, and it's even more likely in a blended family, especially if the children are close in age and thus are competing with each other. So set the ground rules that it's okay to disagree but that it must always be done with respect for each person in the family so no one feels stepped on.

2. Don't assume it will be easier to have a blended family with a spouse and five children than it is to be a single parent of two. If you are not yet remarried, ask yourself the question, "Have we fallen in love, or have we fallen in need?" It's typical for people who have divorced or lost spouses in another way to say to each other, "You have two kids and I have two, so why don't we get married? It'll be easier for all of us." Sure, it may be easier financially with all of you living in one home with one mortgage, but emotionally and relationally, will it be easier? Acquiring "instant children" can also mean acquiring instant problems.

3. Mom and Dad must stand shoulder to shoulder—united together as parents—in order for the marriage and blended family to survive. Think of it this way. Most couples date for only two years before they decide to retie the knot. The relationship each of those spouses have had with their respective children is usually much longer. So is it reasonable to believe that a two-year relationship between a husband and wife who have remarried is going to outweigh parent/child relationships that have been in existence for several years at least, and in some cases, ten to fifteen years or more?

To paraphrase the old saying, blood in biological families is thicker than the punch served at the remarriage reception. When there's a fight in the family, it usually becomes the mom and her kids against the dad and his kids. And in that kind of warfare, the probability that a marriage will survive is very low. But if you and your spouse decide that you're going to stand together on all issues, no matter what (that means keeping any disagreement between the two of you away from the children's hearing and working it out quietly between you), and that "your children" will always be "our" children, you're giving yourself the best chance of success.

Granted, when children in a blended family are very young, Mom and Dad have a better chance. Suppose stepsisters, ages 1 and 3, join stepbrothers, ages 2 and 4. All their personalities are still in the formative stage, and time is on the parents' side. But make those children a little older—beyond age 5 when the personality is formed—and instead of having instant love and harmony and fun playmates, what you can easily have is instant war and constant competition.

Birth Orders Don't Change

The key to understanding how friction can develop in a blended family is to know that once the grain of the wood (the personality) is set after age 5 or 6, every birth order is set as well. In other words, the firstborn is always a firstborn, a middle child is always a middle child, and so on. Blended families do not create new birth order positions. Because one firstborn suddenly has a stepbrother or sister who is older, that doesn't mean that firstborn stops being typically conscientious, structured, well organized, or perfectionist.

By the same token, a lastborn isn't suddenly going to change his personality because a divorce and remarriage makes him a middle child in the family. He'll still lean toward being a show-off, an attention seeker, a manipulator, a charmer, and a little clown who likes to have fun, even though Mom and Dad would now like him to take on more responsibility because there are younger children around.

So the key to the blended birth order game is this: when a child who is born into one birth order lands on another limb in his blended family tree, do not treat that child as something he is not. He may have to take on different responsibilities and play different roles at times, but never push or force him; never forget who he really is.[5]

> *The key to the blended birth order game is this: when a child who is born into one birth order lands on another limb in his blended family tree, do not treat that child as something he is not.*

Let's go down through the different birth orders and see what happens when they get "repositioned" in blended families. First, we'll take a blended family that winds up with almost all firstborns in one way or another:

Family H

Father—firstborn perfectionist	Mother—special-jewel only child
Male—16	Male—15
Male—14	Female—13
	Female—9

According to what we've already learned about birth order and spacing, here's a blended family whose name might be the Armageddons. Why? Because the family contains five people with firstborn characteristics. And at the top of the heap we have a perfectionist, firstborn father, who will be very demanding and critical of not only his own children but also his stepchildren. And just for fun, we've added in a mother who was a special-jewel only child and will probably be extra sensitive about having things her way.

You don't have to go much deeper into this family to see how tension could arrive from many directions. There is bound to be natural rivalry between the two males at the top who are 15 and 16. And the same could be true of the secondborn female, 13, and secondborn male, 14, who could easily vie for supremacy in their secondborn roles.

What parents must remember is that these kids have nothing in common (other than the fact that they have now been thrust together). Just seeing each other every day reminds them of something very hurtful—the divorce and/or separation from one of their parents. Before this new family was formed, these children were used to making the calls. Now if there is an ax to grind, they can easily find reason to do so in each other. After a bad day at school, if all else fails, they can always pick on their no-good stepbrother or stepsister.

Another way the two oldest males may lock horns is if the mother's firstborn happens to be a neat freak who keeps his room clean (such things have been known to happen). He winds up having to share a room with his 16-year-old stepbrother, who is not that concerned about neatness and, in true firstborn style, doesn't like surprises. What happens when the neat stepbrother decides he's had enough of a sloppy room, cleans up the place, and "puts a few things away"? One word: Armageddon!

> *So what can parents do in a blended family when tensions and frictions arise? Run the family like a small corporation. Have regular meetings.*

So what can parents do in a blended family when tensions and frictions arise? Run the family like a small corporation. Have regular meetings where you all sit down and discuss these questions: (1) How does my behavior in this family affect all the other members of the family? and (2) If my behavior is causing problems, how can I change it?

Will blended families with several firstborns always have their problems? Not necessarily. Let's look at this family, for example:

Family I

Father—amiable middle child	Mother—hard-driving firstborn
Male—14	Female—9
Female—12	Male—7
	Female—4

This family could have some problems, but not as many as Family H might. The oldest male on Dad's side is "king of the hill" in the new blended family, and he's always gotten along quite well with his sister, two years younger. She's the firstborn female of the family and has carved her own path quite nicely. Over on Mom's side, the 9-year-old female isn't going to challenge her 14-year-old stepbrother, and the 7-year-old (firstborn male) is certainly not going to either. All in all, this family has a good chance of making it. If the little 4-year-old on Mom's side plays her cards right, she may be able to charm her older stepbrother and stepsister into treating her like a baby princess.

That's not to say that there aren't some problems that could arise. For example, the 12-year-old on Dad's side has been baby of the family all her life, and depending on how much her dad has spoiled her, she may or may not resent the three new "ba-

> **Quick Rules for Family Meetings**
>
> 1. Every member of the group has an equal say.
> 2. One person talks at a time.
> 3. No one interrupts until the person talking is done.
> 4. The atmosphere of the meeting must be one of mutual respect for all.
> 5. If heated conflict arises, end the meeting to give everyone time to go to their own areas and cool off. But before everyone leaves, set another meeting time in the near future (within a day) to come back to discuss the issue.

bies," all younger than she is, who have suddenly moved in. And on Mom's side, the oldest female has been ruling the roost in her family for as long as she can remember, and suddenly she's been pressed into middle child territory. She probably won't even think about taking on her 14-year-old stepbrother, but if she's a feisty firstborn, she may decide the 12-year-old stepsister is worth a try, especially if the girls have to share a room.

Blending Laterborns

While trouble often arises in a blended family with first-borns butting heads, plenty of friction can occur in the later-born children as well. Let's look at how two laterborn people got together and created a blended Brady Bunch:

Family J

Father—nonconfrontational middle child	Mother—lastborn baby princess
Female—13	Male—14
Female—10	Female—11
Male—7	Male—8

Let's set aside for the moment the obvious friction at the top with the oldest female and the oldest male squaring off for king or queen of the hill. If they are both aggressive first-borns, watch out! One or both of them, however, could be compliant firstborns, and that would make things easier.

But in this scenario, let's focus on the kids down below. The one in the worst position in this whole blended family is the 10-year-old on Dad's side. She has always been sandwiched between an older sister and a 7-year-old prince below her, so she's always felt the typical middle child squeeze. Now all of a sudden she has three more people to contend with, two of whom are older, so the squeeze gets even tighter.

On Mom's side, the one in the best position in the entire blended family is the secondborn girl. She's always been the only girl in her original family, so she brings to the table a very positive attitude about herself and life in general. The bad news, however, is that she may resent the other two females— her stepsisters—and there can be lots of tension there. The child this girl may get along with best, strangely enough, is the 7-year-old stepbrother. This may be the case if she has always had problems with her own brothers and still has an unfulfilled need to "mother" someone. These two could form an "alliance" and get along very well.

Note that down at the bottom of this blended heap, we have two little guys vying for the title of crown prince (or maybe it's clown prince). Both of these babies have been used to the limelight and having things their way. Now they have to share that limelight, and there could be trouble. It would seem that there is room for only one baby in this family, so who will it be? The obvious choice is the youngest one of all—the 7-year-old on Dad's side. But that won't sit well with the 8-year-old on Mom's side. So both parents will need to work together to be sure that both of these babies of the family get their share of attention.

Note, too, the birth orders of the two parents. Dad is a nonconfrontational middle child, and Mom was a lastborn baby princess herself. That means Dad has a contradiction working in his middle child personality. Even though he may have learned some mediating and negotiating skills while growing up, he decided on a lifestyle that is nonconfrontational because that's what makes him more comfortable. This means he won't want to do much mediating and negotiating with the children, so that leaves it to Mom. Mom is a lastborn who may have had a long history of being spoiled and wanting things her way. This will certainly spill over into wanting

> *In order to make their blended family last long term, Mom and Dad need to put their relationship as a couple first and the children second.*

advantages and fair treatment for "her kids" instead of for "his kids."

In order to make their blended family last long term, Mom and Dad need to put their relationship as a couple first and the children second.

Part of a Bigger Picture

Birth order isn't a cookie-cutter process that ensures that firstborns will all march lockstep this way, middle children will universally do something different, and lastborns will all be the family comedians. Instead, birth order is designed to give you clues about what an individual is like and what their thought processes and feelings are.

It isn't hard science that can be measured in a test tube or computed to the tenth power with mathematical formulas. Variables such as when the child is born or the child's sex give birth order a subjective side. And other variables such as the values taught to the child by the parents—who are certain birth orders themselves—also come into play. All these factors will combine and have a lifelong effect on who and what that person turns out to be. He or she will make a unique individual who will *probably* have certain characteristics typical of his or her birth order, but not necessarily. The end result always has to do with the variables that come into play.

However, just as not everything in life fits perfectly and consistently into a mold, so also birth order doesn't always fit perfectly and consistently into neat statistical data banks. That's why some

---

Heat Check

You, as the parent, are the emotional thermostat of your family. You control the temperature of the home.

1. Is it too hot, too volatile? Do children fear sharing their emotions, feelings, and thoughts because of your response when they do?

2. Is your home too cold—not enough interaction, affection, etc.?

3. Does your home swing from hot to cold as you do battle with your kids?

professional colleagues and scholars have turned their six-teen-inch guns on birth order, declaring it's of little more value than the discredited science of phrenology (figuring out someone's personality according to the bumps on his or her head).[6]

In the early 1980s, a pair of Swiss psychologists—Cecile Ernst and Jules Angst—reviewed the results from two thousand birth order research projects and concluded that most of them had been done without enough controls on all the factors involved. They published a book on their studies and at the end concluded, "Birth order influences on personality and IQ have been widely overrated."[7]

A lot of my contemporaries jumped on the Ernst and Angst bandwagon and began saying that you can "overinterpret the importance of birth order,"[8] and that birth order "is significant only in families with more than seven children."[9]

But you can't fool me because I've seen the birth order theory play out with great success as I've counseled thousands of couples and their children over more than thirty-five years. Does birth order explain everything? No, but it has always proved to be a helpful tool when clients understand it and apply it to their lives.

I'll never forget the letter I received from a man who runs a beautiful vacation resort in the Northeast. He invited my entire family and me to spend a month with him, compliments of the house, because of what he learned in *The Birth Order Book*. He wrote, "I spent hours in psychiatrists' offices trying to find out why my brother and I were so different. Then I

> Dear Dr. Leman,
>
> My adult daughter was hospitalized due to a terrible auto accident. It left her temporarily blind and discouraged. I decided to spend some of our time in the hospital room reading aloud from *The Birth Order Book*. It not only made my daughter laugh because the book was so true in pegging our family, but it also helped her feel special and one of a kind, and even aided in her recovery. She told me that for the first time, she saw that she had a unique place in our family—she wasn't just "one of the siblings" anymore. Thanks for helping her—and all of us—make sense of our family.
>
> Miriam, Virginia

picked up your book in an airport. By the time I landed, I had the answer."

What answer did he discover? As the firstborn in his family, he had pursued a typical firstborn career—as a detailed, precise, accurate financial consultant. He even wrote technical financial manuals. His secondborn, baby-of-the-family brother, was carefree, changed jobs at will, and couldn't save money because he was a big-time spender. People kept asking the older brother, "Why can't your younger brother shape up and be more like you?" *The Birth Order Book* finally gave him an explanation that made sense.

It Works for Businessmen Too

Mike Lorelli, a former PepsiCo division president who has also held top posts at Pizza Hut and Tambrands, Inc., is a secondborn child who butted heads with an older brother and came out on top in something of a role reversal. While on a business trip, he read *The Birth Order Book* and became a believer in the birth order theory. He offered me an invitation to speak to a group of his top executives.

Today, as a much-sought-after business consultant, Mike still orders *The Birth Order Book* by the case and distributes it to employees and clients. When I asked him why he thought it was such a useful tool, he told me:

> Everybody who is important to me was born. And when you think about it that way, you can use birth order to categorize people and try to figure out what's the best way to motivate your customers, suppliers, consumers, bosses, peers—whoever.
>
> In business it's not only I.Q. that matters; it's not necessarily great transactions that matter, but there are a lot of "softer sides" that can make a difference between success and failure. Birth order is one of those. It has, for example, helped me win people over and make them allies on my team to help keep the ship afloat.[10]

I believe Mike Lorelli is right when he talks about birth order being one of the "softer sides" that can spell the difference between business success and failure. That's why I do much of my speaking in settings such as the IBM School of Management, the Williams Companies, Pepsi, Pizza Hut, and Cincinnati Financial Insurance Company. I've also talked to the Million Dollar Round Table, the Top of the Table, and the Young Presidents' Organization, where salaries hit well over a million.

I love getting up to address a group of jaded vice presidents and sales managers who rigidly sit there, body language saying in no uncertain terms, *What have they sent us this time?* But a few minutes later the arms and legs relax, and blank faces light up as these high-powered business types get a handle on why it's so important to understand your own birth order as well as the birth order of people you have to deal with.

> Dear. Dr. Leman,
>
> About six years ago I read *The Birth Order Book*, and since then I've used it as instructions and signs to watch for when trying to understand candidates for positions I am trying to fill. I don't assume someone has to be just as the book suggests, but I watch for the tendencies to be so. . . . Thank you for the wisdom you impart in your books.[11]
>
> Bruce Dingman, president, the Dingman Company

Michael C. Feiner, former senior vice president at PepsiCo Europe, has used birth order when filling positions in his firm. Here's what he told me about how he uses birth order when questioning a prospective employee:

> I usually ask one last question: "Can you tell me about your personal background—parents, siblings?" Then I just listen as tons of information begin to pour from the candidate. . . . Because getting things done in a large, complex organization is so dependent on relationships, I probe quite extensively about family relationships and how the candidate carved out his/her own turf with his/her family.[12]

We'll talk more about how birth order principles apply to business in chapter 10.

Born to Rebel

As you've already seen in this book, there's no doubt that birth order theory is valuable in the practical world. Yet "experts" have continued to criticize it. However, in 1996 Frank Sulloway, a research scholar in the science technology and society program at the Massachusetts Institute of Technology, published *Born to Rebel: Birth Order Family Dynamics and Creative Lives*, a book that contained overwhelming statistical evidence that birth order theory does have credence and validity.

Sulloway had been researching birth order for twenty-six years. Using an approach he calls "meta-analysis" (essentially the combining of many research studies by use of the computer), Sulloway amassed up to a million biographical points of information on more than 6,500 people who have lived in the last 500 years. Included were 3,890 scientists who took part in 28 scientific revolutions. Sulloway also studied hundreds of people involved in the French Revolution and the Protestant Reformation, as well as participants in 61 American reform movements.[13]

For instance, here are some of the historical figures he discusses in his book: firstborns Mikhail Gorbachev, Boris Yeltsin, Bill Clinton, Jimmy Carter, Saddam Hussein, Jesse Jackson, Winston Churchill, William Shakespeare, George Washington, and Franklin D. Roosevelt (an only child); middleborns Yasser Arafat, George Bush, Fidel Castro, Napoléon Bonaparte, Henry VIII, Patrick Henry, and Adolf Hitler; lastborns Ho Chi Minh, Ronald Reagan, Mohandas K. Gandhi, and Voltaire.

In the fields of science and philosophy, Sulloway mentions firstborns Albert Einstein, Galileo, and Leonardo da Vinci (only child); middleborns Louis Pasteur, Albert Schweitzer, and Charles Darwin; lastborns Copernicus, Francis Bacon, and René Descartes. Copernicus, you will recall, was the scientist who introduced the revolutionary idea that the world was not flat but indeed round and revolved around the sun—he was the youngest of four children. Charles Darwin, the proponent of evolution, and his disciple, Alfred Russell Wallace, were both the fifth of six children.

Although there are areas where I don't agree with Sulloway, he did a masterful job in disputing the claims that birth order is all hocus-pocus and worthless speculation.[14]

The bottom line to all of Sulloway's mental toil (it makes this baby of the family tired just to think about it) is this: down through history, firstborns have been the ones who were conservative and willing to stick to the status quo and tradition, while laterborns were the ones who wanted to change things and even start revolutions. According to Sulloway (who is a laterborn himself), laterborns are more open-minded than firstborns. They are "born to rebel"—willing to take risks and do away with sacred cows.

None of Sulloway's findings concerning the characteristics of firstborns and laterborns were news to me. They fit right in with what I've been saying for more than thirty-five years. And as you keep reading *The Birth Order Book*, the characteristics of the birth orders will make sense to you too. You'll have those "aha" moments where you say, "So *that's* why I do this, . . . why he does that. Now I get it!"

I guarantee it.

4

First Come, First Served

Firstborns

It's time to take a closer look at firstborns—officially defined as the oldest in the family. But don't forget the variables we just covered in chapters 2 and 3. Firstborn personalities can also be created by being the oldest of your sex, having a five-year (or more) gap between you and the child above you of the same sex, or achieving a role reversal and taking over the firstborn privileges and responsibilities.

If you are a firstborn (or an only child),[1] you are a much different person than you would have been had you been born later. If you are a laterborn, realize that a lot of things would be different—and so would you—had you been born first.

The Four-Corner Birth Order Exercise

In my family and parenting seminars, I start by asking attendees to join one of four groups: only children in one corner, firstborns in a second, middleborns in a third, and lastborns in a fourth. Then I tell the groups, "Just chat a bit but remain in your circle."

Casually I move from one group to another and leave a piece of paper facedown in the center of each group. The papers contain identical instructions:

> Congratulations! You are the leader of this group. Please introduce yourself to the others in your group, then have each person do the same. As you talk together, make a list of personality characteristics that you all seem to share. Be prepared to report back to the rest of the seminar with your composite picture of yourselves. Please start to work immediately.

I return to the front of the room, and all the groups keep waiting for me to give some kind of verbal instructions, but I say nothing. Instead I pretend to look busy as I leaf through papers, waiting for "birth order nature" to take its course. Who will pick up the piece of paper first? Almost invariably, a person in the only and firstborn groups picks up the paper and reads the instructions. Someone in the middleborn group soon follows suit. In no time, three groups in the room are busy with their assignments.

Oh yes, the fourth group? The lastborns are usually still milling around, their piece of paper lying on the floor unread.

I wait a few minutes and make one more announcement: "You have only a few more minutes to finish your assignment. Be ready to report to the rest of the group at that time!"

The onlies and firstborns look up like startled deer and redouble their efforts to finish the assigned task. While the middles don't look quite as impressed, they do try to press on toward the finish. The lastborns, however, are usually having such a good time that they don't even hear what I said. In fact, I remember one seminar where the babies all milled around in the far corner, their circle resembling a figure 8 more than anything else. One man wound up standing on the piece of paper that I placed in the center of his circle, just as oblivious to the proceedings as all the other lastborns in his group.

I'm a lastborn myself, so I'm not trying to make fun of the babies of the family. No doubt if I were put through the same exercise, I'd be the guy standing on the piece of paper! But in the hundreds of times I've conducted this exercise, I can remember only one or two cases when the first person to pick up the piece of paper and start "obeying instructions" did *not* come from the firstborn or onlies circles.

Even the reports from the four groups bear out the classic birth order traits: The firstborns report that a definite leader took charge. Among the confident only children, a power struggle often ensues over who will take charge, but it is finally settled. Of all the groups, the middle children probably enjoy the exercise the most as they get to know each other, have little trouble negotiating who will be leader, and do their assignment with no problem. As for the babies, what can I say? Life is a beach!

Driven to Success

If you recall the little quiz you took in chapter 1, you'll also realize that several typical characteristics of firstborns or onlies are borne out in my lab exercise. Firstborns or onlies tend to be conscientious, well organized, serious, goal oriented, achieving, people pleasers, and believers in authority.

> *Firstborns are often the achievers because they are driven toward success and stardom in their given fields.*

And when you add other signs of firstborns and onlies, such as perfectionistic, reliable, list maker, critical, scholarly, self-sacrificing, conservative, supporter of law and order, legalistic, and self-reliant, you can see why firstborns usually get more ink in the write-ups of life. In fact, I wrote a whole book on the subject of firstborns: *Born to Win*.[2]

Firstborns are often the achievers because they are driven toward success and stardom in their given fields.

The world cannot ignore the firstborns. If you aren't one, you have to deal with them somewhere along the line. It may have started early when your older firstborn brother or sister wound up as your babysitter, something that didn't necessarily sit well with either of you. On the other hand, some firstborns become the guardian and protector of their younger brothers or sisters. That's what happened with me. My firstborn sister, Sally, eight years older, often went out of her way to care for her baby brother.

> **The Qualities of a Firstborn**
>
> perfectionistic, reliable, conscientious, a list maker, well organized, hard driving, a natural leader, critical, serious, scholarly, logical, doesn't like surprises, a techie

For example, when I started kindergarten I cried for the first two weeks because they had me in the afternoon session and I had to get to school by myself—a scary proposition for a little cub. Sally couldn't take me because she was in school herself, and my mom wasn't available because she was working as a superintendent of a convalescent home for children. We weren't your classic *Leave It to Beaver* family that was so prevalent in those days. It seemed I was the only kid in the neighborhood whose mom worked. (In fact, I still have a scar on my knuckle, which I cut on some kid's tooth when he teased me about my mom working.) After two weeks of hearing me sniffle, the kindergarten teacher relented and switched me to mornings so that big sister Sally could bring me to school.

One of my early memories is sitting on Sally's bike, barely making the pedals turn because my legs weren't long enough, as Sally and her friend Martha walked beside me for over a mile, helping me steer.

Sally was always sacrificing for me. I'll never forget the time when I was about 8 and Sally and I took the bus from our home to the Buffalo city limits, eight miles away. Our destination was a low-budget department store called W. T. Grants, which had a luncheonette. Sally offered to treat me to whatever I wanted, and as I looked at the menu, I saw hamburgers for thirty cents and turkey sandwiches for eighty cents. We seldom got real sliced turkey at our house, and my mouth watered.

"Can I have the turkey sandwich?" I asked.

"Of course you can. I'm treating," Sally said as she dug into her hard-earned babysitting money.

I have never forgotten how good that sandwich tasted and how she spent what was then "big bucks" to make me happy.

Sally also used to throw little tea parties with me as the honored guest. In the summers we'd have them on our lawn; in the winters we would stay inside. But summer or winter, Sally did make her baby brother do something to help with the party. I had to make a one-mile round trip to Hildebrand's store on foot to get the goodies for the party, which were always the same: Pepsi and potato chips.

Now that we're adults, Sally still goes out of her way for her little brother. Every fall, after we've returned to Tucson for the coming school session, she goes out to our summer house on Chautauqua Lake, not far from her home in Jamestown, New York, and covers all the furniture for the winter.

The Compliant, Nurturing, Caregiving Firstborn

Sally, you see, has always been what is called a "compliant firstborn." She wants to please. Because I have been painting firstborns with some pretty broad brush strokes as organized, goal oriented, achievers, critical, and so on, you may think they are basically all bossy types who want to run the show. Many firstborns do fit the description of strong willed and aggressive. But there are plenty of firstborns who are compliant—they're the model children who grew up to be pleasers of others. They still have all those firstborn qualities, but they're always in a very reliable, conscientious, "how can I please you?" package.

Compliant firstborns tend to be good students and good workers because they started out with a very strong need for Mom and Dad's approval. Then, of course, they need the approval of other authority figures: teachers, coaches, bosses. When asked to do something, their response is, "Yes, Mom . . . yes, Dad . . . yes, sir . . . I'll be glad to do it." Who doesn't want a few children or employees like that around?

A classic example of a compliant firstborn is my wife, Sande. Once we were at a five-star restaurant in Tucson, and our meal had been served in the usual impeccable and precise manner. As I ate with gusto, I glanced over at Sande. She was simply picking around the edges of her poached salmon.

"How's your dinner?" I asked. "Does everything taste okay?"

"Oh . . . yes. Everything's great. Isn't this one of the nicest restaurants you could ever ask for?"

I went back to eating, but Sande continued picking and not really getting into that poached salmon. Finally I voiced my suspicions: "Honey, is your salmon really done to your liking?"

"Well, it's really not quite cooked in the middle . . ."

Actually, the poached salmon was so raw it should have still been swimming upriver to spawn. As a baby of the family, I've found that compliance has never been one of my strong suits. I quickly let the waiter know the condition of the salmon, and he as well as the maître d' and chef were horrified. In no time, an entirely new serving of salmon appeared, cooked to perfection. And a little later, the chef sent out a peace offering in the form of a giant baked Alaska dessert, "compliments of the house with apologies to madam for the inconvenience."

The story of the uncooked salmon nicely illustrates Sande's "I'd rather not complain about it but just grin and bear it" nature. Like my sister, Sally, Sande is a pleaser, a nurturer, and a caregiver, all classic characteristics of the compliant firstborn. And if you're thinking that Cubby Bear Leman is lucky to have two women like that in his life, you are absolutely right!

The downside of being a compliant firstborn is that you can attract the great white sharks of life. I often counsel compliant firstborns who are getting chunks taken out of them by a spouse, a boss, or friends. The classic scenario includes a compliant firstborn working in middle management for a superintendent or manager who has a way of piling on the work. As he drops little projects on this firstborn's desk, he also manages to mention that "evaluations are coming up soon."

> *The downside of being a compliant firstborn is that you can attract the great white sharks of life.*

While having a wife and four kids at home to feed and clothe is an obvious motivation, an even bigger one for the compliant firstborn is the psychological hammer that's been pounding on him ever since childhood. He's always been the responsible one that had to get everything done—take out the garbage, mow the lawn, wash the dishes—because his brothers and sisters were too little or perhaps undependable. Parents have a way of relying on (and taking advantage of) their firstborn child. I call it the "let Ryan the firstborn do it" syndrome.

Many other such scenarios could quickly be sketched. Team up the compliant firstborn with a selfish, narcissistic, or insensitive boss or spouse and you have the making of trouble in River City in a hurry. Compliant firstborns are well known for taking it and being walked on by a world that loves to take advantage of them. They are also known for nursing their resentments quietly, and then venting with one grand explosion. And that's usually when they come to see me.

Aggressive Firstborns: Movers and Shakers

While compliant firstborns have a strong need to be conscientious, caregiving servants, there is another brand of firstborn who is assertive, strong willed, a high achiever, and a hard driver. These assertive firstborns set high goals and have a strong need to be king or queen pin. And along the way, they often develop badgerlike qualities—in other words, they can scratch, claw, and bite.

One classic example of the hard-driving, assertive firstborn is the executive who goes around uptight and immersed in his or her work for fifty weeks a year. Then, while on a two-week vacation, this same executive becomes a new person. I

> *Assertive firstborns set high goals and have a strong need to be king or queen pin.*

have had wives tell me, "When we go on vacation, Harry is just great. He relaxes and lets go. He's almost normal with the kids and with me. But about two days before vacation is over, he gets his game face back. Even before we get home, his old hard-driving personality is in high gear."

In recent years a growing part of my practice has included conducting seminars for groups of corporate executives. I make it a point to do a little surveying to see just how well firstborns are represented in these groups. In one CEO organization, nineteen of the twenty attendees were firstborns. In a meeting of the Young Presidents' Organization, twenty-three of the twenty-six dynamic men and women present told me they were firstborns in their family.

Exacting, Precise, and Picky

While some firstborns become powerful leader types, others stay in the background doing exacting work like editing, bookkeeping, and accounting. Over the years while publishing more than thirty-five books, I have had twenty-seven editors, all firstborns or only children, with one exception. He turned out to be the secondborn male in his family who had done a role reversal on his older brother and was, in effect, a functional firstborn.

Being a baby of the family, I deeply appreciate editors and what they can do to save me from disaster. But I really don't know much about them except that they love red pencils and ask lots of picky questions, such as, "What is this sentence that starts on page 33 and ends on page 35?"[3]

One of the most striking examples I ever saw regarding firstborns and exacting professions occurred when I spoke to the Ohio Society of Accountants. After being introduced, I stood looking at 221 accountants, who were either giving me baleful stares or glancing at their watches. Deciding I needed to loosen them up a bit, I said, "Will all of you firstborns and only children please rise." I wasn't too surprised when almost the entire room stood up! So I asked those remaining to stand up next, and in that small group we counted nineteen middle children and lastborns. Before letting them sit down, I had one more question: "What are *you* doing *here*?"

Everyone roared with laughter, and had the evening ended right there, it would have been a success. It isn't often that you can get more than two hundred accountants to smile, much less laugh aloud!

Accountants take their jobs seriously. In fact, many a CEO will tell you that a company rises or falls based on how careful a "bean counter" they have. Harvey Mackay, chairman and CEO of Mackay Envelope Corporation and author of many bestsellers on business, including *Swim with the Sharks without Being Eaten Alive*, believes that the first person you need to hire (after yourself) is a good accountant.[4]

When I interviewed Mackay, his powerful aggressiveness came out immediately. Firstborns are typically analytical and love to ask questions. My interview with Mackay was over the telephone, and while I couldn't see him, I quickly became convinced I was talking to a firstborn (he's the firstborn male in his family). After ten minutes, he was still asking me the questions, and I was the one who was supposed to be conducting the interview.[5]

Guess Who's the Oldest

You can find firstborns as leaders in all kinds of situations. For example, if I asked you to name one of the Mandrell sisters, chances are you'd think of Barbara, and there's a good reason for that: she's the oldest, resourceful, outgoing, and definitely the leader. Few people mention Louise or "the other one," Irlene.

Among contemporary actors working today are the four Baldwin brothers. Which one can you name? Probably Alec, who is, of course, the oldest.

What about the Smothers brothers? Did you think of Tommy? That's not surprising because he's the oldest, even if he does act like a hypersensitive baby while on stage. My wife, Sande, and I have had dinner with the Smothers brothers, and let me assure you, Tommy is the real leader of this duo. In fact, Dick confided that he had moved to the other end of the country just to get away from Tommy's "controlling nature." I looked at Tommy, and he just smiled.

Here's one more example of two brothers—the ones who are credited with making the first successful flight in an airplane. If I asked you to name one of the Wright brothers, odds are good that you'd say, "Wilbur." Strange, but he was the oldest by four years. Think about how hard it is to name professional athletes who are siblings and who excel in the same sport. I love sports, and I can name only a couple: Venus and Serena Williams, professional tennis players; and the Manning brothers in football. Indeed, siblings tend to go in different directions.

Sixty-four percent of the US presidents have been firstborns or functional firstborns. There was Jimmy Carter, a serious, studious, overachieving governor of Georgia who out-and-out worked his way to the presidency of the United States. But standing in stark contrast to this firstborn was his baby brother, Billy, who got his own share of the spotlight for his beer drinking and rude, off-the-cuff remarks, many of which were designed to embarrass his big brother.

Living High on Stress

Outstanding leaders and achievers they may be, but hard-driving firstborns often pay the price. If their bodies don't break down, relationships with family or friends usually do. I doubt if it's a coincidence that Lee Iacocca, one of the most capable and successful CEOs who ever lived, has gone through three divorces. In fact, it's practically a birth order rule of thumb, particularly for firstborns: the very traits and abilities that enable you to succeed at work, at church, or in other organizations will often work against you in your close personal relationships.

> *The very traits and abilities that enable you to succeed at work, at church, or in other organizations will often work against you in your close personal relationships.*

While on an American Airlines flight, I was fortunate enough to sit across the aisle from Robert Crandall, former chairman of the board and president of American Airlines. As we got acquainted, I learned that he was a firstborn, which didn't surprise me at all because of his well-known, hard-driving, levelheaded leadership abilities.

Later I had the opportunity to interview Crandall for a business book I was writing. When I asked him what he thought of the maxim "Put your spouse first," he responded, "Yes, that's true. On the other hand, you have to have a spouse who recognizes that the number of times she can ask to be first is limited." He went on to say that putting one's spouse first doesn't have much to do with business, that it's more of a "personal values set" than a "business values set."

And therein lies the rub. Trying to separate business from the family often results in the family getting the short end of the stick.[6]

Because I fly so much, I make it a habit to do informal surveys of airline pilots regarding their birth order. Flying is such an exacting task that demands perfection, so it doesn't surprise me that pilots are usually firstborns. In fact, out of ninety-eight men and two women, my informal survey revealed that 88 percent were firstborns or only children. On a recent United Airlines flight, the captain came out of the cockpit and came down the aisle greeting passengers, including me. So I asked him, "How is the firstborn captain doing today?"

He gave me the strangest look. "Have we met?"

"No, but you *are* a firstborn, aren't you?"

"Well, yes, I am," he said, and in less than five minutes we were talking about a lot more than what a lovely day it was in the friendly skies. As the tears rolled down his cheeks, he told me about his third wife serving him with divorce papers. He was one of the best in the high-stress business called flying, but at home he had crashed three times.

Sometimes the hard-driving firstborn personality can go beyond neglecting family or friends and all the way to the ultimate tragedy. Do you remember Cain, the first murderer in recorded history? He thought his sacrifice was every bit as good or better than Abel's. But God didn't, and he wouldn't accept it because it was the "fruit of the ground." So driven, aggressive, firstborn Cain lured his secondborn brother, Abel, out into the fields and killed him. When the firstborn, who is a goal-oriented achiever, starts thinking, *Winning is everything*, he can shove aside values like being law abiding, loyal, or self-sacrificing. Instead, he will do anything to win.

What Makes the Firstborn Tick?

Whether compliant or powerful and assertive, there are at least two good reasons why firstborns come in such downright upright (and often a little uptight) packages. Those two reasons are Mom and Dad. Oldest children serve as "guinea pigs" for parents who have never done this kind of thing before. No wonder the kids have more than their share of stress. Brand-new parents are typically a bundle of ambivalence—one side overprotective, anxious, tentative, and inconsistent; the other side strict, disciplined, demanding, always pushing, and encouraging better performance.

> *Oldest children serve as "guinea pigs" for parents who have never done this kind of thing before. No wonder the kids have more than their share of stress.*

Everything about a firstborn child is important. While little Fletcher or Maddie is still on the way, the very air is charged with expectancy in more ways than one. With grand anticipation, young parents celebrate with baby showers, picking out names, choosing wallpaper for the nursery, and buying baby clothes and toys. (And if the parents are firstborns or onlies themselves, add to that list "starting piggy banks, insurance policies, and college funds.")

Few will deny that the family overdoes things with the firstborn. Parents as well as grandparents record every cry, look, whim, or move with a video camera. They're sure to fill the family photo album with dozens (even hundreds) of pictures. Research indicates that firstborns walk and talk earlier than laterborns. No surprise there. With all the coaching, prodding, and encouragement they get, they probably do it in self-defense!

That firstborn children often go on to become the leaders and achievers in life isn't necessarily their idea, but with only parents (and maybe grandparents, aunts, and uncles) for role models, they naturally take on more grown-up characteristics. This is why firstborns are often serious and not much for surprises. They prefer to know what's happening and when; they thrive in being in control, on time, and organized— all characteristics that stand adults in good stead.

Also remember that a child's personality is pretty well formed by the age of 5. When the firstborn is very young—starting before he is even 12 months old—he is already observing his parents and noting the *right way* to do things. When you think about it, firstborns basically learn only from adults—those big, perfect people who do everything correctly. No wonder they're so willing to break their necks to be right, on time, and organized.

> *Research indicates that firstborns walk and talk earlier than laterborns. No surprise there. With all the coaching, prodding, and encouragement they get, they probably do it in self-defense!*

Perks and Privileges

Anything firstborns do is a big deal, so this attention encourages firstborns to achieve. Because family and friends take the firstborn seriously, he or she often develops greater confidence. It's no wonder that firstborns go on to become president of the club, the company, and even the country. While over 64 percent of US presidents have been firstborns or functional firstborns, only 5 of them have been true babies. As I have contemplated why so few babies have made it to the White House, it occurs to me that maybe they just couldn't find it!

With their strong powers of concentration, patience, organization, and conscientiousness, firstborns have a distinct advantage in many professions. I have often asked at seminars, "If you were manager of a bank and were hiring more tellers, whom would you choose?" Many answer they would take the lastborn children, because they would be so friendly and outgoing as they work with the public. I always have to disagree, however, because while it helps to be friendly with the public, it would be all too typical of a lastborn bank teller to turn to the teller next to her and say, "Helen, could you please take over for me? I've got to have a Coke, and there are still fourteen people in my line."

And then there is that lastborn problem of losing things: "Let's see, I know that $135,000 is around here someplace. . . ."

Before I go any further with this illustration, let's remember the variables and the exceptions. I'm not saying that all babies of the family are automatically less conscientious or careless. I'm saying that the law of averages reveals that the firstborn is a much better bet to be careful, conscientious, and perfectionistic—all important traits for someone entrusted with a lot of responsibility. By their very nature, firstborns hate to make mistakes. They are careful and calculating and sticklers for rules and regulations. In a fussy, precise place like a bank, these characteristics are not only useful, they're almost imperative.

Pressures and Problems

The other side of the coin for the firstborn, however, is that all that attention—the "oohing" and "ahhing," the spotlight, and the responsibility—adds up to *pressure*. For one thing, ask any firstborn for memories of what he used to hear from Mom or Dad when he was a child and those other big role models he was always trying to emulate. Bet you a hundred bucks the firstborn will remember hearing things like this:

"I don't care what *he* did—you're the oldest!"

"What? You don't want to take your little brother (or sister) with you? Fine—stay home!"

"Couldn't you keep your little brother (or sister) out of trouble?"

"What kind of example is that?"

"Will you please act your age?"

"When are you going to grow up?"

"He's littler than you. You should know better!"

Many firstborns who remember comments like these can put them in perspective. They smile wryly or just shake their heads and grin. Others aren't quite so easygoing about it, such as the firstborn woman I received a letter from: "Excuse me, I remember all the pressure of being the oldest, but where was the privilege? I seem to have missed that along the way."

One thing many firstborns can tell you is that, while they had to toe the mark, their younger brothers and sisters got off easy, or, as I often hear, "got away with mur-der." Firstborns do take the brunt of discipline as parents work themselves into their parenting role.

> *All that attention—the "oohing" and "ahhing," the spotlight, and the responsibility—adds up to pressure.*

Along with getting the most discipline, firstborns also get the most work. When you need something done in the family, who ya gonna call? That dependable firstborn is likely to get the assignment, whether it's running down to the corner for a loaf of bread or picking up the dog plops.

And then, of course, there's the infamous task that most firstborn adults can remember: being left in charge of younger brothers and sisters instead of being able to go off with their own friends. Invariably the firstborns wind up being in charge a lot. Older sisters particularly are very dependable and con-scientious as a rule, and many mothers take advantage of this. Firstborn girls often get labels like "mother hen" or even "the warden."

Yes, it's possible that some firstborns do enjoy the babysit-ting role, but sooner or later—usually sooner—it turns into a drag. And it's not unusual for older children to try to ditch younger ones who tag along with them. In the dedication of this book, you may have noticed my special recognition for my brother, Jack, who often tried to lose his baby brother (me) in the woods!

Poor Jack. Sometimes I think he's still mad because Mom and Dad bought me a new Roadmaster bike complete with kickstand when I was 6, and he had to make do with his old fenderless model. What really got to him, though, was that I wouldn't use my kickstand. I'd just throw my shiny new bike down on the driveway when I cruised into home base.

The bottom line is that parents expect too much of firstborns. They are often forced to be the pacesetters and standard-bearers of the family and are urged to follow in Father's and Mother's footsteps into professions or ways of life they really don't want. Today the age-old conflict between father and firstborn son still rages. The father wants the son to take over the family business or accomplish something he never accomplished. The son wants to start his *own* business raising earthworms or maybe become a fry cook at Denny's, a shepherd, a chicken rancher, or just a vegetarian.

Firstborn boys are usually pressured to be the "crown prince" of the family, and firstborn girls get almost as much pressure to be the "crown princess." It's no wonder, then, that you can hear firstborns saying as they are growing up or even after reaching adulthood:

Good Rules of Thumb

1. Don't expect your older children to be babysitters for the younger ones. (Yes, I realize there are finances, unforeseen emergencies, and overloaded schedules. Sometimes it will happen. But don't do it as a rule. It's not fair to the firstborn.)

2. Don't make your firstborn do more than his or her share of the work. Everyone in the family—even little children—can help out according to their age. Don't make your firstborn responsible to pick up the tasks that your other children don't complete.

3. Remember that your child is a child, not an adult.

"Everyone depends on me."

"I can't get away with anything."

"It's tough being the oldest."

"I was never allowed to be a kid."

"If I don't do it, it won't get done."

"If I don't do it, it won't get done right."

"Boy, if I acted the way my little brother does . . ."

"Why do I have to do it? No one else does anything around here."

A Firstborn's Worst Nightmare

I've saved the worst nightmare for most firstborns (and only children) for last. I'll just mention it here and then give it full treatment in the next two chapters. I'm talking about perfectionism. Ironically, many discouraged firstborn perfectionists challenge me, saying they can't possibly be perfectionists because they are so messy. These little scenarios often go something like this:

Firstborn Frank: Your birth order system doesn't fit my family at all—you say firstborns are neat. Well, I'm a firstborn and I'm known for having the sloppiest desk in the office. In fact, the last time anyone saw the top of my desk was the day before I started working for the company. So what do you say to that, Dr. Leman?

Dr. Leman: That's interesting. What do you do for a living?

Frank: I'm an electrical engineer.

Dr. Leman: Sounds like a very structured area—lots of math and mental discipline?

Frank: True enough, but how do you account for the sloppy desk?

Dr. Leman: So your desk is sloppy. Can you find what you need on it?

Frank: Of course. I usually know what's in every pile.

Dr. Leman: So you have order within your disorder. You are in a very disciplined occupation—engineering. And while your desk is sloppy, you still feel you are organized. My guess is you are something of a perfectionist, and perfectionists are known for having sloppy desks as a means of covering their discouragement for not always having life go just the way they want. Another thing about perfectionists—when they find one thing that is wrong or imperfect, they tend to generalize that one inconsistency and want to throw out the entire package. Maybe you're trying to throw out the birth order baby with the bathwater.

Frank: I believe in being consistent and doing things right. I'm never satisfied—I always think I could do a little better job. I'm always trying harder.

Exactly. Frank has described a discouraged perfectionist (himself) to a T. But Frank is only one example of discouraged perfectionism. I get challenged by many others:

"You don't know my husband. He's the oldest in his family, but he can't fix anything around the house. Every time he takes something apart, he loses half the pieces. The only thing he has ever perfected is how to ruin the plumbing, the lawn mower. . . . Whatever he tries to repair is doomed."

"You should live with my wife. She's a firstborn, but the only way I can get her anywhere on time is to tell her we are due thirty to sixty minutes earlier than the actual appointment."

I still say that people like that husband, wife, and, of course, firstborn Frank, are odds-on favorites to be discouraged perfectionists. I'll even go so far as to say all firstborns and only children are perfectionists—many of whom become discouraged. In over thirty-five years of counseling, most of my clients have been firstborn or only children

> *"I'm never satisfied—I always think I could do a little better job. I'm always trying harder."*

who have been masking their perfectionism with behavior that doesn't seem to fit. Perfectionism is the major problem for almost all firstborns and only children. At worst, it can be a curse, and at best, a heavy burden. That's why I'm dedicating the next couple of chapters to those of you who never feel good enough.

Assessing Your Strengths and Weaknesses

Are you a firstborn? Are you a compliant or an aggressive firstborn? In what areas do you struggle? In what areas do you succeed? As we end this chapter, take a look at the chart "Strengths and Weaknesses of Firstborns" below.

1. Set aside a few minutes to consider each trait. Decide if each trait is a strength or a weakness for you.
2. If the trait is a weakness, what changes could you make to improve in that area?
3. If it's a strength, how could you capitalize on that strength or develop it even further?

Strengths and Weaknesses of Firstborns

Typical Traits	Strengths	Weaknesses
Leadership ability	Take charge, know what to do	May undermine the initiative of those who lean on them too much or may come off as too overbearing or aggressive
Aggressive	Command respect; others want to follow their unflinching leadership	Can run roughshod over others; may be insensitive and tend to be selfish; too focused on the goal and not enough on the feelings of others
Compliant	Cooperative, easy to work with, good team player	Can be taken advantage of, bullied, bluffed
Perfectionistic	Always do things right and leave no stone unturned to do a thorough job	Tend to criticize themselves and/or others too much; never satisfied; may procrastinate because they fear they cannot do a "good enough job"
Organized	Have everything under control; always on top of things; tend to be on time and on schedule	May worry too much about order, process, and rules and not be flexible when it's needed; may show real impatience with anyone who is "disorganized" or not as meticulous; can be upset by surprises

Typical Traits	Strengths	Weaknesses
Driver	Ambitious, enterprising, energetic, willing to sacrifice to be a success	Put themselves or those they work with under too much stress and pressure
List maker	Set goals and reach them; tend to get more done in a day than others; planning the day is a must	May become boxed in, too busy with the to-do list to see the big picture and what needs to be done right now
Logical	Known as straight thinkers; can be counted on not to be compulsive or to go off half-cocked	May believe they're always right and fail to pay attemtion to the more intuitive opinions of others
Scholarly	Tend to be voracious readers and accumulators of information and facts; good problem solvers who think things through	May spend too much time gathering facts when there are other things that need to be done; may be so serious they fail to see the humor in situations when humor is desperately needed

Ask Yourself

1. Am I involved in too many activities? Which ones could I give up?
2. Do I know how to say no? Can I think of a recent example of saying no graciously but firmly?
3. How much of a problem is perfectionism for me? Can I state the difference between pursuing perfectionism and seeking excellence?
4. Am I a slave to my to-do lists, or do I use lists to organize my life and keep it balanced?
5. Have I forgiven my parents for any pressures they put on me while growing up? Can I honestly say there were privileges as well as pressures in being a firstborn?
6. Am I a compliant or aggressive firstborn? What are my best attributes? What are my key faults, and what do I need to do to improve?
7. If I know I'm an aggressive firstborn, am I willing to ask my spouse, children, or fellow workers for feedback on my strengths and weaknesses? What would my family say to me about how much time I spend with them?
8. If I feel jealousy or resentment toward any of my siblings, am I willing to confess and try to make it right? When and where could I do this?

9. Do I care too much about what others think of me? Why or why not? Have I been in any situation recently in which this "caring too much" has come to the forefront and caused trouble for me?

10. How good am I at spotting flaws at fifty paces? Would my family or friends say I am too critical?

5

How Good Is "Good Enough"?

If someone were to ask you, "Just how good is 'good enough'?" what would you say?

Would you rate perfectionism as a problem? Why or why not? After all, couldn't the world use a few more perfectionists instead of putting up with all of the sloppy, slipshod work and service that goes on every day?

So which of the following describes perfectionism best for you?

A. a burden
B. a cause of stress and even disease
C. slow suicide
D. a strength

According to my counseling experience, any or all of the A, B, or C answers is correct. The incorrect answer is D. Perfectionism is not a strength. If you think it is, I hope to convince you otherwise.

But first, you need to get a feeling for how much of a perfectionist you are. Take the "Are You a Perfectionist?" quiz on page 102. Go ahead—I'll wait right here until you're done.

So how did you do? Does your score help you understand why sometimes you don't feel good enough?

Perfectionism in the Personals

My favorite example of a person whom I would rate an extreme perfectionist appears in this ad I once clipped from the personals in a daily newspaper:

> CHRISTIAN, blonde, blue eyes, 5′2″, 100 lbs. prof., Cauc./ female, no depend., wishes to meet Protestant Christian, prof. man in 30s with college degree who has compassion for animals and people, loves nature, exercise and phy. fitness *(no team sports)*, music and dance, church and home life. Desire nonsmoker/nondrinker, slender, 5′7″–6′, lots of head hair, *no chest hair*, intelligent, honest and trustworthy, sense of humor, excellent communicator of feelings, very sensitive, gentle, affectionate, androgynous attitude about roles, giving, encouraging and helpful to others, no temper or *ego problems*, secure within and financially, health conscious, neat and clean, extremely considerate and dependable. I believe in old-fashioned morals and values. If you do, too, and are interested in a possible Christian commitment, write to PO Box 82533. Please include recent color photo and address.

A lot can be read into an ad like this. First of all, let me take a walk on the plank of life and suggest that this woman will be single for a long, long time. Can't you imagine her on a date with a Tom Cruise look-alike and she suddenly spots a chest hair peeking through his polo shirt? End of relationship!

My counselor's eyes suggest the odds are at least 500 to 1 that this blonde, blue-eyed 5′2″, 100-pound professional female is a firstborn or only child. Surely she is a super ex-

Are You a Perfectionist?

If you're a perfectionist, how much of one are you? To find out, fill in the blank next to each question below with 4 for always, 3 for often, 2 for sometimes, and 1 for seldom. Then add up your score.

_____ 1. Mistakes—your own or others'—irritate you.

_____ 2. You feel everyone should be as driven to do his best as you are.

_____ 3. You use the word *should* a lot—as in, "I should have taken care of that," or "We should meet on this immediately."

_____ 4. You find it hard to enjoy success. Even when something goes well, it's easy for you to find the things that could have been just a little better.

_____ 5. One small mistake ruins your day—or at least your morning.

_____ 6. Terms like *good enough* and *just about right* bother you, particularly on the job.

_____ 7. You tend to put things off because you feel you're not quite ready to do the job right.

_____ 8. You find yourself apologizing for something because you could have done it better if you'd had more time.

_____ 9. When in a meeting, working in a team, or in any group situation in the workplace, you prefer to be in control of what's happening.

_____ 10. Realizing your deep need to have all your ducks in a row, you insist that those around you have their ducks in the same row (i.e., think exactly the way you do).

_____ 11. You tend to see the glass half-empty instead of half-full.

Scoring:

0–22: Why are you reading this chapter anyway? You're certainly not even close to being a perfectionist.

23–27: mild perfectionist

28–36: medium perfectionist

37–44: extreme perfectionist (you're too hard on yourself and everyone else) treme perfectionist who would score 30 or more on the "Are You a Perfectionist?" quiz. This kind of personality walks around holding up what I call the high-jump bar of life. She is always raising the bar a little higher and is a master at defeating herself at every turn.

A True Perfectionist at 18 Months

We all develop our particular lifestyle (the way we act, think, and feel) when we are very young, and that includes perfectionists. Sande and I saw the handwriting on the wall with our oldest daughter, Holly, when she was only 18 months old. We were on an R & R trip to California and the seashore, and it was the first time on any beach for Holly. She soon discovered sand and came toddling over, holding up one finger with three or four grains of sand stuck to it.

"Ugh, ugh," she grunted, very displeased with all this "mess" and wondering if there wasn't something we could do about it. Before our eyes—at the tender age of 18 months— Holly was displaying signs of the true perfectionist. Despite our best efforts to encourage and reinforce Holly rather than find fault or pick flaws, she has grown into a mature woman who seeks perfection in all she does. And that's why, as I mentioned earlier, her high school literature students get detention when they come to class unprepared. Holly knows she would have had her assignments in on time (she always did in high school and in four years of college), so she wants her students to do the same.

But while Holly is far from being a slob, she is hardly the neatest one in the family. That honor goes to her sister Krissy, our secondborn middle child (more about her in chapter 8). But I don't find it odd at all that our perfectionist, firstborn daughter acts a bit out of character and isn't always concerned about having a perfectly neat room. It's her own way of covering her frustration with life's less-than-perfect warts and bumps.

People who score in the medium-to-extreme perfectionist range on the quiz usually fall into the category I call "discouraged perfectionists." They go through life telling themselves the lie "I count only when I'm perfect." It becomes their lifestyle. I'm not talking about lifestyle in the sense of what you wear, drive, eat, or drink. *Lifestyle* is a term coined by Dr. Alfred Adler, who used it to refer to how people function psychologically to reach their goals (more on this in chapter 12).

Beware the Ultracritical Perfectionist

When the discouraged perfectionist reaches a certain point, she can become ultracritical not only of herself but of others. The person in the want ad, for example, may somehow find a man who happens to meet all her "requirements" and is foolish enough to marry her. But after the honeymoon is over, he will almost certainly find he has an ultracritical discouraged perfectionist on his hands, and he will pay a big price.

Ultracritical discouraged perfectionists hide behind a mask of "being objective." Their favorite motto is: "The good is the enemy of the best!" They are such flaw pickers that they can become a constant irritant to everyone. They can even become toxic, making fellow workers so angry or so worried about their performance that they can't do a job properly or safely.

> *Realize you can never please this ultracritical perfectionist because he cannot please himself.*

I always tell managers and executives that if they have a severely discouraged ultracritical perfectionist on the payroll and he or she is working directly with other people, they should consider strong measures. First, this severely discouraged perfectionist needs a friendly warning and a chance to modify his or her behavior. If the extreme perfectionism continues, the best option is to transfer this person to another area—preferably where he or she can work mostly alone. And if that isn't possible, perhaps this ultracritical perfectionist should be advised to look for another line of work.

Speaking of looking for another line of work, if you are serving under an extremely critical perfectionist who happens to be the office manager, the president, the owner of the company, or some other position of tremendous power, do not get down on yourself because of the constant criticism. Instead,

> *For the perfectionist, nothing is ever good enough, and he or she is never quite finished with the task.*

realize you can never please this ultracritical perfectionist because he cannot please himself. Perhaps the job pays so well that you can hang on and be hammered with the negatives while getting very little positive reinforcement. On the other hand, if self-fulfillment and job satisfaction are really important, it's best to consider moving on.

The Cycle of Perfectionism

For the perfectionist, nothing is ever good enough, and he or she is never quite finished with the task. The cycle of perfectionism generally follows these steps:

1. The perfectionist is the originator of the motto "It's all or nothing." He is sure he must be perfect in everything he does. He tends to be a streak performer; when he's hot, he's hot, and when he's not, he's a mess.
2. This leads to biting off more than he can chew, perhaps the perfectionist's major problem. As a perfectionist, he can always take on one more thing, even when his schedule is absolutely full and running over. This leads toward the next step in spiraling downward to defeat.

3. The hurdle effect causes the perfectionist to panic. He looks down the track and sees all those hurdles ahead, and each hurdle gets a little higher than the last one. The hurdles aren't necessarily there, but they are perceived obstacles, and they are overwhelming. *How did I get into this mess? How am I ever going to get out?* are the typical laments of the perfectionist.

4. As the hurdles seem to grow taller and taller, the perfectionist compounds his problems by maximizing failures and minimizing successes. If a perfectionist makes mistakes, he internalizes them, chews on them, and goes over and over in his mind what went wrong. If he manages to do something right, he thinks, *It could have been better.*

5. When the pressure becomes too great, the perfectionist may bail out, quitting the project or turning it in less than well done with the excuse, "There just wasn't enough time."

6. Whether the perfectionist manages to finish his job or backs out of it because it simply proved too much, he is always left feeling he must try harder. He is the original victim of what I call the "Avis complex." For years, Avis has willingly placed themselves in a secondary position to Hertz. The Avis motto? "Yeah, we're in second place, but *we try harder.*" To me, those words sum up the quandary of the perfectionist: sure that he's number two (or lower), he's never satisfied and always shooting to be better.

The Avis complex doesn't haunt only "average" people. It can be the bane of the celebrity, the highly successful executive, or the genius.

Actor Alec Guinness admitted he was very insecure about his work and added, "I've never done anything I couldn't pull to bits."

Abraham Lincoln presented his Gettysburg Address and then described it as "a flat failure."

Leonardo da Vinci, who was an outstanding painter, sculptor, scientist, engineer, and inventor—actually, one of the world's true geniuses—said, "I have offended God and mankind because my work didn't reach the quality it should have."[1]

Figure 1
The Hopeless Pursuit of Perfection[2]

1. "It's all or nothing. I must be perfect."

2. "There is nothing I can't do or accomplish."

3. "How did I get into this? I'll never be able to get it all done."

4. "It could have been better. I blew it again!"

5. "I am what I do . . . the only thing that counts is results—performance!"

6. "I'll try harder—I know I can do better than that!"

Skilled Procrastinators

This six-step cycle (see diagram above) can be repeated several times a day, depending on what the perfectionist is doing. While going through this cycle, the perfectionist often slips into the habit of procrastinating.

Have you ever known a real procrastinator? (Perhaps you know one all too well.) The procrastinator has a real problem with time, schedules, and deadlines. A major reason behind the procrastination is the perfectionistic fear of failure. The procrastinating perfectionist has such high expectations that he or she is afraid to start a project. He or she would rather stall and rush to get something done at the last minute. Then the procrastinator can say, "If there had been more time, I could have done a much better job."

Recently I did an entire radio show on the topic of perfectionism and feeling that you are not good enough, cannot jump high enough, and can never do anything really well. We had many callers that day who struggle with perfectionism, procrastinating, and just feeling like they don't measure up in life. One of them was Michael, who complained that he never got things accomplished and never finished things (a sure sign of a procrastinating perfectionist). He started projects with his wife or his kids and didn't finish them. He felt overcommitted and admitted he had definitely been biting off more than he could chew.

Michael sounded like the very person I had in mind when I wrote *When Your Best Isn't Good Enough*,[3] a book that zeros in on perfectionism and how to conquer it. While we were on the air, I told Michael I could describe him and his family without ever seeing any of them. I said:

> Sometimes you'll be asked to do something and you'll say no because you'll look at the big picture and say, *This is impossible, I can't do it.* And then you'll move on to something else. Or, as you've already admitted, you will do some things to a certain degree or a certain point and either lose interest or turn left or right at the last minute.
>
> My big guess is that you grew up in a home where criticism reigned. In other words, you had a critical-eyed parent, so you protected yourself from criticism by not finishing things. Your thinking was, *If I don't finish it, how can anyone criticize me?* This, of course, is where self-deception comes in and we become great at lying to ourselves.

Michael replied, "That's almost exactly who I am and what I do. Some days I'll look at the problem and think, *You know, this has eight or nine steps. I can't do this.* Or some days I'll even do two or three steps and then, as you said, turn right or turn left and just walk away from the problem. And that's one of the biggest issues I have—that walking away. I need to stop and say, 'I've committed to this. This is something that needs to get done.'"

As is so often the case, Michael knew the answer to his problem. It was simply a matter of following through and changing his behavior. I asked him if he had liked building models as a kid, and he said that indeed he did—"model cars, stuff like that." I told Michael I found that guys who really struggle with procrastinating and perfectionism usually loved building models or assembling puzzles—anything where all the parts come together.

"Here's the kicker," I added. "You're a very competent person, more competent than you've ever believed yourself to be. If I talked to people who know you well, I believe they would say, 'He's a guy with such great potential. It's unbelievable!'"

It turned out Michael was production manager of a ceramics shop—a very exacting kind of work that is a natural for a perfectionist. I said I was quite sure that people had told him he had done beautiful work on certain ceramic pieces, but inside he was saying, *If you only knew about that little flaw* . . .

"Very, very true," Michael answered. "You know, I recycle a lot of ceramics because of that."

What did Michael need most of all? The permission to be imperfect! I urged him to flaunt his imperfections before his children and to be the first to say to them or to his wife, "Honey, I'm sorry. I was wrong. I shouldn't have said that."

As for getting things done, Michael needed to set some time limits for finishing projects. He had to make the limits

109

reasonable, but at the end of the time stop and accept the job the way it was without trying to perfect it.

So many people who struggle with perfectionism will say things such as, "It's no good," or "Oh, it isn't much—it's really nothing." Those are sure signs of a perfectionist who is fending off criticism. I urged Michael not to be so quick to put himself down. Instead, he needs to start telling himself the truth—that he has really been given a wonderful gift and needs to use that gift in the most positive way he can.

George and the IRS

One of the most unusual procrastinators I ever counseled was a man we'll call George. He came to me because he had not filed his income tax for the last four years. I asked him why. It turned out he had such an elaborate system for keeping records and receipts that reporting his income tax had become an insurmountable task. His family room contained several picnic tables nicely covered with shelf paper. Overflowing on each table were neatly stacked piles of receipts, notes, and bills of sale.

> So many people who struggle with perfectionism will say things such as, "It's no good," or, "Oh, it isn't much—it's really nothing." Those are sure signs of a perfectionist who is fending off criticism.

George kept telling himself the lie that he was dedicated to details and getting things right. Meanwhile, he couldn't sleep because of having all those unpaid taxes hanging over his head. (Or, more precisely, the IRS hanging over his head!)

I wasn't surprised to learn that George's wife was the critical kind (and a perfectionist) who was always on his case about getting things fixed around the house. When she asked him to fix the toaster or the doorjamb or whatever, his reply was standard: "Don't worry, honey. I'll do it tomorrow." Of course, tomorrow came, and the toaster and other things remained unrepaired.

George had so many uncompleted tasks staring him in the face that all he could do was tread water in the swimming pool of life. But no one can tread water forever, and finally George came to see me. He knew he was in trouble, and he wanted some help. After a number of sessions, I finally got him to attack his problems one at a time.

> *Commit to finish one thing before starting another.*

He had to commit to fixing the toaster on a Monday, the door-jamb on a Tuesday, and so on.

We agreed on one inviolate rule: he had to finish one job before he could start another. That's always the key to helping the discouraged perfectionist who procrastinates: commit to finish one thing before starting another. I know that sounds overly simplistic, but it's a basic principle that can do wonders if the procrastinating perfectionist has the commitment to carry it through. As I told George, "Beautiful cathedrals are built one brick at a time."

George must have heard me because he did manage to change. He even committed to a definite schedule for cleaning up his taxes, one step—and one picnic table—at a time. The final irony of this story is that, after paying necessary penalties, George learned that the government owed *him* some money!

Spotting a Flaw at Fifty Paces

Remember my firstborn sister, Sally? I think you could tell from my description of her that she's something of a perfectionist. She continually tries to keep the world straightened up, cleaned up, or shaped up. Here's just one example of what I mean.

A few years ago I bought a boat—a nice nineteen-foot ski boat that I was looking forward to enjoying on Chautauqua Lake in the summertime.

111

I was as proud as any lastborn could be as I backed my new toy into the water and then secured it to the dock. I couldn't wait to show my big sister what I'd purchased, and I didn't have to wait long. Sally drove out from her home in nearby Jamestown and quickly came down to the dock to take a look at baby brother's brand-new toy.

I didn't say a word. I just stepped back and beamed, waiting for her comments.

Sally looked into the boat, and the first words out of her mouth weren't "Gorgeous!" or "First-class!" or any number of other things that would have blurted out of my mouth had I been gazing on such a beauty for the first time. No, Sally's first word was "Footprints!"

Footprints? What was she talking about?

Then I looked down to the boat, and yes, there they were—muddy footprints on the maroon carpeting. While launching the boat, I had apparently stepped into some mud and tracked it on the carpet and on some of the seat cushions as well.

Now if anyone else but Sally had made this rather critical appraisal on seeing my boat for the first time, I would have been irritated. Instead I just did my best impression of Mr. Rogers and said, "Yes, Sally, those are footprints. Can you say 'footprints'?" And then I bent down and brushed the dried mud away with my hand.

My sister and I had a good laugh then, and we still do every time we remember the story. We both know that it's her tendency, as a perfectionistic firstborn, to pick out the flaw in any situation. It isn't that she's mean or disrespectful. She just can't help it—and, by her comments, she was actually trying to help.

Handling Failure

Fortunately, Sally's perfectionism really leans more toward seeking excellence (more on this in the next chapter), even though she does have that flaw-picking quality. She hasn't become a discouraged perfectionist by any means. But a lot of perfectionist flaw pickers *do* become discouraged and depressed, especially if they fail in any regard.

How about you? When you spot a flaw in your performance or appearance, do you equate it with failure and get down on yourself? Do you tell yourself that you've "done it again" or that you'll never amount to anything?

> *When you spot a flaw in your performance or appearance, do you equate it with failure and get down on yourself? Do you tell yourself that you've "done it again" or that you'll never amount to anything?*

What I try to tell perfectionist clients (usually firstborn or only children) is that every human being who ever lived has failed at one time or another. It doesn't matter how intelligent, talented, or fortunate you may be; the only way to avoid failure is to sit back and do nothing. But that's a form of failure too, and it's often what happens when a perfectionist becomes incapacitated by the fear of messing things up. What you do with occasional failure is strictly up to you. You can see failure as your deadly enemy, which holds you back and threatens your very existence, or you can see failure as a teacher and, in some cases, a blessing because it leads down another trail that brings you to success.

> *The only way to avoid failure is to sit back and do nothing.*

Be Objective

The key to handling failure and making it a teacher rather than a destroyer is to look at it in a detached, objective way. Now I know that's easier said and done by a lastborn who doesn't have a perfectionist cell in his or her body. So if you're a firstborn or an only child and failure really bugs you, you have to attack it systematically with what I call *cognitive discipline*: a methodical, organized approach to problem solving.

REFUSE NEGATIVE SELF-TALK

Don't respond with "I knew this was going to happen! It always happens to me!" If you hear yourself thinking that kind of thing, stop and instead look closely at the situation. What caused the failure? What was your first mistake, which led to the second, and so on? Did you go against your better judgment? What can you do differently next time? As you analyze your failure or mistake, you will automatically be learning and setting yourself up to improve in the future.

DON'T LISTEN TO NAYSAYERS

Of course, it's hard when you fail and you get fired on by critics—your spouse, others in your family, your boss, your friends, or that busybody neighbor who seems to know everything you do. Remember that you're under no obligation to believe or even listen to the people who are criticizing or condemning you.

If you're a firstborn, keep in mind that you've been busy all your life living up to everyone else's standards. You may have never even stopped to figure out exactly what you want out of life. You've been living up to the expectations of your parents, your teachers, your spouse, and so on. When you try to live up to everyone else's expectations, you tend to believe what everyone else says about you.

We would never have heard of some of the world's most famous people if they had listened to their critics early on:

Sir Winston Churchill, the prime minister who kept England afloat during World War II strictly on the strength of his brilliant oratory, was at the bottom of his class in one school and failed the entrance exams to another.

Pablo Picasso, the brilliant painter whose works command mind-boggling prices, was barely able to read and write at the age of 10 when his father yanked him out of school. Then a tutor came in to instruct him but gave up and quit in disgust because Pablo just didn't have it.

Louis Pasteur was not the top student in his chemistry class.

Publishers told Zane Grey he could never be a writer.

Thomas Edison's teachers concluded he was a few bricks short of a full load and tossed him out of school. His mother ended up homeschooling him.

There was that composer named Beethoven, whose teacher called him a "hopeless dunce."

And let's not forget Albert Einstein, whose theory of relativity changed the scientific world. He performed badly in almost all of his high school courses and even flunked his college entrance exams![4]

I have often imagined how it was for Einstein while growing up. The teacher would be leaning over little Albert at his school desk, saying, "Albert! What *are* you doing? You're supposed to be practicing your multiplication tables. What on earth is this capital E and that equals sign and the little mc with a 2 after it? Can't you handle 6 x 7?"

Refuse to Feel Guilty

One more thing to remember as you battle failure: you are almost certainly battling guilt as well. Just ask yourself, *Do I feel guilty much of the time?* For most perfectionists, the answer is almost always yes. I have counseled many people whom I sometimes call "the

---

Are You Good Enough for Yourself?

Ask yourself:

1. How do I handle failure?
2. What do I say to myself when I do fail?
3. How do I let others' opinion of me influence my opinion of myself?

guilt gatherers of life." The common mistakes they make include:

> piling one infraction on top of another
> letting their children manipulate them
> taking the blame when others are responsible
> giving in to depression
> believing they deserve to suffer
> judging themselves by what others think of them
> suffering rather than taking steps to change things

I have written extensively on dealing with guilt in other books. For more information, see *Pleasers* and *When Your Best Isn't Good Enough*.[5]

6

Perfect—or Excellent?

All right, so reading the last chapter has convinced you that perfectionism is not a healthy way to live. You're now aware (if you weren't before) that you are a perfectionist to some degree, and you're concerned that you may be in some trouble or even on thin ice.

Congratulations! You've made the first step toward making a change that could literally save your health or your life. It may even save you some friends. Discouraged perfectionists are often stubborn, opinionated, and strong-willed types who become known for telling it like it is. And what happens when you tell everyone like it is? People suddenly are too busy for lunch—and for much of anything else. Even your enemies don't want to hang around long enough to insult you.

> *What happens when you tell everyone like it is? People suddenly are too busy for lunch—and for much of anything else. Even your enemies don't want to hang around long enough to insult you.*

And unless you can change your perfectionistic attitude, it won't do any good to tell yourself you'll just keep your mouth shut and put up with it. Try that and you will really lose your health. Your perfectionism will cause anxiety, and that anxiety, whether conscious or unconscious, has got to come out somewhere. Certain parts of your body will pay the

Dear Dr. Leman,

I can't remember when I laughed so much while reading a nonfiction book. Laughed—I *howled* at some paragraphs in *The Birth Order Book*. You've answered several questions that have haunted me for a long time. . . .

Want clues to my birth order? I bought your book after wandering into a New York bookstore last Saturday, while fretting that the scarf I purchased a month earlier was navy blue—not black as I thought—and didn't match my new black top coat. . . .

If that's not enough: in my closet, dress shirts are on blue hangers, dark shirts on the left, lighter-colored shirts on the right; sport shirts are on brown hangers. I'm laughing so much thinking about this, I can hardly continue writing.

Surely you've guessed: I have no siblings. But here's something curious that I discovered several years ago and wanted to alert you to: virtually all of my close friends are firstborn or only children. And with two exceptions, all fall in the much-younger, much-older groups—something that has always been apparent to me but I never understood until reading your book.

Of course, I've always known that I was not a perfectionist—far from it. Proof: my desk has, throughout my career, been a mess most of the time (but I can find anything within sixty seconds). I could never figure out why I lost control of my desk so often. Thank you for telling me the answer to something that has bugged me for years.

Nonetheless, it is a bit spooky having a stranger—you—know so much about my personal life. Good grief! Dr. Leman, you will never know how much enlightenment your book has given me. Thank you.

Edwin

(Interestingly, Edwin is a former newspaper reporter who rose to become one of five vice presidents with a publicly traded telecommunications company. His letter is a choice example of a perfectionist who has begun to see the light.)

price. That's why so many firstborn or only children wind up going to see psychologists, and the first symptoms they notice are migraines, stomach disorders, or backaches. They are the worriers of life, the ones who develop colitis, ulcers, facial tics, and cluster headaches.

Now right here you may be thinking, *C'mon, Dr. Leman, you're laying it on a bit thick, aren't you?*

Well, yes and no. I admit that not all perfectionists wind up with serious medical and psychological problems. Some perfectionists function very efficiently, but underneath the polished, seemingly flawless exterior is usually a person who wonders how long he or she can stay ahead of the posse. And that person is continually frustrated, perhaps wondering, *Why do I do these compulsive things over and over?* Whatever your degree of not being good enough, I know it's a burden and certainly a source of stress. And I also know from working with hundreds of perfectionists that the answer lies in controlling your perfectionism and turning it in an entirely new direction—even if it's one baby step at a time.

Perfect versus Excellent

Many perfectionists would stop me right here and say, "Yes, just what do I do about my perfectionism? Shoot for mediocrity and failure?"

Of course not. The key is to learn the difference between the hopeless pursuit of perfection and the satisfying seeking of excellence.

Do you know the difference? Take the "About You" quiz on page 120. Again, I'll wait right here while you take it before we go on.

It isn't too hard to see that in each pair, the first statement is that of the perfectionist and the second statement that of the seeker of excellence. Here's why:

About You

Each question has two statements. Read each pair of statements and label one of them E (for excellence) and the other P (for perfectionism).

1. I aim for the top. _____
   I strive to do my best. _____

2. What counts is the bottom line. Everything else is just talk. _____
   I did my best, and whatever happens, I'm happy with me. _____

3. What's the use? I can't do what I know I'm capable of. _____
   This one hurts, but I'm staying with it. _____

4. I blew it! How could I let this happen? _____
   What a bummer! But I see what went wrong. Next time . . . _____

5. What if I slip up again? What if something happens I can't control? Everyone will laugh. _____
   Here I am with the same opportunity. This time it's going to be different. _____

6. I play to win. No one remembers who finished second. _____
   I strive to do my best. I'm happy with that. _____

7. Why do people have to be so negative? Don't they know how long I've worked on this project? _____
   They may be right. I don't like it, but there may be something in what they say. _____

8. Let's not kid ourselves. They love me around here because I produce. _____
   Everyone likes to win, but it's playing the game and being part of the process that counts. _____

1. Those who chase perfection are always reaching beyond their grasp—for the top. They set impossible goals. Pursuers of excellence set goals too, according to their own high standards, but they put those goals within reach.

2. Perfectionists base their value on their accomplishments. They have to produce or else. Seekers of excellence value themselves simply for who they are.

3. Perfectionists are easily dismayed by disappointment and will often throw up their hands in total defeat, be-

cause if they can't be perfect, why even try? Seekers of excellence can be disappointed and hurt by a setback, but they don't give up. They keep moving toward their goal.

4. Perfectionists regard failure as the ultimate evil and let it devastate them. Pursuers of excellence are always learning from their mistakes and failures so they can do a better job in the future.

5. Perfectionists remember their mistakes and chew on them the way a dog gnaws a bone. They are sure that everyone else remembers them too and that they're ready to pounce. Seekers of excellence correct their mistakes and let them fade from memory so they aren't inhibited in the future.

6. Perfectionists can settle only for being #1. Pursuers of excellence are happy with themselves as long as they are sure they tried as hard as they could.

7. Perfectionists fear and hate criticism and will either avoid it or ignore it. Seekers of excellence don't enjoy criticism but they welcome it because it may help them improve.

8. Perfectionists have to win or their self-image plunges to zero. Pursuers of excellence can finish second, third, or even lower and their self-image remains strong.

How to Control Perfectionism by Seeking Excellence

Following are some suggestions I've seen work wonders in the lives of perfectionists I've counseled.

Take perfectionism seriously. Perfectionism isn't some little "psychological glitch" in your makeup. It is your deadly enemy. I call it slow suicide, and that's not even half facetious.

The perfectionist is always trying to avoid criticism or failure, both of which he sees as totally unacceptable. My advice is this: realize you will always have critics with you, and everyone fails now and then. When you don't succeed, analyze the situation. What is the worst that can result from your failure to do what you had hoped to do? Maybe you need to fine-tune your goal setting and not reach so high. Remember, there are many major league baseball players in the Hall of Fame who failed seven times out of ten. In other words, they batted .300 and made the Hall.

> **Realize you will always have critics with you, and everyone fails now and then.**

A good hitter—someone who bats at least .300—doesn't get down on himself if he strikes out or if his sharp line drive is speared by the shortstop and he's robbed of a base hit. Instead, he hitches up his pants and tells himself, *Next time I'll get a hit.* Whatever you're doing, the moral is clear: Give it your best shot, and then *live with your best shot* and be satisfied. Or to put it another way: the real winners in life take their cuts, and even if they strike out, the next time up they get back in the batter's box of life and keep swinging.

Recognize that you have an almost desperate need to be perfect. And at the same time, recognize the fallacy in this kind of thinking. Since you are *never* going to be perfect, why not give yourself permission to be *imperfect?* Do it one day at a time. Every morning, start off by giving yourself permission to be imperfect.

Of course I'm not suggesting that you settle for mediocrity. I am a firm believer that the world needs a certain number of perfectionists who are very good at their job. For example, when my stomach began acting up and the pain wouldn't go away, I wound up in the emergency ward headed for a gall bladder operation. Just before they put me under, I told the anesthesiologist (whose last name sounded like Rumpelstiltskin backwards) that we were going to talk about his birth order. He said to me in broken English, "Birth order? I am unfamiliar with term *birth order.*"

I said, "You are the firstborn son, aren't you?"

"No," he replied.

"Noooo . . . ?" I was flabbergasted.

He said firmly, "I'm the *only* son."

I said, "Proceed!"

As you know, I like to poll airline pilots to see if they are the firstborn, and they usually are. One day, however, I had to take a small commuter plane to a parenting seminar in Santa Maria, 140 miles up the California coast from Los Angeles. The commuter plane was so small that I wound up sitting barely three feet from the two guys flying the plane, and I couldn't help noticing the lead pilot's digital watch.

"You're a firstborn, aren't you?" I said.

"No, actually, I'm a baby of the family," he replied.

I started getting a little nervous and asked, "How about your buddy?"

After conversing briefly with his copilot, he turned and said, "He's the youngest too!"

We were taxiing for takeoff, and

> *The real winners in life take their cuts, and even if they strike out, the next time up they get back in the batter's box of life and keep swinging.*

two babies were flying the plane! I almost bailed out right there, but the day was saved when I learned that the pilot had a gap of twelve years between him and the next oldest child in the family. And the copilot had a six-year gap between him and his older brother, who was a pilot as well.

I calmed down and decided to stay in my seat. The law of variables may have put two lastborns in the cockpit of the plane, but they were really a functional only child and a functional firstborn, and that was good enough for me. (We made it to Santa Maria with no problem, and both pilots did a beautiful job, even when the air got a little rough.)[1]

My point in telling you about the anesthesiologist and the two pilots is that some personality types are better fitted to certain jobs than others. So I don't mind if anesthesiologists, pilots, surgeons, and the like allow themselves to be imperfect—particularly at home with the wife and kids—just so they're seeking excellence while on the job!

Make a conscious effort to go easy on criticizing yourself and others. In fact, start going easy on others first. If you have to give someone feedback, try to separate the deed from the doer, which is not easy. A good approach is not to say, "*You* did this" or "*You* did that," but practice talking about what happened instead. Say, "Now you're getting it. That looks great!"

> **As you lighten up on others, you will learn to lighten up on yourself!**

A strange thing will happen: as you lighten up on others, you will learn to lighten up on yourself!

The destructive feeling that many perfectionists have is self-directed anger. That is why they are so self-critical. You can learn to be less critical if you add a margin for error to your tasks and remind yourself that everyone makes mistakes.

Have the courage to admit out loud, "I was wrong." This may be the most difficult sentence any perfectionist has to utter because your whole code goes against the idea of ever being wrong, "less than," or not perfect. And as you make progress on "I was wrong," also try two other short sentences that may be even more difficult: "I'm sorry" and "Will you forgive me?"

These three sentences total nine words—the toughest nine words any birth order has to utter, but particularly hard for firstborn perfectionists. When perfectionism is your goal, admitting that you have missed that goal is difficult. It's an admission of failure, and failure is anathema to the perfectionist. But admitting mistakes makes you human and approachable.

Work on developing a thicker skin. Be aware that perfectionists are sensitive, admit that this is an ingrained pattern, and deal with it, but don't expect to get rid of it overnight.

Instead, watch for those times when you catch yourself being very sensitive or being defensive about criticism, whether it comes from others or from within yourself.

You will do a lot of the "two steps forward, one step backward" shuffle. At the end of the day, you may look back and say, *I really didn't need to get so upset over forgetting to mail that important letter or to make that call.* But even

> **Admitting mistakes makes you human and approachable.**

to be aware of how upset you got over something that really wasn't worth it is making progress. Ingrained patterns are not changed overnight.

Also, sensitive perfectionists need to do nice things for themselves. As the hair color ad puts it, "You're worth it." But perfectionists have a hard time believing that. One woman I counseled had a habit of going to the local department store, buying new clothes, and then returning them a few days later. This woman was an extremely discouraged perfectionist who always returned whatever she bought, giving the excuse that something "just wasn't quite right."

I told her that what wasn't quite right was that she thought she wasn't worth the new clothes because she wasn't meeting her perfectionistic standards. We had to work on two problems: (1) She really needed new clothes. (2) She really needed to understand that it was okay to buy something new and keep it. Finding fault with what she bought was really a cover-up for her belief that she didn't deserve a new dress.

> **Sensitive perfectionists need to do nice things for themselves.**

Finally we had a breakthrough. She bought a new dress and actually kept it. Then she got a new sweater and kept that. I knew we were out of the woods when her husband finally called me and complained about all these bills he was getting for his wife's new clothes!

Bite off smaller chunks of life. In other words, don't take on so much at once. That's when the big picture becomes overwhelming—a typical plight of the perfectionist. So work at doing one thing at a time. Finish A before going to B. Yes, there will always be those things that come up—phone calls or emergencies, minor or major. The thing to do is avoid putting a major task into a tight schedule (a typical problem for the perfectionist because he or she is always doing too many things and thinking there will be time for all of them). Always leave room in your schedule for the interruptions and the emergencies.

> *Work at doing one thing at a time. Finish A before going to B.*

Expect less of yourself. Perfectionists are famous for unrealistic expectations and for setting goals that are way out of human reach. What you may want to try is what I call "negative motivation." I once worked with a professional baseball pitcher who was an extreme perfectionist. As long as he was ahead in the count, he could usually get batters out, but if he got behind—three balls and one strike, for example—he would more often than not walk the hitter. And if someone made an error in the field behind him, he'd usually fall apart.

After I worked with him for several sessions, he got traded to another team. One day I was fortunate enough to be in the same city where this player's team had a game. I went to the ballpark and managed to get down near the dugout and get his attention. He was pleasantly surprised to see me, and I was pleased to learn he was five wins and no losses to that point in the season.

"Don't worry, Doc," he said with a grin, "I never forgot what you told me. Every time I walk out to the pitcher's mound, I tell myself, 'Maybe today's the day I'm going to blow it.'"

That may sound like crazy advice, but for this extreme perfectionist it worked. It helped him acknowledge that there were going to be days when he would go out there and blow it. Once he accepted that, he was able to relax and pitch up to his potential because he literally expected less of himself and wasn't paralyzed by his perfectionism.

Become skilled at saying no. This is especially important if you are a firstborn or only child who wants and needs the approval of others.

Perfectionists get trapped in situations where they say yes when they really want to say no. Not being able to say no raises the perfectionist's frustration level to the point where he or she is literally ready to explode.

But if you can't say no, you'll never be able to say yes to life. In other words, you'll not have a life of your own because too many people will be taking advantage of you and pulling you in a dozen different directions to get what they want out of you. I'm not talking about fair-weather friends or even enemies. These people who make unreasonable demands on your time are often your own family. And it's hardest to tell a husband or a child, or maybe your mother or father, "No, I can't do that," or, even better, "No, I really don't want to do that—it's not me."

> *If you can't say no, you'll never be able to say yes to life.*

But it's amazing what will happen if you learn to say no in a very respectful and gentle way. You will stop saying yes to headaches and stomach problems, and people will start backing off and will not try to take advantage of you as much.

Work on becoming an optimist. Perfectionists usually see the proverbial glass as half-empty. Change this pessimistic view to one that sees the glass as half-full. Positive thinking is not just a cliché that turned Dr. Norman Vincent Peale's books into bestsellers. It really works because it can be one of the most powerful psychological forces on earth. So start using it in simple ways. Think about and meditate on things you are thankful for. More importantly, think about people you are thankful for and why.

When you are tempted to think about what went wrong today, remind yourself of at least three things that went right. If you can't think of anything that went right today, go back a day in time. The key is to focus on the good, not the bad. And think about what can happen during the coming days and coming weeks that will be enjoyable.

Change your self-talk. I mentioned this in chapter 5, but it bears repeating because it's a key to controlling perfectionism. Here are some examples of changing negative self-talk to positive self-talk:

Instead of saying, "I hate these staff meetings," say, "I'm not much for staff meetings, but I'm looking forward to this one because I may learn something."

Instead of saying, "I can't do this; I'll make a fool of myself," say, "I can do this. I don't have to be afraid because the other people there won't be judging me."

Instead of saying, "I can't talk in front of a group," say, "Talking to groups isn't my favorite sport, but I'm prepared, and what I have to say this time is important."[2]

Positive self-talk is a great tool for dealing with feelings of inadequacy and not being liked. Instead of dwelling on your weaknesses, make a list of your strengths and dwell on those. As for your imperfections, keep telling yourself that imperfect people can be very approachable and likable.

> **When you are tempted to think about what went wrong today, remind yourself of at least three things that went right.**

Get rid of grudges. So you were insulted, or your lovely work was not appreciated as much as it should have been. A grudge is a heavy burden, and all it does is sap your energy. Realize that people make mistakes and sometimes say things they don't mean or they regret. The world still goes on, so why waste your time and energy carrying that grudge? Give yourself—and the other person—a break and move on.

Don't let life blow out your candle. Stop for a minute and think of five to ten of your early childhood memories. (For more on why this is so important, see *What Your Childhood Memories Say about You.*[3]) They may be only faint glimpses, scenes that flash across your mind, but those little glimpses still mean something. If not, they wouldn't have stuck in your memory for all these years. Part of Adlerian psychology says that early childhood memories are consistent with the way a person sees life as an adult. In fact, these early recollections of life—what happened, good or bad—are usually symbolic of a person's entire lifestyle.

> *Make a list of your strengths and dwell on those.*

When I asked a man in his twenties for an early childhood memory, he spoke of looking out the window and watching the other boys flying kites in a stiff breeze. It seemed to him that ever since he could remember, he had been standing on the sidelines watching other people have fun. That was one of the reasons he had come to see me for help. He was still basically watching life go by and not doing much with his potential, even though he was gifted in several areas. He was always wishing he was like others who were involved, active, and successful—the people he admired and envied.

Of course, you already guessed the young man's birth order. He was the oldest in his family, and you've probably already guessed what his parents were like—perfectionists and overly demanding. The reason this man lacked self-confidence to try much of anything was obvious: his parents had blown out his candle at an early age.

Not all firstborns and only children wind up like this young man. But he is a good example of how firstborns or onlies can become discouraged perfectionists. They have so much going for them—ambition, strong power of concentration, excellent organizational and planning skills, and creative thinking. They are precise, meticulous, and have excellent memories. They usually come across as leaders and are looked up to by the rest of us. In short, they have it together.

But having it together is not a guarantee that you can't get out of balance and become a victim of your own perfection- ism. Perfectionists constantly have to work at being open, tolerant, and patient—with others and themselves. It won't happen overnight, but every step you take toward pursuing excellence, instead of perfection, will reap rewards in every area of your life.

7

The Lonely Only,
Super Firstborn

Only Children

I f you are a typical only-child perfectionist, you may have turned to this chapter muttering, "About time—it's already page 131 and the only child has barely been mentioned—just sort of lumped in with firstborns like some kind of vestigial organ." (And of course, as an only child, you're using words that the rest of us have to look up in the dictionary.)

If that's what you're thinking, I understand. Lonely onlies tend to be critical—and even more than a bit self-centered. After all, the only child has a unique advantage/disadvantage: he or she has never had to compete with siblings for parental attention, favor, or resources.

In this distinction there is good news and bad news. The good news is that it helps make the only child more confident, articulate, and seemingly on top of things. The bad news is that he or she has never learned to deal with brothers and sisters. The only child doesn't have to share with siblings or to

> *The only child has a unique advantage/disadvantage: he or she has never had to compete with siblings for parental attention, favor, or resources.*

go second sometimes. It leaves the only child self-centered by default, and depending on how he or she was parented, the confident outer shell may hide someone who feels inferior, is rebellious, and is always trying to prove he or she is good enough. And that brings us right back to the classic signs of being a discouraged perfectionist.

A Bad Rap

Only children still get a bad rap. One survey of college students seemed to prove that only children are perceived as more self-centered, attention seeking, unhappy, and unlikable than those who grew up with siblings.[1] This survey seemed to echo the label put on only children back in the 1920s by none other than Alfred Adler, the pioneer psychologist who made birth order such an important part of his school of thinking. In one of Adler's most important books, he penned the infamous judgment, "The only child has difficulties with every independent activity and sooner or later they become useless in life."[2]

With all due respect to a patron saint of my profession, I must challenge Adler's statement on two counts. First, it has a slight grammar problem (which to a baby of the family like me is no big deal), but far more important is that what he says about only children as a total group is simply not true.

Exactly how and why Alfie Adler came to this conclusion is hard to say. Perhaps he'd just had a long day counseling an only child—perhaps several only children. Whatever happened, he put a very erroneous blanket label on a birth order that has turned out some outstanding names in all walks of life.

If Adler really believed that only children as a rule would turn out having difficulties with being independent and would wind up useless, he would have had a hard time explaining US presidents Gerald Ford and Franklin D. Roosevelt, the only man to be elected four times; premier journalist Ted Koppel; magician extraordinaire David Copperfield; and football greats Roger Staubach and Joe Montana, legendary quarterbacks in the National Football League.

Other only children who lived fairly useful lives include Leonardo da Vinci, the Duchess of Windsor, Charles Lindbergh, Indira Gandhi, and Isaac Newton.

If we care to look into the business world, we need certainly to consider Robert E. Allen, CEO of AT&T; Carl Icahn, architect of some of the biggest corporate takeovers in history; and T. Boone Pickens, billionaire oil tycoon.

The forty-fourth president of the United States—Barack Obama—is an only child. He's a functional only child because he has a sister

> **Qualities of an "Only"**
>
> Little adult by age seven, very thorough, deliberate, high achiever, self-motivated, fearful, cautious, voracious reader, black-and-white thinker, talks in extremes, can't bear to fail, has very high expectations for self, more comfortable with people who are older or younger

he grew up with. However, his only-child personality was already formed by age 9, when she came into his life, and she was his half sister.

T. Boone Pickens: "Birth Order Makes Sense"

The first time I met T. Boone Pickens, we were on the same TV talk show, pushing books we had just written. As we sat in the green room waiting to go on, he saw me holding a copy of *The Birth Order Book*.

"What's birth order?" Boone asked.

Since walking in, I had been watching Boone, so I thought I'd take a shot at guessing his birth order: "Well, you're probably an only child, aren't you?"

Boone looked at me rather strangely and said, "Why, yes! How did you know? Have we met?"

"I'm a psychologist, and birth order is something I use in my work."

We started talking about birth order, and after ten minutes of my instruction, Boone was suggesting uses for birth order I'd never thought of!

A typical only child, Boone has a mind like the proverbial steel trap. He travels with an entourage of people, but something unique occurred that day. Boone went on first, before me. After his six-minute spot on the show, his entourage got up to head for the limo that would take them to the airport. But Boone said, "Everybody sit down. Dr. Leman's on next, and we're going to learn something about birth order."

> *The first person you want to understand completely is you.*

When I finished with my segment, Boone said something I'll never forget: "You know, this makes sense. Big business and industry would be smart to pay attention to everyone's birth order, I would think—especially when assigning certain jobs within the organization."

Needless to say, my encounter with T. Boone Pickens made my day and then some. In a few minutes he had grasped what I had been trying to tell people for years. Boone could see that the first person you want to understand completely is *you*.[3] It's too bad T. Boone Pickens and Alfred Adler couldn't have met and had a chat about only children being doomed to a useless life!

The bottom line is that it's never a good idea to stereotype any birth order into some kind of slot or rut because of what you've heard, read, or even observed. Of course, some only children do come out spoiled, selfish, lazy, aloof, and even dependent and useless. But I've counseled middle children in that boat and also lastborns who fit the same description.

Some Lonely Onlies I Admire

Although I'm a lastborn (and nothing like an only child), certain lonely onlies are among people I admire most in this world. One is Ted Koppel, the succinct, do-things-exactly-right former host of *Nightline*. I know the guy's retired. But when I think of interviewers who were some of the best, he immediately pops into my mind. Sure, he looked a little bit like Howdy Doody, but he was the best of the best.

I also have the highest regard for humorist and songwriter Steve Allen (the original host of *The Tonight Show*), who turned out something like ten thousand tunes. One of my joys in life was doing a couple of autograph parties with him. For an only child, he had a great sense of humor.

One of America's leading developmental psychologists, Dr. James Dobson, is a person I've known and admired for years. Listen to his program and you'll never hear a mistake. As an only child, he doesn't allow them!

Nor can I forget to mention Charles Gibson, former cohost of *Good Morning America*, where I have been a frequent guest as "family psychologist."[4] Gibson goes by "Charles" or "Charlie," and it's easy to see why he can't quite make up his mind. According to his ordinal birth order, he is the lastborn in his family, and that accounts for the "Charlie" who is easygoing and engaging. But the sibling just above him is more than ten years older, which automatically qualifies him for functional only child. And that accounts for the "Charles," who has such a confident, in-charge manner.

And right here in Arizona we have Pat McMahon. Those of us who reside in the Grand Canyon state know he is one of the best radio/television personalities in the business.

The Secret Is Why

I could go on with my only-child Hall of Fame, but perhaps I need to stop and ask some obvious questions:

1. Where has all this criticism of onlies come from over the years?
2. What is the only child's downside, or should I say "dark side"?

The secret to understanding an only child is knowing *why* he or she is an only. And there are two major reasons, either of which determines the only child's fate to a great extent.

The Special Jewel

You may be a "special jewel" only child, meaning that your parents wanted more children but could have only one, and all their energy and attention (along with a certain amount of doting and spoiling) went into you. If you're a special jewel, most likely you were sheltered from reality (including the consequences of your actions) in your earlier years. And you may well have developed a typical trait of many only children—feeling overly important. Now that you're an adult, you may have to cope with what could be a lifelong problem—being self-centered—because it's hard to break that pattern molded long ago by Mom and Dad. Special jewels often arrive when parents are older—usually in their thirties or upward in age—and they make their only child the center of the universe.

> *The key to understanding an only child is knowing why he or she is an only.*

I tell special jewels not to take the self-centered label too hard. They must keep in mind that they never had to learn how to share with siblings, so it's natural enough to feel overly important. Adult only children need to balance two extremes: believing they really are more important than others and thinking they're being treated unfairly when things don't go their way.

Parental Plan

The other reason you may be an only child is that your parents planned for only one. In the late '60s, when I was getting started in counseling, the planned-for only child was often the victim of very structured, tightly disciplining parents. They treated their lonely only as a little adult, always pressuring him or her to be grown-up, mature, responsible, and dependable. This kind of only child can appear very confident, cool, and calm on the surface, but just beneath, he or she is seething with inner rebellion. All your life you may have resented having to be the little adult, and now, having reached adulthood, you may be ready to indulge (or are in the midst of indulging) yourself in one way or another.

> *Adult only children need to balance two extremes: believing they really are more important than others and thinking they're being treated unfairly when things don't go their way.*

Today, things have changed. Families have been growing ever smaller, and many parents are opting for only one child. According to a survey the US Census Bureau released in 2009, the average number of children in a household under the age of 18 is one.[5] These only children aren't as pressured as they used to be. They're the beneficiaries of better parenting and often turn out to be well-adjusted, pleasant people with great initiative and high self-esteem.

One social psychologist who teaches at the University of Texas at Austin says, "The view of only children as selfish and lonely is a gross exaggeration of reality."[6] The more recent assessment of the only child is that he or she may have great initiative and good self-esteem. It's also often the case that the only child never felt all that lonely either.[7]

They Want to Do It Right

Whether special jewels or planned, only children are excellent candidates for growing up to be ultra perfectionists. They want things just so, and when things don't go their way, they get frustrated, antsy, and even angry. They become very im-

> *Only children are excellent candidates for growing up to be ultra perfectionists.*

patient with, or very intolerant of, people who don't measure up to their standards. Only children often quietly (and sometimes not so quietly) wish they could move in, take over, and "do it right."

The single personality type I see far too much of in my office is the "discouraged perfectionist," the person who thinks he or she has to be perfect (see chapter 5). These people are very structured, with high expectations for themselves and others. Only children suffer the most severely from this problem, but firstborns are not far behind.

Discouraged perfectionists come in different makes and models, but one of the most prevalent is the woman who wants to be everyone's rescuer. She agonizes over the problems of others and always wants to move in, take over, and solve everything. I call this the "nurse mentality," and it is no coincidence that nurses are often only children, or at least firstborns in their family.

Discouraged perfectionists need to realize the gap between their ideal self and their real self. The ideal self is the person you'd like to believe others see. The real self is the person you actually are. Here's how Kathleen, a 41-year-old discouraged perfectionist only child, compared her ideal self with her real self.

Ideal Kathleen	Real Kathleen
organized and efficient	inefficient and unorganized
happy and cheerful	negative and grumpy

Ideal Kathleen	Real Kathleen
uplifting, able to bring out the best in those around me	nitpicky, discouraging to those around me
have realistic view of time and how much can be accomplished	begin things that won't fit in time slot—can't possibly finish
good housekeeper	always behind
able to manage household efficiently	can't get it together or get others to help
energetic and eager	mostly tired and force myself to do things
sexually aggressive and expressive	tired and mechanical
have realistic love expectations	have unrealistic romantic expectations, wanting to be pursued like before we were married
beautiful on the inside so the beauty can flow out	full of anger inside
self-confident no matter what others think	wonder what others are thinking
make steady progress toward goal	procrastinate, put everything off till the last minute
finish projects	have many unfinished projects
have clean closets at home	too much clutter, can't part with anything
short and to the point	could go on and on and on
self-assured	need approval of others
feel secure	need to be needed

Even after Kathleen made such an exhaustive list, she let me know she could have gone on—and on! For a nonperfectionist baby of the family like myself, it was not only exhaustive, it was exhausting! But it proved my suspicions. Kathleen was, indeed, a classic discouraged perfectionist. She knew exactly what she was supposed to be like, but she couldn't measure up.

Her husband, Russ, described her as depressed, full of guilt, much too sensitive, a worrier, under a lot of pressure, constantly on the go, always catching up on projects, always having to do the right thing, always biting off more than she could chew—and always feeling like a failure.

After I looked at Kathleen's real/ideal exercise, I gave her a suggestion for the next time she began to think discouraging thoughts: take off her high-heeled shoe and rap herself on the side of the head a few times. "I'm sure you've heard of the bestselling book *How to Be Your Own Best Friend*," I said. "Kathleen, you could easily write *How to Be Your Own Worst Enemy*!"

What's Ideal? What's Real?

1. On the left-hand side of a piece of paper, make a list of the ways you would like others to see you. Label the list "Ideal Me."

2. Now label the right-hand column "Real Me." For each item in your left-hand list, write the ways you actually are and appear to others.

3. Evaluate your lists. How much discrepancy is there between the ideal and the real?

4. Would you call yourself a discouraged perfectionist? Why or why not?

Kathleen was wallowing so deeply in her discouraged perfectionism that she didn't even see the humor in what I was trying to tell her—or the truth. I went on to explain that she was her own worst enemy because she let several different enemies live right there inside her head. The first thing she had to understand was that by comparing the ideal with the real, she could get to the very crux of the defeated perfectionist personality. One of Kathleen's enemies was the idealism that had made her set extremely high goals. When she couldn't reach those goals, her *perception* of her real self made her feel like a failure on every count. She really wasn't as bad as her "real Kathleen" column seemed to say, but she *thought* she was, and that trapped her in her own prison of unfulfilled perfectionism.

Combating the Flaw Finder

Kathleen's prison had been created mostly by the way she had been parented. An only child, she grew up in a family with a very detached father who would never praise her for anything—but he was very good at finding her flaws. Kathleen always felt that she could never measure up no matter how hard she tried.

For example, at age 13 she single-handedly built a brick wall that went around the back of her home and encircled a small patio. It was a major task for anyone and practically impossible for a 13-year-old. But in her own way she pulled it off and did an exceptionally good job. Everyone who saw the wall marveled at her work—except her father.

When Dad came home from a business trip and found the wall, he was enraged. Everything Kathleen had done was wrong. He couldn't find one thing right with the wall or with her.

Things were bad enough growing up, but Kathleen fortified her perfectionist prison by choosing to marry Russ. He was smart, good at his job, and very successful. He was also a firstborn child and very insecure, because he also always felt as if he couldn't quite measure up. Russ was an interesting combination, almost a paradox—he was very critical and flaw finding, but at the same time he didn't want any conflict. The result was that he disapproved of Kathleen but never said much. Communication was almost zero.

And so Russ was absolutely inept at providing what Kathleen really needed in life: a husband who could share intimate thoughts and feelings with her. Kathleen's forte, however, was getting her hopes high and then having Russ fall short of her expectations. But instead of confronting Russ, she turned the evidence on herself and became all the more convicted of not being a good person. Whenever Russ didn't measure up to her lofty expectations for a husband, she didn't tell herself Russ was terrible; she told herself she was terrible and if she could be a better person, Russ would behave differently!

As part of the counseling program, we brought Russ into the office, and I helped him learn how to articulate his feelings, first with me alone and then later in front of Kathleen. It was a revelation to him as he became aware that he was full of feelings but had just never learned to let them out. He had always quietly "disapproved" of Kathleen, and she had sensed it, only driving her deeper into discouraged perfectionism. When they finally got to talking, a lot of things cleared up fast.

One thing they learned together was that Russ was a controller and that Kathleen was a pleaser. (See chapter 12 for more on controllers and pleasers.) One of the reasons behind Russ's reluctance to show feelings was that he was afraid if he ever told his wife how he felt, she would reject him. This is a classic characteristic of some controllers who have a hard time sharing their feelings, because they are afraid if they ever do they'll be rejected.

On the other hand, as a pleaser Kathleen was sure she could never say no to anyone, that she had to do everything for everyone, and that she had to continually put herself second and the entire world first. It was exceptionally gratifying to help Kathleen and Russ find out they could share feelings with each other and love each other just the way they were.

Because Kathleen was such a super pleaser, an important part of her therapy was getting her to learn the word *no*. Her inability to say no led her into the overwhelming propensity to commit herself to more than she could handle. I had to literally argue her into agreeing to weed things out of her life that were really too much for her. She was extremely active in her place of faith and in her community, she had decided to homeschool her two children, and she was attempting to hold down a part-time job of twenty-two hours a week.

There was, of course, no way any human being could do all this very satisfactorily. Kathleen had no time for herself, not to mention time for Russ. But it was her style, and she drove herself to the brink. That's when she came to see me.

"How will I ever catch up?" Kathleen asked me in one of our sessions.

"My general prescription, Kathleen, is that you drop some things, or you will drop dead yourself."

Kathleen had some tough decisions to make, and it all started with treating herself better. Of all the changes she made, the ones that were most significant centered on backing off and saying no to a world that was constantly pressuring her with requests such as, "I know you're busy, but you're really the one person we know who can handle this."

Before she sought help, Kathleen was in danger of fulfilling Alfred Adler's prophecy that only children feel useless and lack independence. I find it ironic that, while Adler was so negative on only children, one of my clients—an only child—fulfilled another one of his claims: It isn't important where you were born in your family. Your particular birth order means only that you've had a certain environment in which to develop. As an adult, you can recognize your characteristics and take practical steps to emphasize your strong points and strengthen your weak ones.[8]

Kathleen, the discouraged pursuer of perfection, became a much more relaxed seeker of excellence. She proved there is *always* hope, even for an only child whose unfeeling, critical father turned her into a totally discouraged perfectionist. I count Kathleen as one of the real victories of my counseling career.

How Edwin Got over the Hump

Another success story, in which I like to think I played a part, is that of Edwin, the super perfectionist only child you met in chapter 6.

After Edwin read *The Birth Order Book* and wrote to thank me for explaining why and how he was such an only-child perfectionist, I asked him if he would care to contribute some thoughts about using birth order principles in the business world. He didn't reply for several months, and I thought perhaps he'd forgotten about it. So I dropped him another note to renew my request.

Two weeks later Edwin wrote back, listing in breathless fashion an incredible array of assignments, tasks, and crises that he had been handling as a busy vice president. He said that my first letter had been resting safely in one of his piles, this one being next to his couch. But now the deadlines and crises had passed, including his housekeeper hanging his dress shirts on *blue* hangers instead of *brown* hangers. He had kept the housekeeper despite this glaring error and had gotten rid of all of his brown hangers so that now all his shirts, dress or sport, were on blue hangers. Finally he was ready to deal with the questions I had sent and said I would hear from him soon.

Frankly, I wasn't too optimistic. It was obvious Edwin was still going at a frenetic pace and saying yes to too many of life's insatiable demands. And he seemed to be enjoying all of the pressures, which is often true of perfectionists, until they start to reach burnout. Still, I could see Edwin was making a little progress. Switching to all-blue hangers for all of his shirts sounds humorous and a little eccentric, but I saw it as a baby step toward less structure.

It turned out that "soon" took several more months, suggesting that Edwin was still hanging on to the perfectionistic habit of procrastinating. Finally he did send answers to my questions, including this one: "You're a vice president. How do you see your perfectionism helping or hurting you on the job?"

Here is his insightful reply:

> It helps to strive for perfectionism because you quickly build a reputation for doing quality work. When the boss has an especially important assignment, to whom is he or she going to assign it? That's right, the person who, based on past experience, will do the best job. . . .
>
> Early in my career I recall being given a series of assignments. I was not able to complete them in the normal, eight-hour work days, and put in a considerable amount of noncompensated overtime. I was criticized for this by coworkers. I thought nothing of the additional hours—I simply wanted to do the best possible job I could. I honestly didn't even think about this work leading to a promotion or a raise

(which it did). I was just trying to do the best job that I was capable of doing.

Perfectionism hurts, however, because you demand the same perfection from your co-workers and subordinates. Occasionally, resentment can result. I used to be easily disappointed and upset when I saw that someone just didn't give 100 percent. Now I realize that, for whatever reasons, not all people have the same motivation.

When I asked Edwin if he thought he was making any progress with his messy desk (and couch), he said:

Until I read *The Birth Order Book*, I thought that I lost control of my desk because I switched from project to project during the day, putting files on top of other files in a desperate attempt to keep the flow of work moving and not interrupt the momentum by taking time to refile things.

However, now I understand that this is merely my defense mechanism to try to convince the world that I am not really a perfectionist. That way I am less likely to be criticized. Only children, you know, don't want to be criticized, even if it is for being a perfectionist! And I don't criticize myself for a messy desk either. I've improved my desk since I've read *The Birth Order Book*.

Edwin will always struggle with perfectionism, but he's making real progress that goes beyond improving his "messy desk." When he took the "Are You a Perfectionist?" quiz (see page 102), Edwin scored in the high 20s, meaning that he was close to an extreme perfectionist, but when he did the "About You" quiz (the comparison of perfectionism and excellence on page 120), he clearly showed he knew the difference and was coming down on the side of excellence much more often than he used to. He told me:

I seek excellence, not perfection. There is a difference. I strive for excellence, knowing that perfection means flawlessness.

Let's say we are considering an acquisition, and time is short. My "briefing report" for the acquisitions group will be thorough and complete—covering all of the research and facts—but it may not be perfect. I may include my hand-drawn charts (I'm a lousy artist), not slick, computer-generated charts; some of the Ts may not be crossed, but the information will be correct, thorough, and timely. That will be an excellent report, but not a perfect one.

The last line of Edwin's note above clearly tells me he is over the perfectionist hump. He can do a less-than-perfect report that includes a typo or two and even hand-drawn charts and still call it excellent, because it does what it's supposed to do—deliver information. Edwin finally sees the point. His goal is to do the best job possible with high standards rather than turning every job into a monument that glorifies his perfectionism.

If I ran a larger operation that needed Edwin's skills, I'd hire him in a heartbeat. Any company would be lucky to have him as vice president or even as CEO because his struggles with perfectionism—and less-than-perfect co-workers—have made him a more understanding, well-rounded person who still wants to do the best job he can.[9]

> *Lower your high-jump bar of life.*

But, of course, Edwin isn't perfect. If you want a bloody nose, just try calling him Eddie. It's interesting—when you think about firstborns and only children, a Jennifer, a Robert, or a Suzanne may come to mind who loathe being called Jenny, Bobby, or Suzie.

A Final Word

A piece of advice that I give to all perfectionists and especially to only children is this: Lower your high-jump bar of life.

Others haven't put that bar up so high—*you* have, as you have reached for perfection and made real success impossible. When you learn to settle for excellence, however, life will be more satisfying, happier, and more fulfilling, as you clear the bar and then some!

Assessing Your Strengths and Weaknesses

Are you an only child who struggles with perfection? In what areas do you struggle? In what areas do you succeed? As we end this chapter, take a look at the chart "Strengths and Weaknesses of Only Children" below.

1. Set aside a few minutes to consider each trait. Decide if each trait is a strength or a weakness for you.
2. If the trait is a weakness, what changes could you make to improve in that area?
3. If it's a strength, how could you capitalize on that strength or develop it even further?

Strengths and Weaknesses of Only Children

Typical Traits	Strengths	Weaknesses
Confident, self-assured	Trust own opinion, not afraid to make decisions	May be self-centered from being treated by parents as "center of universe"; also fearful, ambivalent about trying new things
Perfectionist	Always do things right and leave no stone unturned to do a thorough job	Tend to criticize themselves and/or others too much; never satisfied; may procrastinate because they fear they cannot do a "good enough job"
Organized	Have everything under control; always on top of things; tend to be on time and on schedule	May worry too much about order, process, and rules and not be flexible when it's needed; may show real impatience with anyone who is "disorganized" or not as meticulous; can be upset by surprises
Driver	Ambitious, enterprising, energetic, willing to sacrifice to be a success	Put themselves or those they work with under too much stress and pressure
List maker	Set goals and reach them; tend to get more done in a day than others; planning the day is a must	May become boxed in, too busy with the to-do list to see the big picture and what needs to be done right now

Typical Traits	Strengths	Weaknesses
Logical	Known as straight thinkers; can be counted on not to be compulsive or go off half-cocked	May believe they're always right and fail to pay attention to the more intuitive opinions of others
Scholarly	Tend to be voracious readers and accumulators of information and facts; good problem solvers who think things through	May spend too much time gathering facts when there are other things that need to be done; may be so serious they fail to see the humor in situations when humor is desperately needed

Ask Yourself

1. Am I learning to bite off less and not expect so much of myself? What recent examples can I think of?

2. Am I building time and space for myself into my schedule? How do I know?

3. Am I developing friends among younger or older people rather than only my own age level? (List the ages of your friends. Who gives you strokes? Who argues with you?)

4. How selfish and self-centered am I, really? What can I do to put others first, help others more, and be less critical?

5. Do I understand and really believe that no one is perfect?

6. Do I understand and really believe that my naturally high standards need to be more reasonable and less excessive?

7. Do I understand I really can't do it all myself? What recent examples of depending on others can I think of?

8. I am working on my self-talk. What recent example of turning negative self-talk to positive self-talk can I think of?

8

I Never Did Get No Respect

The Middle Child

We've been spending a lot of time on firstborns and only children and their nemesis, perfectionism. But if you're laterborn and fall somewhere in that nebulous "middle child" category, you might be a little upset by now (but not surprised) with the lack of attention. You might even be saying, "He's likely to get to me *last*. What else is new? That's the story of my whole life!"

It's quite normal for middle children to feel left out, ignored, and even insulted. After the first edition of *The Birth Order Book* came out, I received several letters of mild complaint from middleborns. Here's a sample:

Dear Dr. Leman,
   I counted the number of pages in *The Birth Order Book*, and fewer are devoted to middle children than any other birth order! What gives?
   Feeling ignored,
   Middle Child Reader

Going along with what I always thought was a middle child attempt to poke a little fun, I would respond to these complaints by writing back a bit tongue in cheek:

> Dear Middle Child:
> So what? What's the big deal? Besides, you're used to it! Get a life!
> Happy family photo albums,
> Dr. Leman

A Bit Mysterious

But kidding aside, the middle child does get fewer pages in this book than the other birth orders.[1] One reason for this little oversight is that we psychologists don't know that much about middle children. They are, in fact, a bit mysterious.

Although I counsel fewer middle children than lastborns or babies, I have talked to enough of them over the years to see a classic pattern emerging: the official definition of a middle child is a person born somewhere between the first, or oldest, in the family and the last, the actual baby of the family. This results in the middle children feeling they were born *too late* to get the privileges and special treatment the firstborn seemed to inherit by right. And they were born *too soon* to strike the bonanza that many lastborns enjoy—having the parents lighten up on discipline.

I'm not alone in saying that middle children are a mystery. Many articles and books have been written about them, one of the best being *First Child, Second Child* by Bradford Wilson and George Edington. These authors admit that of all birth order positions, "'middleness' is the most difficult to define, let alone describe or generalize about in any meaningful way."[2]

One reason for all the fogginess is that the term *middle* can mean many things. The typical middle child can be the second of three, or the third of four, or the fourth of five, and so on. Some authors go into great detail on categorizing different middleborn children. In my own counseling, however, I have discovered that middleborn children and *secondborns* have a great deal in common and are often one and the same because many families stop at three. For the purposes of this chapter, we'll group the secondborn and middle child together and refer to them as "middle children." In chapter 14 we will discuss the secondborn of two children in a more thorough way when we talk about parenting the two-child family.

> Each child looks above, sizes up the older sibling, and patterns his life according to what he sees.

The Branching-Off Effect

When talking about the middle child, the most critical factor is the branching-off effect that is always at work in the family. This principle says the secondborn will be most directly influenced by the firstborn, the thirdborn will be most directly influenced by the secondborn, and so on. By "influenced," I simply mean that each child looks *above*, sizes up the older sibling, and patterns his life according to what he sees.

The secondborn has the firstborn for his role model, and as he watches the firstborn in action, the secondborn develops a style of life of his own. Because the older brother or sister is usually stronger, smarter, and obviously bigger, the secondborn typically shoots off in another direction. If, however, he senses he can compete with his older sibling, he may do so. If he competes successfully enough, you can have a role reversal, something we discussed earlier in the variables of birth order.

The secondborn can, for all intents and purposes, take over the firstborn's prestige, privileges, and responsibilities. That's what happened with Richard Nixon, secondborn of five boys. Because his older brother by four years was sickly, the mantle of responsibility often fell on Richard's shoulders. But in another sense, Nixon retained several "middle child" qualities that stood him in good stead later in life.[3]

> *Any time a secondborn child enters the family, his lifestyle is determined by his perception of his older sibling.*

Any time a secondborn child enters the family, his lifestyle is determined by his perception of his older sibling. The secondborn may be a pleaser or an antagonizer. He may become a victim or a martyr. He may become a manipulator or a controller. Any number of lifestyles can appear, but *they all play off the firstborn*. The general conclusion of all research studies done on birth order is that secondborns will probably be somewhat the opposite of firstborns.

Think "Contradictions"

Because laterborn children play off the ones directly above them, there is no surefire way to predict which way they may go or how their personality will develop. I've looked at many charts listing characteristics of middleborn children and found them to be an exercise in paradox. An example of one of these charts appears below, containing two columns with words and phrases that can all be very typical of the middle child. The left- and right-hand columns have been arranged to illustrate some of the direct contradictions you can find in this birth order.

The Middleborn: Inconsistent Paradox

Loner, quiet, shy	Sociable, friendly, outgoing
Impatient, easily frustrated	Takes life in stride, laid-back
Very competitive	Easygoing, not competitive
Rebel, family goat	Peacemaker, mediator
Aggressive, a scrapper	Avoids conflict

The bottom line is that the middle child is "iffy"—the product of many pressures coming from different directions. More than any other birth order, you must look at the entire family to understand a particular middle child. How he or she finally turns out is about as predictable as a Chicago weather report. In many ways, the middle child remains a mystery.

> **Qualities of a Middle Child**
>
> Mediator, compromising, diplomatic, avoids conflict, independent, loyal to peers, many friends, a maverick, secretive, unspoiled

Middles Know How Rodney Feels

One thing, however, that's not such a mystery about middle children: they usually feel the squeeze from above and below. You may have noted that the title of this chapter paraphrases comedian Rodney Dangerfield's famous line: "I don't get no respect!" Many middle children would say they understand.

A number of middleborns have told me they did not feel that special growing up. "My older brothers got all the glory, and my little sister got all the attention, and then there was me" is a very familiar assessment.

Somehow there just doesn't seem to be a great deal of parental awareness of the middle child's need for a spot in the pecking order. The following scene comes from a work of fiction, but it is all too true for many middleborns:

When Mama introduced Sylvie . . . she always said, "This is Sylvie, my oldest child." . . .

When Mama introduced Rufus . . . she said, "This is Rufus, the baby in the family."

And when Mama introduced Joey to people, she would say, "This is Joey, my oldest son." . . .

But when Mama introduced Jane, she just said, "This is Jane." Because Mama had not figured out that Jane was the middle Moffat. Nobody had figured that out but Jane.[4]

If I want to get a rise out of middleborn children, all I have to say is "family photo album." They laugh, but it's usually sardonic laughter. The family photo album often contains solid proof that Mom and Dad relegate the middle child to the background. There will be two thousand pictures of the firstborn and thirteen of the middle child. Secondborn children in particular seem to fall victim to this strange phenomenon. It's almost as if Mom and Dad had their first child and snapped pictures left and right. Then, when the secondborn came along, either they went on welfare and couldn't buy film, or the camera got broken and wasn't fixed until "baby princess" arrived.

> If I want to get a rise out of middleborn children, all I have to say is "family photo album."

Picture the scene (no pun intended). Thirteen-year-old girl falls in puppy love for the first time and wants to give her boyfriend her picture. She goes to her mother and says, "Hey, Mom, are there any pictures of me without *her*?" Mom looks a little chagrined and has to shake her head no. So the new boyfriend gets the photo—carefully trimmed so older sister's armpit barely shows!

The Importance of Friends

Middleborn children often hang out more with their peer group than does any other child in the family. That's really no surprise because middles often feel like fifth wheels who are out of place and misunderstood at home, or like some kind of leftovers that always get bypassed and upstaged by the younger or older siblings.

No wonder, then, that friends become very important to the middle child, because friends make him or her feel special. At home the firstborn is special because he or she is first. The last-born is special because he or she means the end of the line. The middle child? He's "good old John" or "just plain Mary."

There is a psychological theory that says human beings operate according to three natural motivations:

1. to obtain rewards and recognition
2. to avoid pain and danger
3. to get even[5]

Every birth order has these three motivations operating in life, but it's especially interesting to trace their effect on the behavior of the typical middleborn.

To obtain rewards and recognition, the squeezed-out middleborn goes outside the family to create another kind of "family" where he or she can feel special. Firstborns typically have fewer friends. Middle children often have many.

How sad, you may say, that the middleborn child has to go outside the family to get recognition and feelings of acceptance. But weep not for our social butterfly. All these relationships will pay off later, as I'll explain in a moment.

> *Firstborns typically have fewer friends. Middle children often have many.*

To avoid the pain and danger of being an outsider in his family, the middle child leaves home the quickest. I don't mean she runs away or volunteers for boarding school, but she makes friends more quickly at school and in the neighborhood. Tired of being told "You're too young" when she seeks the same privileges as the oldest, and weary of hearing "You're too old" when she whines for a little TLC like that given the youngest, the middle child goes where she is "just the right age"—to her peer group.

To get even, at least a little bit for those feelings of rootlessness, the middle child becomes a bit of a free spirit. She gives herself the right to reject the family's dos and don'ts, at least in part, by choosing some other group's values for a measuring stick. It may be a team (middle children are great team players), a club, or a gang of kids who hang out together.

The important thing is that the middle child experiences the group as *hers*, something her family can't control or squeeze in any way.

Because of this early search for friends and recognition outside the home while growing up, the middle child may be the one who moves away from the family as an adult. This was graphically illustrated during one of my guest appearances on *Oprah*. Three sisters were also on the show as an example of how birth order plays out among them. When I happened to make the point that the middle child is most likely to move away from the family, the oldest and youngest sisters howled with delight. They had always lived in New Jersey, close to their parents and the rest of the family. The middle daughter, who had many friends, had taken off to make a life for herself in California.

They're Often Good Mediators

Of course, some middle children choose other ways to meet their needs for obtaining recognition, avoiding pain, and getting even. They may prefer becoming mediators and even at times are manipulative. Because they couldn't have Mom and Dad all to themselves and get their way, they learned to negotiate and compromise. And these obviously aren't such bad skills to have for getting along later in life. (If you are getting the message that middle children just may turn out to be the best-adjusted adults in the family, you're right, but more on that later.)

But if the middle child is very compliant and not at all interested in confrontation or conflict, the propensities to negotiate and compromise can backfire. I've had more than one middle child super mom and super wife come to me for counseling with the same problem: the husband is having another affair (with a younger, more attractive woman, of course), but secondborn wife is sticking it out—again.

She has many options—moving out, serving papers, confronting the other woman—but she doesn't really want to do anything. She grew up a pleaser, always trying to avoid rocking the boat. Now she has become a victim and indulges in victim thinking. She will hang tough with her cheating hubby until the bitter end, and he knows it.

Donald Trump: Deals Are His Art Form

On the other hand, the aggressive, competitive middle child may use his or her negotiating and mediating skills to become a skilled entrepreneur. Possibly the most outstanding example of this is Donald Trump, one of the more flamboyant real estate wheeler-dealers of the twentieth and twenty-first centuries.

Trump is the fourth born of five who looked above at two older sisters and a firstborn big brother, Freddy Jr. Father Trump was grooming Freddy Jr. to take over and follow in his footsteps as a hard-driving builder and manager of huge apartment buildings in New York City, but there was a problem. Freddy Jr. was a complacent, compliant firstborn who wanted to please. Donald, eight years younger than his oldest brother, took over the position of successor to his father more or less by default, and his career in real estate was launched.

This sounds like a role reversal, but it isn't. To have a true role reversal, Donald would have to be within two years of Freddy. Instead, because there was an eight-year gap between Freddy, the firstborn son, and Donald, the next son to be born in the family, Donald was able to develop a lot of firstborn qualities of his own despite having those two older sisters above him. The Trumps are a good example of how a large gap between same-sex children can make a huge difference in the roles they eventually play in the family.

When I'm doing a seminar, people sometimes come up to me and say, "I'm a middle child, but I feel I have an awful lot of firstborn qualities as well." When I start to probe a little in their family relationships, I usually discover a situation with similarities to what happened with Donald Trump, who became a functional firstborn due to certain variables at work in his family.

In his autobiography, Trump speaks of making deals:

> I don't do it for the money. I've got enough, much more than I'll ever need. I do it to do it. Deals are my art form. Other people paint beautifully on canvas or write wonderful poetry. I like to make deals, preferably big deals. That's how I get my kicks. . . . The real excitement is playing the game. I don't spend a lot of time worrying about what I should have done differently, or what's going to happen next. If you ask me exactly what the deals . . . all add up to in the end, I'm not sure I have a very good answer. Except that I've had a very good time making them.[6]

Nixon and Bush Sr.: Skilled in Diplomacy

If I were to ask you to name two US presidents of the latter twentieth century who were considered skilled in foreign affairs and diplomacy, who would come to mind? Many political observers would say Richard Nixon or George Bush. It just so happens that both men were middle children.

You may recall that I mentioned how Nixon did a role reversal on his older brother because of the older brother's ongoing illness. Nonetheless, Nixon also grew up learning how to negotiate and mediate. A major reason for this may have been that his younger brother was born only twelve months after him, which meant that baby Richard got very little experience at being the baby of the family. Instead, he was quickly thrust into the middle child role.

> **Middle children are the most secretive of all birth orders.**

Secrets about the Middle Child

Although middle children are not as easy to paint in clear and vivid colors as firstborns or only children, we do know some things that can help adult middle children function with a better understanding of themselves and how they relate to others.

You are more of a closed book than an open one. Studies show middle children are the most secretive of all birth orders.[7] If this applies to you, realize you could be displaying the "burned child" reaction. The burned middle child experiences the world as paying him less attention than it did his older or younger siblings. This leads you to play it closer to the vest with your relationships.

As a rule, you do not choose to confide in very many people. This is not necessarily a minus; in fact, in some cases it may be the wise thing to do. But it can also backfire. It's interesting to note that President Nixon got into all kinds of Watergate troubles because of being secretive. His effort to cover up what had gone on eventually led to his impeachment.

For one of the times I appeared on Leeza Gibbons's TV show, the program dealt with birth order and was titled "Born First, Born Last . . . What's My Destiny?" One of the families that appeared on the show included a mother and four daughters who fit into typical birth order stereotypes right down the line. The thirdborn girl was shy, a peacemaker who didn't want anyone in the family to be fighting or mad at one another. She was also very secretive, something I've seen borne out in so many middle children over the years.

This child's destiny will more likely than not include being very secretive in her marriage, and I hope she chooses a man who is very patient and willing to listen and draw her out. Being secretive and closed is not the best quality to bring to a marriage. I have counseled too many middle children who were simply not communicating with their spouse.

You are likely to be mentally tough and independent. While in graduate school, I often heard that middle children are the last to seek the services of helping professionals such as psychologists, counselors, or pastors. After I got out into the real world and began counseling people, I quickly saw that my own caseload bore out exactly what I had learned in school.

Who would show up more often in my office? Firstborn engineers, doctors, people in professions that are demanding and exacting. Why would firstborns (and only children) top the list? One reason, of course, is that firstborns and only children have the most hang-ups (usually caused by overly demanding parents). At the same time, they are logical, scholarly, organized people who are much more likely to analyze their plight and seek help. Because firstborns have always bought into authority figures, they have no problem with coming to psychologists, counselors—people who *know*—for help.

The next largest group to ask for help? Lastborns—the babies who are used to being cared for and helped.

My smallest group of counselees has always been middle children. But I'm not surprised. The reason could lie in the burned-child reaction coming out (or perhaps the burned child wants to stay in hiding). Another explanation is that middle children tend to be mentally tough and independent, qualities they acquired while learning to cope with feelings of rejection and being a fifth wheel while growing up.

It's fine to be tough and independent. It's foolish, however, to refuse to get the help you may need. I urge any middle child who is in a situation where counseling might do some good to sit down and think it through carefully. You might be cutting off your nose to spite your face because you're nurturing a grudge you got way back on that day when your older sister got to go to the beach and you didn't, and then a couple of hours later, you got grounded for a month when you clobbered your little brother for being such a pest.

Teenage middles often run with the pack. If you're a middleborn parent with teenagers, you may well understand why your own children are out running with the pack. Possibly you gave your own parents fits by going along with what they thought was the wrong crowd. (For more help as a parent, read *Have a New Kid by Friday, Making Children Mind without Losing Yours,* and *Running the Rapids.*)

I counsel many families where the parents are worried about a child who seems to be hanging with the wrong crowd. Granted, not all these children are middleborn, but middleborns seem to turn up with this problem more than do those of other birth orders. Firstborns seem to be the least inclined to run with the pack, mainly because they are such natural leaders. Lastborns may run with the pack strictly because they like to explore and take risks, but middle children have deeper reasons. Because of being squeezed and feeling like they don't really fit in at home, middle children have a deep need to belong. The pack fills the bill.

> *Because of being squeezed and feeling like they don't really fit in at home, middle children have a deep need to belong. The pack fills the bill.*

You're likely to be the most faithful marriage partner. Studies also show that middleborns rate as the most monogamous of all birth orders.[8] No surprise here. Middle children grow up feeling they don't fit in that well at home, so when they start their own family, they are extra motivated to make their marriage work.

Another way to say this is that middle children are loyal. They are far more prone to stick to their commitments than other birth orders are. While this is an excellent quality, it can lead to a lot of pain for a middle child spouse who is being taken advantage of by a mate who is unfaithful, abusive, or dominating.

You probably embarrass easily. Again, we can't lay a blanket judgment on any birth order, but studies show that middleborns are much more prone to embarrassment, but of course they will never admit it.[9] Why would the middle child admit to embarrassment? That in itself would be embarrassing!

> Middle children are loyal. They are far more prone to stick to their commitments.

This is one of the areas where the paradox of middle children becomes most apparent. While they are prone to embarrassment, middleborns are often rebellious as far as convention is concerned, something that could obviously put them in embarrassing situations. Alfred Adler characterized the firstborn by saying he or she likes "the exercise of authority and exaggerates the importance of rules and laws." As for the second child, "he will be inclined to believe . . . there is no power in the world which cannot be overthrown."[10]

Middle Ground: Not a Bad Place to Stand

Like any other birth order, being a middle child has its pluses and minuses, but when you add it all up, the middle ground is not a bad spot at all on which to stand. All the research shows that middleborns do not have as many hang-ups or problems as firstborns or only children (and that's obviously one reason why they don't show up in great numbers in counseling offices). Yes, I realize that you may be a middleborn who thinks your siblings got all the privileges or the breaks or the spoiling while you had to toe the mark. But did it really hurt you that much? Maybe it did you some good!

> All the research shows that middleborns do not have as many hang-ups or problems as firstborns or only children.

162

Privileges and breaks are not necessarily that great. There are almost always strings attached. That's why studies show that laterborn children are less fearful and anxious than first-borns. While new parents are handing out all those privileges and breaks to the firstborn, they are also transmitting their fears and anxieties as they wrestle with problems and crises they've never seen before. In addition, they usually have high expectations, which put pressure on their firstborn child.

So by the time you—the middle child—came along, your parents almost certainly were more relaxed than they were when your older brother or sister arrived. That firstborn sibling of yours ran interference for you—what I call "snow-plowing the roads of life."

Granted, not all firstborns simply snowplow the roads of life for their little brother or sister. They may charge down the road so hard and so fast that they leave the middle child feeling left in the dust. Alfred Adler, the father of birth order psychology, was a middle child himself. And while he thought being a middle child was a fairly safe spot, he did admit that he often felt "put in the shade" by his older brother, a true firstborn who always seemed to be outdoing him at every turn. At one point Adler said, "My eldest brother . . . is a good industrious fellow—he was always ahead of me—and for the matter of that he is *still* ahead of me!"[11]

Even if you had to live in the shadow of a crown prince or princess, there is no point in wasting time in self-pity. With true middleborn resourcefulness, be thankful for the experience. At least it gave you empathy for people who don't always get to be the star. Kathy Nessel, a fellow psychologist, is a middle child herself. I like the way she sums up the advantages of "middledom":

Middle children are tenacious adults because we are used to life being rather unfair. Our expectations are lower; consequently, we are more accepting in a relationship. The middle child may say, "Well, this isn't perfect, but it is kind of nice."

We are not as driven as firstborns, but then again neither are we as compulsive.[12]

A middle child client of mine echoed Kathy Nessel's words when he said, "Being a middle child of three wasn't easy, but as an adult I really believe I can cope with problems better because I got a lot of good training in give-and-take while I was growing up. I'm glad I wasn't first, and I'm glad I wasn't last. I'm glad I'm me!"

All of this suggests that perhaps the best word for the middle child is *balanced*. And in this topsy-turvy world, being balanced is not a bad way to fly.

Assessing Your Strengths and Weaknesses

Are you a middleborn? In what areas do you struggle? In what areas do you succeed? As we end this chapter, take a look at the chart "Strengths and Weaknesses of Middle Children" below. Keep in mind that a lot of these may not apply to you since middle children are known for paradox and contradiction.

1. Set aside a few minutes to consider each trait. Decide if each trait is a strength or a weakness for you.

2. If the trait is a weakness, what changes could you make to improve in that area?

3. If it's a strength, how could you capitalize on that strength or develop it even further?

Strength and Weaknesses of Middle Children

Typical Traits	Strengths	Weaknesses
Grew up feeling squeezed and rootless	Learned not to be spoiled	May be rebellious because they don't feel they fit in
Reasonable expectations	Because life hasn't always been fair, they are unspoiled, realistic	Being treated unfairly may have made them suspicious, cynical, even bitter
Social lion	Relationships are very important; they make friends and tend to keep them	Friends can be too important and not offending them may cloud judgment on key decisions

Typical Traits	Strengths	Weaknesses
Independent thinker	Willing to do things differently, take a risk, strike out on their own	May appear to be bullheaded, stubborn, unwilling to cooperate
Compromising	Know how to get along with others; can be skilled at mediating disputes or negotiating disagreements	Can be seen as willing to have peace at any price; others may try to take advantage of them
Diplomatic	Peacemakers; willing to work things out; great at seeing issues from both sides	May hate confrontation; often choose not to share their real opinions and feelings
Secretive	Can be trusted with sensitive information; know how to keep secrets	May fail to admit it when they need help—it's just too embarrassing

Ask Yourself

1. Is being a middle child comfortable for me? How do I know?
2. Would my family and friends call me secretive or open?
3. How willing am I to seek help from counselors, doctors, and other authority figures?
4. How do I recall my older sibling or siblings? Did they snowplow the roads of life for me, or did they make the roads even rougher to travel? If the latter, have I made peace with that—and them?
5. In the process of give-and-take (at home or at work), I would rate myself as A (excellent), B (good), or C (fair to poor). What are my reasons for that rating?
6. If I felt squeezed and felt that life was not always fair while I was growing up, how have I adjusted to that as an adult? Is that legacy a strength or a weakness today?

9

Born Last but Seldom Least

The Baby of the Family

First of all, I want all you babies of the family to know that I'm on to you. I know you just skipped the first eight chapters and started right here. I understand. Like any lastborn, I would have done the same thing. I hope you'll go back later to read some pretty important stuff you missed (it'll sure help you understand everyone else in your family, your friends, and your co-workers), but meanwhile let's begin with a little story of how Cubby Leman found his true calling in life.

The year is 1952. The scene is a hot gymnasium at Williamsville Central High School in western New York. A hard-fought basketball game is in progress, and a skinny little 8-year-old kid is out on the floor trying to lead cheers during a time-out. Pinned on his sweater is an image of the team mascot—a billy goat.

The game is as close as the air. The place is packed with screaming fans, but at the moment the fans aren't screaming for the "Billies." They're all laughing at this little kid, who has gotten the cheer completely backwards and has forgotten what comes next. His big sister, captain of the Williamsville cheerleaders, looks embarrassed, but she has to laugh too, because this little kid is pretty funny. But is the little 8-year-old guy embarrassed? He doesn't seem to mind at all. In fact, he's looking up at the crowd and kind of enjoying the fact that they're all laughing!

Loving the Limelight

I was that little kid—born last in a batch of three—nicknamed "Cub" when I was 11 days old. The name stuck, and as I became a toddler and a preschooler, I instinctively became aware of how to always be the "cute little Cubby" in the family. The youngest may have been born last, but he has a sixth sense that tells him he's not going to be least!

Youngest children in the family are typically the outgoing charmers, the personable manipulators. They are also affectionate, uncomplicated, and sometimes a little absentminded. Their "What? Me worry?" approach to life gets smiles and shakes of the head. Lastborns are the most likely to show up at the elementary school concert or the Sunday school picnic unzipped or unbuttoned in some delicately obvious area. Without doubt, they can be a little different.

It stands to reason, then, that the family clown or entertainer is likely to be the lastborn. No one told me that—I just naturally assumed the role. That was my thing in life— getting people to laugh or point or comment.

No wonder, then, that when I turned 8 and my cheerleader sister, Sally, invited me to become the mascot for the high school team, I jumped at the chance. Hundreds of people came to those games, and they would all be looking right at me! I loved every minute of it, even that embarrassing scene when I forgot the cheer and the crowd roared with laughter.

Qualities of a Lastborn

Manipulative, charming, blames others, attention seeker, tenacious, people person, natural salesperson, precocious, engaging, affectionate, loves surprises

In fact, at that moment in the Williamsville High School gym, I made a decision. In my 8-year-old mind, at least, a star was born. I decided to be an entertainer.

Yes, I know I came out a psychologist who is practicing family therapy. I enjoy my chosen profession and get deep satisfaction from helping families, but my cherished avocation is making people laugh, and I do it whenever and wherever I can.

The Dark Side of Being a "Clown"

A typical characteristic of the lastborn is that he is carefree and vivacious—a real people person who is usually popular in spite of (because of?) his clowning antics. Get the family together for the big Thanksgiving or Christmas photo. Work tenaciously to maneuver everyone into place and to snap the picture when everyone looks halfway sane, and—whoops! Who's that over on the left with the crossed eyes trying to touch his nose with his tongue? Yes, it's lastborn Fletcher (who in this picture may be 26 years old) doing his thing for a laugh.

Or maybe Fletcher is doing his thing for other reasons. There is another strain of characteristics in most lastborns. Besides being charming, outgoing, affectionate, and uncomplicated, they can also be rebellious, temperamental, manipulative, spoiled, impatient, and impetuous.

I can relate to this dark side of the lastborn. Without question, part of my motivation for being "clown prince" of the Leman family was that I wasn't born crown prince or princess. Sally and Jack had beaten me to it. It seemed to me they had all the talent, ability, and smarts. Five years older, Jack was 9.75 in everything he did. Eight years older, Sally was a perfect 10.0. Ever since I could remember, it seemed that I scored around 1.8 in comparison to their abilities and achievements. In short, they had all the firepower, and I was a dud.

So it's no surprise that I took the Dennis the Menace route to get my share of the attention. As a 5-year-old, I went to a relative's wedding and became forever established in her memory bank when it came time to throw the rice. Everyone was throwing rice but Kevin. I was throwing gravel.

> *They had all the firepower, and I was a dud.*

These are typical feelings and actions of the lastborn child. Lastborns carry the curse of not being taken very seriously, first by their families and then by the world. And many lastborns have a "burning desire to make an important contribution to the world."[1] From the time they are old enough to start figuring things out, lastborns are acutely aware that they are the youngest, smallest, weakest, and least equipped to compete in life. After all, who can trust little Festus to set the table or pour the milk? He's just not quite big enough for that yet.

Those Born Before Cast a Long Shadow

I like the description of lastborns by Mopsy Strange Kennedy, a family therapist who has written on occasion for various magazines. Mopsy is a lastborn herself, and that's no surprise. Only a lastborn baby of the family is likely to grow up, get a degree, become a therapist, and still keep a handle that sounds like a nickname or pet label of some kind. So Mopsy speaks

> *From the time they are old enough to start figuring things out, lastborns are acutely aware that they are the youngest, smallest, weakest, and least equipped to compete in life.*

169

from experience when she observes that the babies of the family "live, inevitably, in the potent shadow of those who were Born Before."[2]

I understand when Mopsy recalls how her early achievements (tying shoes, learning to read, telling time) were greeted with polite yawns and murmurings of "Isn't that nice" or, worse, "Bryan, do you remember when Ralph learned to do that?" Ralph, of course, is the big brother born first.

> Parents get all "taught out" by the time the lastborn arrives. The tendency is to let the lastborn sort of shift for himself.

Lastborns instinctively know and understand that their knowledge and ability carry far less weight than that of their older brothers and sisters. Not only do parents react with less spontaneous joy at the accomplishments of the lastborn, but they may, in fact, impatiently wonder, *Why can't this kid catch on faster? His older brother had this down cold by the time he was 2½.*

Part of the reason for this is that the parents get all "taught out" by the time the lastborn arrives. The tendency is to let the lastborn sort of shift for himself. It's not unusual for babies of the family to get most of their instruction from their brothers and sisters in many areas. The parents are just too pooped for any more pedagogy.

Obviously, receiving instructions from older brothers and sisters does not ensure that lastborns are getting the facts of life (or anything else) very straight. Lastborns are used to being put down or written off.

> It's no wonder the lastborn grows up with an "I'll show them!" attitude.

The older kids always laugh at the babies, who still grope blindly with fantasies like Santa Claus and the Tooth Fairy. It's no wonder the lastborn grows up with an "I'll show *them!*" attitude.

The Checkered Academic Career of Kevin the Clown

In *First Child, Second Child,* Wilson and Edington comment:

> Some lastborns become very adept at charming the world in various ways, while others grow up with a feeling that the only way they can gain anybody's attention is by making a mess; by being a problem child or a pest or a rebel who enjoys shooting spitballs at City Hall. If you are a typical lastborn, you have a fair share of both the charmer and the rebel in your makeup, and other people are often caught off guard by the fact that you can be endearing one minute, and hard to deal with the next.[3]

The above paragraph describes me to the last untied shoelace. To "really show them I mattered" was one of my main motivations while growing up, and I was indeed a charmer one moment and a spitball-shooting rebel the next. I have to say that Sally and Jack didn't make fun of me a lot. Indeed, Sally became something of a second mother. But both of them certainly had it all over me in the achievement categories. I often describe the three of us in the same terminology used for reading groups at school. Sally, the A+ student, and Jack, the B+ student, were the "bluebirds" of the family. I took one look at all this and decided to become the "crow." Reading bored me, and studying anything was the last thing I wanted to do—and I usually did it last, or not at all.

But I wanted—and desperately needed—attention, and I got it by clowning, teasing, and showing off. I wasn't your classic juvenile delinquent. I could actually be quite diplomatic, which probably saved my life a few times when I went too far with big brother Jack.

When I could tell that he was getting ready to land on me, I'd go into one of my cute little self-deprecating speeches and say things such as, "C'mon, Jack, you're so handsome, you're the king, you're the best. You wouldn't hurt a poor little guy like me, would you?" My ploys usually worked—at least, they reduced Jack's wrath to a sharp punch on the arm instead of something more serious that might have rearranged my teeth.

Another thing you will read on the characteristics charts for lastborns: they are suckers for praise and encouragement. A little pat on the head, a slap on the back, and a "Go get 'em—we're counting on you" is enough to keep a lastborn going for hours, if not weeks.[4]

> A little pat on the head, a slap on the back, and a "Go get 'em—we're counting on you" is enough to keep a lastborn going for hours, if not weeks.

That was certainly the case when I was the mascot for the high school team. One of my most legendary feats involved a sneak attack on another school's mascot. Amherst Central High School was our mortal enemy in athletics, and their cheerleading squad included two guys who dressed up in a tiger suit and danced around on the sidelines during the basketball and football games. One night, as I watched from our side of the gym, a fantasy formed. What if I could sneak up on the tiger, yank off its tail, and run as fast as my 8-year-old legs could carry me back to our bench before anyone could stop me? Well, I did just that, and I made the high school paper with the banner headline DEMON LEMAN DEFEATS AMHERST TIGER IN HALFTIME BOUT.

With that kind of clipping, a lastborn barely needs food. He's living on praise.

But it's hard for a leopard (or a billy goat) to change its spots. Once I started getting all that reinforcement as a kid, I went on to develop clowning (as well as being a problem child) into a fine art. By the time I hit high school (literally), I was a master of sorts at getting laughs while driving teachers crazy.

I did all the dumb tricks: crawling out of class on my hands and knees, setting wastebaskets on fire, getting everyone in school to bring alarm clocks set for 2:00 p.m. and put them in their lockers. Today principals and teachers would shake their heads and go back to worrying about the newest dope pusher or gang member seen on campus. But in the 1960s, wastebasket arson was a big deal, and that kind of caper got me all kinds of laughs. It got so the other kids would come into a class on the first day of the term, see me, and start nudging each other and smiling. Yes, this class was going to be a blast. Leman was in it!

> *By the time I hit high school (literally), I was a master of sorts at getting laughs while driving teachers crazy.*

No Joy to Have in Class

When some birth order charts talk about a lastborn's charm, they mention that he or she can be "a joy to have in a group or a class." Not for my teachers I wasn't. Not only was I a constant disruption, I refused to learn anything either.

As a high school senior I took a course called consumer math, a fancy term for bonehead arithmetic. They stuck me in there because it was the last term of the year and they didn't know what else to do with me.

The first six weeks I got a C, and the second six weeks I pulled a D. During the third six weeks, I was getting an F and was thrown out, but not before I had driven the teacher out as well. And I didn't just drive the teacher out of class; I drove her out of teaching. She quit and didn't come back!

The poor woman just didn't know how to handle powerful attention getters like Leman. She thought I was out to get her. Not really—I was out to get laughs, admiration from my schoolmates, and the limelight. Very few of my teachers

> *I didn't just drive the teacher out of class; I drove her out of teaching. She quit and didn't come back!*

understood this, but one exception was an English instructor who kept me in line quite easily. He was so direct and businesslike that I knew my clowning would never work. As far as he was concerned, it was "shape up or you're out of here!" I shaped up. How can you get attention if you're not even there?

That instructor probably had never heard the term, but he was an expert in *reality discipline*, which is what I really wanted all the time, even more than the laughs and the attention. Lastborns especially want and need reality discipline, which deals directly and swiftly with their problem and/or attitude and demands that they be accountable for their actions.

Miss Wilson Saw through My Facade

I should have been a much better student—I had the ability—but the schools I grew up in did not hold me accountable. They just pushed me through. They wanted to get rid of guys like Leman—and the sooner the better. Very few of my teachers saw through my lastborn charade. I have mentioned the no-nonsense English instructor. There was also a math teacher who wasn't fooled. As I came down to my last semester in high school, Miss Wilson pulled me aside, looked me in the eyes, and asked, "Kevin, when are you going to stop playing your game?"[5]

"What game is that, Teach?" I asked. (Yes, I actually did call her "Teach." After all, this was 1961 and we were "cool.")

"The game that you play the best." She smiled. "Being the worst!"

I laughed and tried to act as if I didn't care, but she had me. Her words began to turn my life around, and they are still with me today. Years later I talked with Miss Wilson and thanked her again for sounding the challenge that woke me up. She smiled and said, "Oh, I did very little, Kevin. You did it yourself. You were a challenge all right, but I knew what you could do if you wanted to!"

What a beautiful, unselfish lady. And rather modest too. She didn't even mention how she had tutored me at her home during those final weeks when I was making a last desperate attempt to graduate.

"College? I Couldn't Get You into Reform School!"

When Miss Wilson blew my cover, so to speak, I went to the high school counselor and said, "I've been doing some heavy thinking, and I want to go to college."

The counselor, Mr. Masino, looked up at me over the top of his glasses and without hesitation replied, "Leman, with your record, I couldn't get you admitted to reform school!"[6]

His response was, you might say, a bit discouraging, but I could understand where he was coming from. I ranked fourth in my class—fourth from the bottom—going into my final semester.

"Okay, I'll show you," I muttered as I was leaving his office. "I'll get into college on my own!"

In those days there were no community colleges, so either you went to a four-year college or you went to work. I had a real aversion to the latter, so I chose school—*any* school. But because I didn't know quite how to begin, I turned to the college admissions center at Evanston, Illinois, a commercial firm that for twenty-five dollars would submit a student's "credentials" to 160 different institutions of higher learning.

My application went to schools of all kinds—ones with outrageous tuition fees and ones no one had ever heard of. Someone in the registrar's office at Upper Iowa University wrote back and told me he couldn't get me into UIU, but he had a brother-in-law who ran a refrigerator repair school, and would I be interested?

The bottom line is that my counselor was right. All 160 colleges and universities turned me down, even the one connected to our church denomination, North Park University in Chicago.

But I wouldn't give up. I decided to focus in on North Park, hoping that church ties might overcome my puny grade point average. I kept writing back to North Park and called in reinforcements to bombard the school with their letters too. My brother, Jack, who had attended North Park for two years and later graduated from another college, sent a letter extolling my change of heart and determination to make it in college if given a chance. With my mother's help, I persuaded my pastor to write a letter, then added my own final argument: the Bible verse on the virtues of forgiving a wrongdoer seventy times seven times.

> All 160 colleges and universities turned me down. But I wouldn't give up.

Nine days before the semester started, North Park relented and let me in on probation, with the understanding that I carry a twelve-unit load. My dad cashed in some life insurance policies to pay for room, board, and tuition, and I was on my way to college!

During the first year, the "fear factor" (fear of having to go to work) kept me going. Despite woefully weak preparation in high school, I eked out a C average. But then I ran out of gas. I guess I thought I didn't have anything left to prove. In my sophomore year I fell behind and started failing fast.

I also failed in areas other than academic. Reverting to my high school habits, I sought attention by teaming with my roommate to rip off the ice cream conscience fund (established because of a faulty machine in our dorm that dispensed free ice cream) and buy pizza for our entire floor. We saw our crime as more of a prank than anything else. In fact, we made sure we told everyone we had done it. How can you get attention if you don't advertise?

Two days later I attracted the kind of attention I didn't want. The dean called me in and asked if I knew anything about the theft of the conscience money. In true lastborn fashion, I manipulated things a bit and said, "Yes, sir, I have heard that unfortunately some inconsiderate person has stolen the conscience-fund box."

Well, the dean knew I was lying through my teeth, and he had no choice. He suggested that I'd had a hard year and I needed a rest—permanently—from North Park. I thought about his offer, and it seemed like an appropriate time to leave. I was failing my courses, and the dean had completely failed to see any humor in the conscience-fund caper. Besides, spring weather is always nasty in Chicago, and my parents had just moved to Tucson, Arizona, where it was nice and warm.

I Struck Gold Selling Magazines—for a While

So I left school and went home to Tucson, where I spent the summer trying to find a job, but to no avail. That fall I enrolled in a night course at the University of Arizona and continued trying to find work. Jobs remained scarce; the minimum wage was about $1.10 an hour, but then I saw the ad in the paper: EARN $90 A WEEK, GUARANTEED.

I answered the ad and found myself applying for a job selling magazines door-to-door. I got the job, but selling magazines door-to-door was something I had never done, so the company gave me an "intensive" training course that lasted all of one afternoon. I learned a basic pitch that involved getting the customer to believe he or she was subscribing to three magazines and getting four additional ones free. The customer had to put $7 down and then pay $2.95 a month—for 26 months.

Even a Consumer Math flunky like me could figure out that this would amount to a final total of $83.70 (including the original $7 down). Obviously customers weren't paying for three magazines and "getting four free." They were paying what amounted to $12 a year for each of seven magazines. But my bosses taught me to count on the very basic human desire to "get a good deal" and buy on impulse.

Training completed, I reported back the next morning. I was driven out to a middle-class Tucson neighborhood, dumped on a corner, and told, "Okay, see what you can do and be back right here at 1:00 p.m. sharp."

With real eagerness, I started knocking on doors, giving the pitch, taking orders, and collecting the seven dollars up front. The morning flew by, and I looked at my watch just in time to get back to my pickup corner by 1:00. Back at the office, I handed my sheaf of orders to my immediate supervisor. I thought I had done fairly well and was anxious to see what she'd say. Joyce looked at all the papers in her hand and said, "What are *these*?"

"Well, they're my orders," I stammered, thinking that somehow I had really blown it and that my sales career was over.

"You mean you got *all* these orders this morning?" she said with disbelief in her tone.

"Yep," I said with a sheepish smile.

"You better come with me," Joyce directed, and we walked back to the manager's office. She waved the orders in his face and said, "Larry, look! Look at what Calvin did!"

I was feeling so good that I didn't even bother to correct her on my name. She was holding *twenty-seven orders* for magazines, a new one-morning record for Tucson, if not the entire nation, as far as that company was concerned.

And what was my big secret to magazine-selling success? Well, it didn't hurt to be wearing a University of Arizona T-shirt. And all those stay-at-home moms felt sorry for me as I stood hot and sweaty on their doorstep. Occasionally I'd be invited in and handed a lemonade, and then my baby-of-the-family personality just took over. I never was pushy or hard sell. I used the soft-sell approach—what I call "bringin' your dancin' shoes"—and I usually left with an order.

With some money coming in, I continued my night course at the University of Arizona and sold magazines by day. While I had excellent intentions, the double load proved too much, and I started falling behind in my schoolwork. That bothered me, but something bothered me even more. For a young kid, I was making really decent money selling magazines, but I kept having a gnawing feeling about what I was doing.

> **I kept having a gnawing feeling about what I was doing.**

It wasn't really robbing people, but it was all just a little bit too slick. I talked to my supervisor, Joyce, about quitting, and she couldn't believe it. "Why would you want to do that?" she asked. "You're the best salesman we've got. You're doing very well and you're just a kid."

I thanked Joyce for the compliment and said I still thought I'd better quit. Getting people to spend money on magazines they didn't necessarily need or want was starting to bother me.

"Sorry to lose you, Kevin," she said with a shrug. "You're a natural-born salesman if I ever saw one."

As I left the dingy apartment that served as the magazine sales office, I was glad that I had discovered that I was a "natural-born salesman" and that Joyce had even finally gotten my name right. At the same time, was I just going to waste my talent and never amount to anything? Where was I going to find a job that would pay as well as selling magazines?

Deep down, however, my conscience told me I had done the right thing. I had decided to use my abilities to serve people, not slicker them. I have never been sorry. Eventually I went on to get degrees that led me into my present, very people-centered profession—counseling and teaching.

Cleaning Urinals Put Me Nose-to-Nose with Reality

I knew quitting the magazine sales job was the right thing to do, but I still had problems. I tried taking another night course at the U of A and also flunked that. My parents were impressed with my high ideals and ethics, but they let me know that I still needed to earn some money so I could pull my weight while living at home. I eventually found employment—as a janitor at the Tucson Medical Center. I kept thinking about going back to school, but I'd always put it off with one excuse or another.

After a few months of cleaning urinals, however, the realities of life hit baby Kevin right between the eyes. Yes, I had a year of college behind me, and I knew I could do it if I wanted to. On the other hand, I had tried two courses at the "big school" and flunked them both. Now here I was, a janitor making $195 a month full-time. I knew that cleaning toilets wasn't really what I wanted to do with my life, but I remained stuck in limbo.

> *My first words were, "Pardon me. How would you like to go to the World's Fair with me?"*

One day as I emptied the trash into my cart at the men's restroom door, I was mulling over the possibility of winding up being a janitor all my life. Then I looked up, and around the corner of the hallway came my wife. Of course, she wasn't my wife yet, but she was a very beautiful nurse's aide who was working in the building, and she looked like great wife material to me.

My first words were, "Pardon me. How would you like to go to the World's Fair with me?"

She laughed and said, "Excuse me?"

"Would you like to go to the World's Fair with me?"

She sort of laughed again and said, "Well, I don't know about that."

Realizing I wasn't getting a flat no for an answer, I said, "Well, how about lunch then?"

Sande didn't quite know what to make of this weird fellow who was emptying trash, but being a nurse's aide, she thought I might need help, so she agreed to a lunch date. We wound up at McDonald's, where we split a twenty-cent cheeseburger.

We kept dating, and soon we were going steady. Sande could tell I was searching for something else in life, and she shared with me her personal faith in God. It was through Sande that I made some spiritual commitments that at last turned me in the direction my math teacher had pointed way back in high school. I took another course at the University of Arizona, the same one I had flunked. This time I passed with a solid A—the highest grade in the class of six hundred. Now *that* was a miracle!

> *She agreed to a lunch date. We wound up at McDonald's, where we split a twenty-cent cheeseburger.*

From there I went on to get my undergraduate degree in psychology, followed by master's and doctorate degrees. And I was on the dean's list most of the way through. A lot of things motivated me: memories of my English and math teachers, memories of getting a start at North Park and blowing it with stupid pranks, meeting Sande, and getting my life squared away by finding a real faith in God.

But there was also a remark made by Sande's supervisor in her nursing ward that motivated me. This middle-aged lady pulled Sande aside one day and said, "Don't associate with that janitor—he'll never amount to anything." A comment like that is enough to spur any lastborn on to greater heights. From that day on, I was driven with one thought: *I'll show her!*

> *From that day on, I was driven with one thought: I'll show her!*

Long before now you noticed that I'm not bashful about using illustrations from my own family, not to mention my own life. But I turned this chapter into a mini autobiography for a reason. My antics as a kid and on up through high school are a classic demonstration of many typical lastborn traits that can go to seed and become destructive. Frankly, before my math teacher nailed me that day in the hallway between classes,

I was headed for real disaster. But Miss Wilson made me realize that getting attention was not enough. Somehow this registered in my teenage brain: *The limelight is fun, Leman, but what do you do for an encore?* And that drove me on to a goal I had never even thought about—a college degree.

I like to describe myself as one of the few licensed psychologists I know who went through college and postgraduate work—thirteen years in all—without the benefit of a high school education. I literally did not learn much of anything in high school, a fact that hardly makes me proud. After earning a doctorate, I arranged to speak at a summer camp and told the teenagers my story. I did this for several years, emphasizing that my behavior as a youth was hardly the kind they wanted to imitate. In fact, I let them know, just as my math teacher had let me know, that being best at being worst is a stupid game for anyone to play.

> *I was headed for real disaster. But Miss Wilson made me realize that getting attention was not enough.*

Why Car Salesmen Are Often Lastborns

After confessing to using my sales skills to trick people into buying magazines, I need to clarify that there's nothing wrong with selling if you do it with the right motives. If I had stayed in the sales profession, I could have easily found myself selling cars. I have learned over the years that it's a line of work that attracts babies of the family in profusion.

Have you ever walked onto a used car lot to be greeted by a guy with a big smile, white shoes, matching white belt, dark blue pants, light blue shirt, and dark blue polka-dot tie? Maybe he wasn't quite that flashy, but he probably said, "Well, what would it take to put *you* in *that* car today?"

If you've ever had such an encounter, it's likely you were dealing with the baby of the family. You have to be careful with these guys—they'll sell you your own house and throw in a paint job by the owner to boot!

I jest a bit, but essentially it's true. Your good salespeople are often lastborns.

I do some consulting with businesses, and one of my favorite stops is a car dealership. I was visiting a local car agency one day and started talking casually with one of the salesmen about birth order. It turned out he was a lastborn, and so was just about every salesman in the agency!

And what about the manager? I went with the odds and guessed he was a firstborn. Right again. Firstborns often wind up in positions of leadership. This manager was an excellent salesman in his own right, but as a firstborn he had risen to what he really wanted to do: cross every *t*, dot every *i*, and enter those nice black numbers on the bottom line.

Not surprisingly, this firstborn manager was having trouble with some of his lastborn salesmen. They just weren't attending to details such as filling in reports on time. His superstar salesman was a lastborn and was in the most hot water with the manager. I sat down with the manager for a cup of coffee and had him consider this: "What do you really want this guy to do—sell or do paperwork?"

The manager's answer boiled down to "both."

I recommended to the manager that he stop trying to turn a baby of the family into a paragon of well-organized efficiency. Why not alleviate the problem by arranging to have one of the secretaries or clerks do the paperwork and turn his salespeople loose to do what they do best—sell!

The manager took my advice and assigned a clerk to fill in the salesman's paperwork for him. Naturally enough, his sales went higher than ever, and it meant more money for the dealership.

> *Babies of the family can feel on top of the world on Monday and at the bottom of the pile on Tuesday.*

Lastborns Live with Ambivalence

In *First Child, Second Child*, an excellent book I quoted earlier, the authors observe that growing up the youngest can turn a person into a bundle of uncertain ambivalence. Lastborns are on a seesaw of emotions and experiences that they find hard to explain or understand.[7] My own life as a lastborn bears this out. We babies of the family can be charming and endearing but then turn rebellious and hard to deal with. We can change from powerhouses of energy into basket cases who feel helpless. We can feel on top of the world on Monday and at the bottom of the pile on Tuesday.

I'm not sure about the exact reasons for this ambivalent streak that we babies of the family carry through life, but here are a few clues: Lastborns are treated with ambivalence—coddled, cuddled, and spoiled one minute, and put down and made fun of the next. In self-defense, we babies of the family grow up with an independent cockiness that helps cover all our self-doubt and confusion. We say to ourselves, *They wrote me off when I was little. They wouldn't let me play. They chose me last. They didn't take me seriously. I'll show them!*

> *One of lastborns' major traits is persistence.*

Because we lastborns want to show the world we can do it, one of our major traits is persistence. One hundred fifty-nine colleges turned me down, but I persisted and finally got in the one hundred sixtieth. Quite a few years later, after I had written *The Birth Order Book* and was hoping to get it publicized on national TV, I wrote to *The Phil Donahue Show* (yes, before there was Oprah, there was Donahue). I enclosed a copy of my book and asked if they would be interested in having a birth order psychologist on their show. The first turndown came as a form letter, telling me that they appreciated my suggestion but had no use for my idea at that time.

Undaunted, I wrote again and, of course, sent another copy of *The Birth Order Book*. Again, the same kind of form letter came back, but I wouldn't give up. I kept trying. I tried thirteen times to get on the *Donahue* show, and somewhere along the line they quit sending me form letters. Instead, they went to postcards, a sample of which appears below:

Dear DONAHUE Correspondent:
Because of the great volume of mail received in our office, we're sorry we cannot answer your letter personally.
Your suggestion has been reviewed. However, we do not plan to use your idea for a DONAHUE program.
Thank you for your interest in our show.

THE DONAHUE STAFF

But finally, almost miraculously, I was accepted. I'm not sure if they simply wanted to get me out of their hair or if they felt sorry for me, but I did get to appear on *Donahue*. It was one of the first really big talk shows that I had ever done. Just before I was scheduled to go on, the producer called and asked, "Will you be nervous? After all, you're it; there's nobody else who is scheduled to appear."

"No problem," I replied. "In fact, if Phil ever has a day when he doesn't feel good, I'll be glad to sub for him."

Was that just lastborn egomania talking? Partly. But there was also a lot of the lastborn desire for attention that makes a lastborn bold enough to do things that might make other people quail or even run for cover.

> *The lastborn desire for attention makes a lastborn bold enough to do things that might make other people quail or even run for cover.*

Oh yes, and the show went so well that it made the "Best of Donahue" list. Phil was impressed, and I was out of my lastborn mind as sales on *The Birth Order Book* skyrocketed.

Lastborns "Just Do It"

I wouldn't be surprised if a lastborn wrote that well-known line for Nike. Beneath our veneer of independence and persistence is that inner rebel who gets away with murder. We lastborns are impetuous and brash, vowing that we will get attention; we will make our mark. We will show our older brothers and sisters, our parents, and the world that we are a force to be reckoned with. We go ahead and *do it* and worry about repercussions later.

I'm sure that's what drove me to be such a little demon while growing up. I couldn't compete with a 10.0 sister and a 9.75 brother, but I could get their attention by driving them crazy.

> I couldn't compete with a 10.0 sister and a 9.75 brother, but I could get their attention by driving them crazy.

Possibly my finest hour came when Sally got married. She was in her early twenties and I was a teenager. Sally couldn't figure out how to involve me in her wedding. She couldn't trust me to be an usher—who knows what I would pull right in the middle of the ceremony? So she assigned me to take care of the guest book.

The night before her wedding, we all attended the traditional rehearsal dinner at a fashionable downtown hotel. Even I showed up dressed to kill in a suit and tie. As custom would have it, Sally gave everyone involved in the wedding a little gift. I opened mine and discovered a pair of bright plaid Bermuda shorts. Another fantasy formed, and Leman the demon could not resist. I slipped out and did a quick Clark Kent change in a nearby restroom. Moments later I reappeared in the swank hotel dining room attired in suit coat, tie—and the shorts!

Sally's face turned bright red as her perfect evening dissolved into her guests' guffaws and menacing looks from the maître d'. But I was happy. Once again I was the center of attention. I would pay the price later when I faced Mom and

Dad at home, but it was worth it. I had struck a blow for all the last-borns who have ever vowed, "I'll show them!"

So how about you? Do any of the stories I've told in this chapter resonate as part of *your* story? Have you gained some understanding of why you do what you do? Why you crave and seek attention? Or do they help you understand the baby of your family just a little bit more? If so, I've accomplished my purpose.

> *Once again I was the center of attention. I would pay the price later when I faced Mom and Dad at home, but it was worth it.*

Assessing Your Strengths and Weaknesses

Are you a lastborn? In what areas do you struggle? In what areas do you succeed? As we end this chapter, take a look at the chart "Strengths and Weaknesses of Lastborns" below.

1. Set aside a few minutes to consider each trait. Decide if each trait is a strength or a weakness for you.
2. If the trait is a weakness, what changes could you make to improve in that area?
3. If it's a strength, how could you capitalize on that strength or develop it even further?

Strength and Weaknesses of Lastborns

Typical Traits	Strengths	Weaknesses
Charming	Likable, fun to be around, easy to talk to	Manipulative, even a little flaky; seeming to be too slick and a bit unbelievable
People oriented	Read others well and know how to relate and work well one on one or in small groups; social settings and events are their cup of tea	May come across as undisciplined, prone to talk too much and too long, the kind who talks a good game but can't always produce
Tenacious	Keep on coming with tireless persistence, not taking no for an answer	May push too hard because they see things only their way

Typical Traits	Strengths	Weaknesses
Affectionate and engaging	Caring, loveable, wanting to help; like to get strokes and to give them	Can be gullible, easily taken advantage of; make decisions too much on feeling and not enough on thought
Uncomplicated	Appear relaxed, genuine, and trustworthy—no hidden agenda	May appear to be absent-minded, a little out of focus—like an airhead
Attention seeking	Entertaining and funny, know how to get noticed	May appear self-centered, unwilling to give others credit, having a big ego, temperamental, spoiled, and impatient

Ask Yourself

1. Am I a mature adult, or are people still saying or thinking, "Why don't you grow up?"
2. Part of growing up is learning to pick up after yourself. Do I have trouble with this?
3. Do I enjoy working with people, data, or things? Do I need to consider changing my line of work?
4. If I have a love for the limelight (attention seeking), do I let it slip over into self-centeredness, when I'm always thinking about me and not about others? How do I know? What would my friends tell me?
5. Do I use my ability to make people laugh strictly to get attention, or do I use it to make others feel good and enjoy life?
6. Do I control my tenaciousness and persistence, not letting it get out of hand? Or do I become overbearing?
7. Would people say I am a good listener? Or do I just try to "read" people and not really listen to what they say? Do I need to improve my listening skills and take time to listen to others without thinking about what I am going to say next?

10

The Winning Edge in Business

Getting Behind Others' Eyes

My father had only an eighth-grade education, but he was successful in raising a family and running his own small dry-cleaning business. It's funny, but the older I got, the smarter Dad became. Unfortunately I had to get quite a bit older—well into my thirties—before I understood his message to be concerned about making sales.

In the early years of my counseling career, Dad would ask, "Kevin, did you have any customers today?"

"Dad," I would protest, "they're not customers; they're *clients*!"

"Do they pay you money?" he wanted to know.

"Yeah, of course they do."

"Then they're customers."

And of course he was right. My dad had a simple intuitive knowledge of human nature. Our practical little conversations eventually helped me realize that my clients were indeed my customers. And once I had that straight, it wasn't much of a stretch to see that what I had learned in my psychology courses, particularly about birth order, could be invaluable.

As a counselor, I was basically selling people help—help with their problems, questions, and anxieties. But the more I counseled, the more I understood that you can't help people unless you really know them—particularly how they see life.

Fortunately because of the product I was trying to sell—counseling—I was forced into knowing my customers better and better in order to help them more and more. In fact, I soon learned that after I obtained a client (i.e., customer), I wasn't through making my sale; I had only begun. The real job lay ahead—selling those I counseled on buying ideas and suggestions to make real changes in their lives.

> *Know your customers, and selling your product will take care of itself.*

So as a psychologist, I have constantly been in the business of sales. And that's why I can state the following with confidence: know your customers, and selling your product will take care of itself.

I'm convinced that a little basic knowledge of birth order can be of great help in the business world, particularly in regard to sales.[1] But can a basic knowledge of birth order literally increase a sales representative's effectiveness? I'll let Harvey Mackay, one of America's top CEOs and writer of many business bestsellers, answer: "When you get right down to it, the salesperson who hits the top of the charts is the one who understands human nature the best."[2]

Obviously I believe that a working knowledge of birth order is one of the most effective ways to know your customers. Am I saying that birth order will *always* work and guarantee you a sale? Of course not. No method *always* works. As I counsel, I don't always "make the sale" in trying to get people to change their dysfunctional and destructive ways. But that doesn't stop me from learning all I can about them—what I call "getting behind their eyes" to see the world as they see it. If I can do that, I can sell them the ideas I have to offer, which can make a difference in their behavior and their lives.

Every single one of us is a salesperson in some arena of life. We can all benefit by getting behind others' eyes.

Part of learning about people includes learning their birth order. When a client sits down with me for the first time, I can ask about his or her birth order, as well as a lot of other "psychological" questions to gain insight into this individual's personality. The average person, however, doesn't have this luxury, and frankly, it's not advisable to ask customers direct questions about their birth order. For example, do not say something such as, "You're always so well dressed and nicely groomed—tell me, are you the firstborn in your family, or at least the firstborn male (or female)?" This kind of question will make you sound like either a first-year psychology student doing research for a term paper, or a mental case.

> *Every single one of us is a salesperson in some arena of life. We can all benefit by getting behind others' eyes.*

A much better approach is to engage the other person in conversation and ask casual questions such as, "Where did you grow up? Where's home for you?" As you get the customer talking about where he grew up, you have him talking about his family. From there you can ask what his family did. Were they farmers? Was there a family business? Did he have any brothers or sisters? Was it a large or a small family?

The other person may respond, "It was just me and my sisters and my kid brother."

To this you can comment, "I'll bet the kid brother got away with murder."

More than likely the other person will say, "Yeah, he did, as a matter of fact."

How to Buy a Car

If you're a firstborn

Read *Consumer's Report* and *Car & Driver* magazine, search the Internet for months for specs on the car of the year, go to the annual car show downtown to check out the possibilities, visit at least four dealerships, get price quotes, and then go home to methodically think it all over and study in detail the various luxury/comfort packages offered.

If you're a middleborn

Do some research (mainly ask friends which cars they like the best, read a few magazines, or search online), walk into a dealership, fall for the pitch given by the celebrity the car manufacturer has hired, and leave with that model of car.

If you're a baby

Decide you want a car, walk onto a car lot that day, and say something profound such as, "Shazzam! Do you have a teal one? . . . You do? . . . And it's got gold trim? . . . I'll take it!" Then, fifty-nine car payments later, you wonder why you bought that stupid car.

"So you had to do most of the work?" you say. "Tell me, who was oldest in the family—you or your sisters?"

With this kind of an approach, you always want to be casual, with your goal being to form a relationship first and get birth order specifics later. Keep making mental notes as you build a case for whatever birth order this person may be.

Another approach is to bring up something about your own family rather casually. For example: "I saw my older brother over the weekend. He and his family came down for the holidays. Do you have any siblings who descend on you at holiday time?"

As you engage in discovering a person's birth order, you will learn all kinds of other things: hobbies, favorite sports, favorite teams, favorite restaurants. The possibilities are almost endless.

The more personal knowledge you can gain about a customer (or someone you hope to make a customer), the better, because it will all help give you some clues about that person's "private logic." All of us have a private logic—how we see life, how we see others, and how we see ourselves. It's part of our total lifestyle.

Our private logic is more or less our personal agenda. Each of us views life differently. If you doubt this, call two or three of your siblings or close friends with whom you have shared a memorable experience in the past. Simply ask, "Do you remember the time . . . ?" Describe the experience in a few words, then sit back and listen as you hear amazingly different views on what happened.

Always be aware of your customer's private logic. As you try to understand his or her point of view, you will really get behind your customer's eyes. It is here that you learn about the person's real biases, preferences, and desires.

> *All of us have a private logic—how we see life, how we see others, and how we see ourselves. It's part of our total lifestyle.*

As you call on your clients, keep making mental (and later written) notes about their birth order characteristics. Soon you will have an invaluable record in your Blackberry that will remind you of how they think, what they like, and how they want to do business. This information can become a gold mine, but of course the bottom line is how you mine that gold—that is, how you use the information in actual sales situations.

I have used the following "secrets" for years as I've dealt with firstborns, middle children, and lastborns. Whether I'm selling myself as a speaker or counseling a client about how she can change if she chooses to do so, I use these simple, commonsense concepts. You can use them to "sell" anything. Just try them, and you'll see what I mean.

Secrets to Selling to a Firstborn

Selling to a firstborn (or the only child who is a super firstborn) is a little like clearing a minefield. You need to proceed with caution, but you want to get in and out as quickly as possible.

Keep in mind that when talking to a firstborn, you're talking to Mr. Nuts and Bolts, Ms. Specifications Page. They are not

> *Keep in mind that when talking to a firstborn, you're talking to Mr. Nuts and Bolts, Ms. Specifications Page.*

likely to be overly impressed with flashy four-color brochures and lots of bold claims. The firstborn basically wants to know: What is your product or service going to do for me? How much will it cost?

Proceed with caution with firstborns and watch out for red lights.

Getting in the Door and off the Ground

All right, you have arrived a few minutes early (never even a minute late) for your appointment with Mr. Hennesey. The moment has come, and you are being ushered into his office. To grab his firstborn attention switch, you must be prepared. Remember that Mr. Hennesey is a very direct, no-nonsense, bottom-line kind of guy. If you don't get right to the point, he may just point you to the door.

So have your sales pitch planned and follow it to the letter. Don't ramble; don't try to fake it. Just say your piece—preferably in five minutes, but three would be even better.

Why a Firstborn Hates Why

As you give your presentation to a firstborn, you may hear him asking questions such as "Why?" along with "What?" "When?" "Where?" and "How much?"

Be ready to answer all those questions, of course, but whatever you do, try not to ask the firstborn any questions beginning with *why*. Naturally, you're probably wondering, *Why not?* It's because the question *Why?* is confrontational and puts the other person on the defensive, at least a little bit—but sometimes more than a little bit.

For the firstborn, especially, a question beginning with *why* is a threat to his or her being in control. Always remember that firstborns like to be in control, and they are not at all pleased by surprises or questions that may put them on the defensive.

It's also good not to press the firstborn for a decision. I'm not saying you shouldn't try to close a sale (we'll get to that in a moment), but remember that firstborns like plenty of detail, so encourage questions as you proceed.

One other thing to remember is that firstborns have substantial egos. When you have an opening, you may want to ask firstborns what makes them or their com-

> *Firstborns like to be in control, and they are not at all pleased by surprises or questions that may put them on the defensive.*

pany successful. Be cautious, however, about saying anything that sounds like insincere flattery. In fact, if you really want to impress Mr. Hennesey, try to do some homework on his company before you arrive. If the company is listed on the stock exchange, you can call a broker and try to get updated on the latest action regarding that firm.

Closing the Sale with a Firstborn

As you wrap up your presentation, always keep in mind that firstborns want to know the cons as well as the pros, the negatives as well as the positives. Don't try to fool them by claiming that what you are selling is absolutely foolproof and flawless. You know better, and so do they.

Instead, use the psychological principle of "oppositional attraction." It's the same thing that I've often used with small children in counseling situations. Way back in graduate school, we learned that if you move *toward* the average 2-year-old, saying, "Come here; come to me," she will usually go the other way—as fast as her little feet will carry her. But if you want to get the average 2-year-old to come to you, you *back up* and say, "Come, come to me." When I first heard this, I didn't believe it would work, but in nine cases out of ten it actually does. There is something about backing up that leaves the child feeling in control and not as fearful.

And what does handling 2-year-olds have to do with handling 45-year-old purchasing agents or CEOs? A great deal. The idea is that you don't just make your sales pitch by saying, "Please sign with me and my company." Instead, as you move toward your close, you will want to let the firstborn know he is in control—he's the one who will make the decision.

One of the best ways to do this is to state the obvious pluses and minuses. For example: "Now I know that you've been with this other company for seven or eight years and that they've been giving you good service. I'd be lying if I said only we give good service—lots of companies give good service. But what I'm excited about is the new dimensions of what we offer. We are ahead of our competitors in several areas. We've not only broken ground; we've established ourselves, and we have proven product [or service]."

> All you're really trying to do on this first call is get your toe in the door. Your foot can come later.

Then leave it with the firstborn. You've made your pitch, and he will make his own decision. If things have gone well, you may hear him say something such as, "I want to think this over. I know someone [across town, in the next state] who uses your product [or service]. I think I'll shoot him an email and see what he thinks."

On the other hand, you may hear a polite, "Thank you very much. I appreciate your presentation, and we'll let you know."

In many cases, especially with firstborns, the latter comment is probably what you will get when making a first call. All you're really trying to do on this first call is get your toe in the door. Your foot can come later.

As a group, firstborns are formidable but reachable. They're impressed by efficiency and a concern for their time and busy schedule. With firstborns, remember: Don't try to get chummy. Just get done and get out.

If you're a firstborn yourself and would like more help in the area of business, read chapter 9 of *Born to Win*.

> *With firstborns, remember: Don't try to get chummy. Just get done and get out.*

Secrets to Selling to a Middle Child

Probably no other birth order is more sensitive to the axiom "Sales are relational" than the middle child. Middle children are relational by nature because they have a hunger for it. As you will remember, they are the ones who go outside the family first to find friends and groups where they feel somewhat in control and aren't squeezed as they are at home.

As you prepare to call on a middle child, you want to remember that he is a good team player, reliable, steady, and loyal. And unlike the firstborn, he actually enjoys being asked questions—in fact, the more questions, the better. Why is this? It's simple: he never got asked that many questions while growing up at home. He was simply ignored.

> *He actually enjoys being asked questions—in fact, the more questions, the better. Why is this? It's simple: he never got asked that many questions while growing up at home. He was simply ignored.*

While most middle children tend to be more laid-back and relational than others, there are exceptions. You can run into a middle child who is something of a buzz saw—very competitive, even a scrappy aggressor type. And instead of seeming to like relationships, the middle child may be a loner, quiet, or shy. But it has been my observation over years of counseling that the typical middle child who winds up in some kind of middle management

> *Middle children like relationships, but on their terms.*

position where he is making decisions regarding purchasing supplies or services is more inclined to be the relational negotiator and mediator.

Some Ideas on Approaching a Middle Child

When calling on a relationship-hungry middle child, you may want to ask her if there is anyone else she would like to bring along—to sit in on the conversation or perhaps go to lunch. With a third party, it's often easier to keep conversation flowing, and this may put the middle child at ease. But it is the middle child's call and not yours. Never bring along one of your own colleagues as a surprise, thinking that the relationship-hungry middle child believes "the more the merrier." Otherwise you could easily wind up making the middle child feel overwhelmed. Middle children like relationships, but on their terms.

Another good idea is to contact the middle child outside the office—at lunch, for example. Do everything you can to make your call less of a sales call and more of a social contact. The middle child usually responds best to a presentation that is slower than you would make to a firstborn and is given with sensitivity. If it's a first call, you may want to leave the impression that you're not there to sell something as much as you are just to make a contact and get to know each other.

Do everything you can to convince the middle child you are concerned about him and his particular interests. If he is a small businessman and your company usually sells to bigger firms, let him know that that doesn't make him any less important to you. For example, you may be able to say, "We've just opened a new division to accommodate small businesses, and I'd like to show you a package that will save you money."

Another effective approach to the middle child is to ask him what his biggest problem or hurdle is. What's the greatest difficulty he faces in business today? Learn how you can help, and then move in to do just that. For example: "I'd like to invite you down to our plant. I'd like you to see what we can do for you." A variation of this could be: "I'd like to invite you down to meet some of our people. I want to show you what we're doing for businesses like yours on a regular basis."

> *Build your relationship slowly; cast out your lines and wait. As a rule, middle children need more lines cast than the decisive firstborns or the more impetuous babies.*

You'll probably have to make more calls on a middle child before you close the sale. Build your relationship slowly; cast out your lines and wait. As a rule, middle children need more lines cast than the decisive firstborns or the more impetuous babies. They are more "go with the flow." They may take longer to sell, but in the end they may be more loyal customers (if you give them good service).

A Middle Child Likes Warm Fuzzies

Again, remember that middle children are more likely to appreciate the old proven ways. Their motto is definitely "If it ain't broke, why fix it?" or "If I've been getting along fine with the product from XYZ Company, why should I switch to ABC Company?" Obviously price can be a factor, but it isn't always the main consideration. Middle children in particular will be looking for service, for relationships, for the warm fuzzy kind of thing that will help them feel more secure and more at home with you as a supplier.

Middle children are not as afraid of (or as disturbed by) change as firstborns may be. Firstborns like the status quo because it helps them stay in control. But because the middle child never had that much control while growing up, he's a little more willing to roll with the punches.

199

And while middle children may not be as much the perfectionists as firstborns, that doesn't mean that you can't find middle children who are perfectionists. Any birth order can succumb to perfectionism. It's just that firstborns and only children are more likely do so because of the tremendous pressure they have been under ever since they can remember.

> Middle children in particular will be looking for service, for relationships, for the warm fuzzy kind of thing that will help them feel more secure and more at home with you.

Closing the Sale with a Middle Child

While the money-back guarantee or no-obligation promises are always powerful tools with any birth order, they are particularly attractive to the middle child. Keep in mind that she is slightly insecure and still rebelling (maybe more than a little bit) against the childhood that had her in the middle, squeezed, left out, and sometimes ignored.

It never hurts to emphasize to middles how they can check with others about your claims and how you will specifically service them if they do buy anything from you. For example, you might say, "We both know there are many companies that do what we do, but I believe that the company I'm representing really focuses on fitting our product [or service] to a customer's needs. We will bend over backward to accommodate specifically what will enhance your production."

> When dealing with middle children, you must always remember three things: Sales are relational. Sales are relational. Sales are relational.

When dealing with middle children, you must always remember three things: Sales are relational. Sales are relational. Sales are relational.

Secrets to Selling to a Lastborn

There is one more birth order that is, in some ways, more relational than the middle child. I speak, of course, of the babies of the family.

> *Babies fly by the seat of their pants and never stay put for very long.*

When you're selling to lastborns, I always like to say, "Bring your dancin' shoes and a weather vane." In other words, be as fun and as charming as you can, and be aware that as the winds change, the lastborn can change as well. Babies fly by the seat of their pants and never stay put for very long.

Sell Them before They Sell You!

As you prepare to approach your lastborn client or potential customer, the more entertaining you can be, the better. It doesn't mean that you come prancing in with party hat and horn. All I'm saying is that your typical baby of the family is looking for fun in life, and while he or she may appear quite businesslike on the surface, this fun-oriented attitude can be right there waiting to come out.

> *Babies of the family like to work hard and play hard. Sometimes they like to do both at the same time.*

If a social environment is good for approaching a middle child, it's even better for the lastborn. Babies of the family like to do everything hard—when they work, they work hard; when they play, they play hard. Sometimes they like to do both at the same time.

As you're chatting with your lastborn customer, be aware that he always loves hearing or telling a good story or joke. Ask, "Would you tell me some of your favorite stories—things that have happened in your business? I'd love to hear them."

When you tell stories, however, stay away from anything even remotely off-color. As much as I love humor, I always follow this rule, not because I think it's a safer way to do business, but because it's the best way to do business in any setting.

Time Counts, So Keep Things Moving

As I mentioned, you need to move fast with firstborns because they are all business and have no time to waste. Lastborns may want to waste a bit of time, but balanced against that is their short attention span. If your lastborn client starts having fun with a story or two, you'd better be well aware of the time. It may be up sooner than you would have liked, and your baby may be gone or halfway out the door, headed for another appointment, before you've had an opportunity to sell your product.

> The typical baby of the family is highly susceptible to being impressed by name-dropping.

As you make your presentation, be aware that the typical baby of the family is highly susceptible to being impressed by name-dropping. It won't hurt at all to mention highly visible people or firms who already use your product or service.

Closing the Sale with a Lastborn

The typical lastborn is 180 degrees from the typical firstborn. You'll remember that firstborns could care less about full-color photos and slick-looking layouts. They want the specs, the numbers, the graphs. Babies, on the other hand, could care less about specs, numbers, and graphs. They love those full-color pictures, the flash, and the glitter. That's how babies arrive at the bottom line.

In other words, the baby tends to ask first, "What does this whole thing really do for *me*? Does it make *me* feel good?" I'm not saying the baby can't make sound business decisions; I am saying that when it comes to weighing the business side of things against personal pluses and minuses, the baby will be giving the personal side significant weight.

Lastborns Are Often Risk Takers

Studies show that the laterborns in the family, particularly babies, are far more likely to be risk takers than firstborns. A professor of marketing from a major university in the South called me on one occasion to say she had just read *The Birth Order Book* and loved it. She speculated that because firstborns are such leaders and the ones who move things forward in so many areas of life, it would make sense to know what firstborns were thinking in order to predict the next trends in marketing.

I was impressed with how she was trying to use what she'd been learning in *The Birth Order Book*, but I had to say, "You're absolutely right, the evidence is overwhelming that firstborns are the leaders of society, but if you're looking for trends, you want to see what the laterborns are doing. They're the ones who are far more likely to be willing to take a risk and change things."

> *If you're looking for trends, you want to see what the laterborns are doing. They're the ones who are far more likely to be willing to take a risk and change things.*

Knowing that lastborns tend to be risk takers can help you as you move in to close your presentation. Because they want to act now, not later, babies are typically spontaneous and impetuous. You can be a little more confrontational and press a little harder for a decision. If the baby of the family is leaning at all in your direction, don't hesitate to ask for a commitment or to sign on the bottom line.

When I bought a Chrysler Sebring convertible, I went in and made the deal I wanted to make, true enough, but the sales manager—a firstborn, by the way, who was a very dapper dresser—also did a good job of recognizing how I was operat-

> *All of us want respect,
> some of us more
> than others.*

ing, and he dealt with me accordingly. For example, he noticed I was in a hurry and impatient. Maybe he even remembered that I tend to be a bit impetuous, because he had dealt with me before. At any rate, he didn't hem and haw. He made the deal, signed me up, and let me drive out the door in a very short time. While he'd never had any kind of course on selling to different birth orders, he sold to me—a lastborn—pretty well.

Selling to babies can be fun, but don't get the idea that they're airheads. Remember, there is that dark side to the baby—the side that says, "I want to *show them*!" Lastborns remind us of a universal truth: all of us want respect, some of us more than others.

The Best-Kept Secret in Business

The secrets to selling to different birth orders are all based pretty much on common sense. But maybe the best-kept secret to making sales, working for an employer, managing your employees, or heading up the PTA or a neighborhood watch group is this: take a personal interest.

As an author, I'm often out on the road pushing my latest book. My publisher sends me on a tour of several cities where I appear on TV and radio and then drop in at the local bookstores to greet and get to know people. I usually enjoy these bookstore stops a great deal. On rare occasions, however, I experience an author's worst nightmare: having a great TV or radio interview and then going downtown to stop at a bookstore and not finding my book anywhere!

I was in a large Midwestern city not too long ago, being escorted about by a very classy lady who not only knows books but knows people, especially the managers of the bookstores. As she took me over to meet the manager of one bookstore that is part of a well-known national chain, she told me about how this manager's daughter had been in an accident. The damage had been so severe it had taken a year for the little girl to recover.

I told my escort I appreciated that information, and a few minutes later, when she introduced me to the bookstore manager, I said, "I hear you're quite a woman. I've heard some good things about you. I know it's been a rough year for you."

Immediately the bookstore manager perked up, and the conversation jumped several levels above the usual perfunctory introduction. The reason was simple. With a couple of comments, I had gone into relationship mode and let the woman know that I understood how it had been for her. Then I added, "You know, I have four daughters myself."

That was all we really needed. The manager and I talked about her daughter's injuries and how her recovery had been slow and frustrating.

Later—quite a bit later, in fact—we got around to talking about why I was supposed to be there—because I was in town on a book tour. It was as if a light went on, and the store manager said, "Oh my, what shows were you on today? Say, I don't think we have your book in stock. I'll order some right away!"

How to Sell a Car

If you're a salesperson, you have to get behind someone else's eyes instead of simply viewing the world from your own eyes.

To a firstborn

Realize he or she is going to ask you every conceivable question known to humankind, so be ready. By asking you these questions, the firstborn is testing what you know about the car. He or she already knows it and has done the research but wants to see how smart you are.

To a middleborn

Help the middleborn weigh the options that are best for his or her lifestyle, but without pressure. Show the middleborn several possibilities, then give him or her the credit of being smart enough to decide.

To a baby

This buyer's main concern is color, flash, and whether he or she can have the car by Saturday for an important date. Encourage the lastborn's enthusiasm and you'll have a fast sale. But don't promise what you can't deliver, or you may have a temper tantrum on your hands.

In a few minutes, she put a sizable order for my book in the computer.

As my escort drove me to the airport, we talked about the conversation I had had with the manager, and she mentioned how impressed she had been with the way I could build a relationship so quickly. I commented, "You know, if you call that lady two years from now and mention my name, she'll remember me. Why? Because I was interested in *her* and *her child*, not primarily in pushing my books."

> *If you always try to treat people the way you'd like to be treated, your motives will be right, and what comes around will almost always be good.*

And that's the point of this little story. Obviously I could go around being interested in bookstore managers (and everyone else) only to manipulate them to get what I want—more book sales. After all, I want more book sales as badly as any author. But I can honestly say that I build relationships because *I am truly interested in the people I deal with*. The benefits that come out of that are obvious and, to some extent, automatic.

As someone said, "What goes around comes around." If you always try to treat people the way you'd like to be treated, your motives will be right, and what comes around will almost always be good. The smart person figures out how to navigate all the birth orders.

Learning to do so is valuable not only for business but for all of life—including marriage, the most intimate relationship of all. To see how birth order can affect any marriage, including yours, turn to the next chapter.

11

Birth Order Marriages Aren't Made in Heaven

I used to think that marriages could be made in heaven. Now, after counseling couples all these years, I know they're made on earth. And you know what my first question is for any couple who comes for marital counseling? "What's your birth order?"

The answer I get most often is, "I'm a firstborn and so is she," or "I'm an only child and so is he."

This is not to say I don't counsel couples who are middle children or lastborns, but over the years as I've counseled thousands of couples, the most competitive, most volatile, and most discouraged are combinations where both spouses are firstborns or, worse, both are only children.

Their relationship is the opposite of the true concept of marriage, which is pulling together, sharing, melding into the unity of one. Instead, they are like mountain sheep, constantly butting heads. They lock horns over something, and neither one will back off.

And what do they disagree about? *Everything.* Firstborns and only children are, by nature, perfectionist flaw finders and nitpickers. There's a country song that goes, "You want things your way, and I want them mine." How true it is!

I Ejected One Couple for Fighting

One pair of firstborns I counseled would spend the first ten or twenty minutes of every session fighting as I sat there and listened. Finally I got tired of it and threw them out of my office.

"No charge for today," I said. "I'm sick and tired of listening to you run each other down. You go home and think it over. When you're both ready to take a run at making a marriage, come see me again."

Admittedly, ejecting this couple for fighting was a harsh counseling tactic, but it's something I've done on rare occasions over the years when I felt the situation warranted it. I didn't hear from this couple for about a month, and I began to think, *You blew that one, Leman. They won't be back.* But a few days later, they called and made an appointment. This time they didn't fight (at least in my presence).

> It's the little things that drive firstborns crazy: clothes in a heap, unentered checks, lights left on, and so on.

What had happened? The couple had made a simple decision that had "unlocked their horns." They had decided to quit butting heads. More precisely, they had decided to quit using their tongues as chisels to chip away at each other and their marriage. They had been at each other over the little things (a true sign of perfectionism). But it's the little things that drive firstborns crazy: clothes in a heap, unentered checks, lights left on, and so on.

They often locked horns when they were going somewhere in the car. Firstborn husband would be driving, taking his familiar route to the freeway, when his firstborn wife would say, "Why did you turn here? We're taking the freeway, aren't we?"

"I always go this way," her husband would reply.

"Well, you should have turned back at Elm Street," the wife would respond matter-of-factly. "It's three blocks shorter."

We didn't really start getting anywhere until I asked them a simple question: "Who's winning this marriage? With all the lambasting that you've been doing to each other, who's coming out on top?"

> *If you're not married yet, and you want better odds for a happier marriage, marry out of your birth order.*

They looked at each other and admitted, "Well, neither one of us wins."

"Exactly," I said. And then I reminded them again that they had married within their own birth order. Once they understood how two firstborns can be a volatile combination, they learned how to give in and accept each other.

They didn't really need any more sessions. I sent them on their way with some final advice: "Remember to never let the sun go down on your anger. Talk about things before you go to bed at night. When either of you gets picky over some little thing, learn to laugh about it, and above all else, take Elm Street to the freeway!"

Over the years I have counseled more discouraged, fast-becoming-destructive perfectionists than anyone else. But a marriage between two middle children can be destructive too, and so can a match with two babies. The first principle (not a rule) for a riskier kind of marriage: marry someone in your own birth order. If you're not married yet, and you want better odds for a happier marriage, marry out of your birth order. We'll discuss that later in this chapter, but right now let's take a look at some examples of couples who married within their own birth orders and see what happened.

Perfectionists and Sex

Shirley, a 38-year-old, and George, a 41-year-old, both first-borns, came to see me with what George called "Shirley's sex problem." The oldest of four children, Shirley grew up in a family with an extremely domineering father, whom she described as intelligent and explosive. According to Shirley, her dad had always tried to run her life. And while still in her teens, she vowed she would "never marry anyone like Dad."

> *The parent of the opposite sex has the most influence on us.*

But of course Shirley had married someone just like Dad. Why? One explanation that usually hits the mark is that, as a rule, the parent of the opposite sex has the most influence on us. And in Shirley's case, domineering Dad had made his mark. Despite all her vows to never marry anyone like him, there was an even deeper drive telling her, *I could never satisfy Dad, so I'll find a man just like him and please him. I'll win yet!*

While George wasn't as explosive as her father had been, he was very demanding and critical. He also wanted sex every day! But Shirley was a classic perfectionist who approached sex like everything else—as a carefully regimented performance. Shirley and George had sex with no deviation in technique, position, or lighting (none).

Shirley had tried to please George, but the demands she had placed on herself to meet his sex drive had caused her to become unable to enjoy sex. She had grown unresponsive to George, who was a perfectionist himself and was constantly nitpicking her about sex and everything else. The nitpicking only made Shirley more uptight and resentful. She saw George as just another domineering male like her father.

The one ray of hope was that Shirley and George wanted to save their marriage. This was greatly encouraging because my approach to every marriage counseling case is the same:

if a couple has stood before God and man and said, "I do, for better or for worse," then they should try everything possible to stay together. So we had two firstborn perfectionists locking horns and banging heads, with the bedroom as their main battlefield. The first step toward unlocking horns was to suggest a less rigid and demanding schedule regarding sex. This really wasn't too hard. Because of all the tension and fighting, they had already dropped down to "only" four times a week.

I gave Shirley and George several suggestions and techniques on how to relax and enjoy each other while they made sex a celebration instead of a performance (i.e., ordeal). (For more suggestions, see my books *Sheet Music* and *Turn Up the Heat*.) Soon they started making good progress as a couple. I also gave Shirley assignments of her own that she carried out very well. First, I had her admit to her perfectionism whenever she saw it popping up. This simple exercise started making her much more aware of the demands she was placing on herself as well as on others.

> **How to Fight Fair**
>
> 1. Choose a setting where you won't be interrupted.
> 2. Only one person talks at a time until he or she is done. Then it's the other person's turn.
> 3. Before you open your mouth, count to ten.
> 4. Hold hands and look each other in the eye.
> 5. Keep whatever is said between the two of you.
> 6. If feelings are too hot, agree to part for a few hours, but set a time to come back to discuss the issue.
> 7. Don't let the sun go down on your anger.

I also instructed Shirley to watch her expectations, to take smaller bites of life. That included learning to say no and refusing to take on more than she could handle. Like Kathleen in chapter 7, Shirley was a classic pleaser who worked outside the home, did all the housework herself, and also served on several volunteer committees in her community. She had been carrying a double load and then some as long as she and George had been married.

As Shirley learned to say no, she learned how to give herself space. She quit living under the tyranny of her to-do list, which she had been literally taping to the steering wheel of her car to constantly remind her of all she had to get done that day. She planned less and managed to accomplish it, rather than finishing each day irritated and frustrated because she "had not gotten everything done."

Just as predictably, the relationship between Shirley and George improved radically, particularly in bed. They started having sex less and enjoying it more!

Something else Shirley had to deal with was her image of George as a very dominating husband. Rather than her playing a passive role to George, I encouraged her to take a certain amount of initiative in their relationship, especially when it came to sex. I suggested things like "kidnapping" her husband from work and getting out of town to a nearby resort for an overnight. Another idea was taking time for a picnic lunch in the middle of a workday.

Perfectionist that she was, Shirley really threw herself into her new assignments with enthusiasm. I remember the delight she had when she told me of the time she picked up George after work for an evening that included a picnic supper, time in a hot tub, and staying at a hotel for the night. She had thought of everything, making the reservations and arranging for Grandma to stay with the kids.

Was George perfect in this relationship? No, I had to work with him on details of his own perfectionism and domineering nature. After all, it's much easier to decide your spouse is the one who needs changing than to realize that you're part of the problem. (For you ladies who long for your man to change, you'll find *Have a New Husband by Friday* an informative and inspiring read.)

But while both spouses had problems, in this case it was Shirley who was the key to getting the marriage back on the right track. As soon as she started dealing positively with her perfectionism, she was able to rearrange priorities. As she started controlling her own expectations and goal setting, the scene changed. By marrying a man much like her father—domineering and critical—she had set herself up for failure. It was like a train that had been roaring full speed toward a washed-out bridge. But Shirley stopped the train, threw a switch, and got herself and George on a track that led to safety and happiness. I'm proud of her!

Sylvia Plus Mark Equaled No Communication

Another birth order marriage that can run into trouble is that of two middle children. As we saw in chapter 8, the middle child shoots off in his own direction, depending on the strengths and weaknesses of the firstborn ahead of him. The middle child can go in a lot of directions, but most middle children develop the ability to mediate, negotiate, and compromise.

In short, middle children are often diplomats, which sounds like a wonderful skill to carry into marriage, but ironically what often happens with two middle children is a tendency to desire peace at any price. They become avoiders—of their problems and eventually each other. Middle children prefer the oceans of life to be smooth. They don't want to make waves, so the result can be a quiet surface with all kinds of storms brewing underneath because they are not communicating.

> *Middle children prefer the oceans of life to be smooth. They don't want to make waves, so the result can be a quiet surface with all kinds of storms brewing underneath.*

Such was the case with Sylvia, a quiet 32-year-old and thirdborn daughter in a family of five children. With two sisters above her and two boys below her, Sylvia got lost in the middle during her childhood and teenage years. She grew up shy, passive, and definitely an avoider of conflict. She

213

tried to please her parents by taking over a lot of the care of her two younger brothers while their mother worked. Mark was 29, the second of three children. His older brother had always been the best at everything, and his little sister got the typical "baby princess" treatment that often left Mark feeling as if he hadn't gotten a fair shake. Mark went outside the family early to find his own friends and social life, another classic mark of the middle child. One of those friends was Sylvia, his high school sweetheart, whom he married soon after graduation. Now, after eight years of marriage, Sylvia and Mark had two children, 7 and 4 years of age.

> **Mark didn't want to make waves. He wanted to avoid conflict whenever he could, so the simplest solution was, "Sorry, I have to work late tonight."**

Sylvia arranged for the counseling, acting on the urging of one of her older sisters, who was tired of hearing her complain about feeling trapped with little children and unable to communicate with her husband. Sylvia was also worried about another woman because during the last few months Mark had been insisting he had to work longer hours at his job.

I talked separately with Sylvia and Mark. It turned out there was no other woman. As you may recall, the middle child is the most monogamous of all birth orders, and this was true in Mark's case. It seemed one woman was all he could handle, especially when he felt she tried to run his life. Sylvia was still operating with Mark the way she had with her two younger brothers. She told him what to do, and Mark resented it, even when it came from a sweet, shy girl like his wife. But as a middle child, Mark didn't want to make waves. He wanted to avoid conflict whenever he could, so the simplest solution was, "Sorry, I have to work late tonight."

Sylvia, on the other hand, didn't know how to approach Mark and could only guess what was going on. Communication was at zero when Sylvia came to me for help. Sylvia and Mark made good progress when they committed themselves to spending time talking after the kids were in bed and they could concentrate on each other. Having Mark share his feelings really helped Sylvia because his silence and secretive devotion to work had bothered her a great deal. Mark learned that he could tell Sylvia how he felt, and she would not reject him.

While Sylvia appreciated the talks with Mark, she admitted it was difficult to verbalize her own thoughts. I suggested that she supplement the talks by writing Mark positive notes now and then. Mark had to travel occasionally for his company, so Sylvia began slipping little notes and cards into his suitcase. Finding these little love notes and brief bits of encouragement between his shirts when he was unpacking in the hotel made the trips much easier for Mark.

Another plus that came out of the new effort to communicate was that Sylvia felt less trapped as the mother of two small children. Mark had his job as an outlet, and he learned to come home and say, "What can I do to help?" Sylvia was thrilled, and as Mark became more willing to be helpful around the house, she learned to back off on her "motherly" little ways of telling him what to do.

As middle children, Sylvia and Mark were really good candidates for marriage. The irony in their situation, however, is what faces any couple when both of them are middleborn. They may not communicate because their urge to avoid conflict and make the oceans of life smooth wins out over their natural tendency to be mediators and negotiators—which sounds like a paradox—and that's how relationships often flounder.

Peter and Mary: Born Last, First in Debt

Marrying your own birth order is usually not a good idea for the babies in the family either. On the positive side, lastborns may have a ball during their courtship because they both have a fun-loving, go-for-broke nature. But once the lastborns are married, one of them better take responsibility for the family budget or they will "go for broke" indeed.

> As a rule, lastborns cannot live on a tight budget.

By the time they came to see me, Peter and Mary, both babies of their families, were in serious difficulties with the bank and several other creditors. They were in their early thirties, had no children, and had a good income, but they were hopelessly in debt. Every credit card balance was well over the maximum, several store bills were overdue, and their car and ski boat were about to be repossessed. The only reason they weren't in trouble on a house payment was that they were renting an apartment. And the only reason they weren't behind in their rent was a no-nonsense landlord who threatened immediate eviction proceedings if the rent was even one day past the ten-day grace period.

All of this fiscal chaos led, of course, to marital warfare. Neither Peter nor Mary had been particularly overindulged as children, but when they got out on their own, as a married couple, they decided to live by the pleasure principle. If they saw something they wanted, they bought (that is, *charged*) it. They blamed each other for their overindulgence. Ironically enough, both were also overweight. There was no control anywhere in sight.

My first step with Peter and Mary was putting them in touch with a financial counselor. He put them on a tight budget, consolidated all their debts, and arranged a payment program. He even had them cut up all their credit cards. As a rule, lastborns cannot live on a tight budget. As a lastborn myself, I understand that perfectly. I leave it to my firstborn wife, Sande, to keep us out of debt.

Peter and Mary saw me only a few more times. Their real problem was money, not their marriage. They loved each other and were committed to staying together. Once they committed themselves to not buying anything on credit for at least two years, and to selling a couple of their "toys," like the ski boat, they were well on their way to stability.

Peter and Mary are typical examples of how lack of order and stability are often weak links in the makeup of lastborns. As we saw in chapter 9, the lastborn child grows up spoiled, overindulged, coddled, and cuddled. This hardly helps them get basic training for running a budget. On the other side of the coin, lastborns are often treated as if they don't know quite enough and are always behind, too young, too small, too weak, and "stupid." Lastborns often develop an attitude that says, *Who cares anyway? I might as well have a little fun while I can.*

Once Peter and Mary realized they could control their spending and still have fun, they enjoyed life with each other a whole lot more.

> **Simple Rules for Babies**
>
> 1. Talk with your spouse about any potential purchases that are more than $100 *before* you make them.
> 2. Agree together that, other than purchasing a house and a car, if you don't have the money in the bank or in your wallet to pay for a certain item, you don't buy it.
> 3. If you see something you want to buy, walk away and wait twenty-four hours. Think, *Do I really need that item? Or do I just want that item? And for how long will I want that item?*
> 4. Agree together with your spouse on a certain sum of money each of you can spend each month for "fun money." Each of you should have that money in cash in your own "fun jar." When the money is gone for the month, it's gone. There's no dipping into the credit card, the checking account, or the savings account.

Which Birth Orders Make the Best Matches?

So what's the best combination for a happy, satisfying, lifetime marriage? Find someone with a different birth order.

Opposites not only attract, they are usually good for one another in a marriage setting. Psychologists have done stud-

> ### *What's the best combination for a happy, satisfying, lifetime marriage?*
> ### *Find someone with a different birth order.*

ies that prove this theory.[1] According to their research, firstborns or only children and lastborns supposedly make the best match. Next come the middle children and lastborns.

Following is a quick rundown on six birth order combinations and why they tend to go wrong or right in a marriage, plus some practical tips for each combination. Keep in mind that there are no guarantees that a certain birth order combination will lead automatically to a successful or miserable marriage. But the point is that there are *indicators* in birth order information that can help a couple deal with any tensions they may have.

Tips for Firstborn + Firstborn Marriage

1. Stop "improving" on things your spouse does or says.
2. Stop "shoulding" your mate.
3. Define roles carefully to avoid arguments over control.
4. Get rid of the we've-got-to-do-it-my-way attitude.

Firstborn Plus Firstborn Equals Power Struggle

As we've already seen with George and Shirley, when perfectionistic firstborns get together, there is a butting of heads (i.e., a power struggle). The issues usually focus on perfectionism and who has control. If you are a firstborn or an only child married to another firstborn or only child, here are some tips for reducing tension and increasing harmony in your marriage:

1. *Stop "improving" on things your spouse does or says.* To a perfectionist, this may be a real trick, but bite your tongue and do it anyway. What your tongue says determines the direction (and often the longevity) of your marriage.

2. *Stop "shoulding" your mate.* For firstborn perfectionists, criticism is second nature. If you are being hard on
yourself and/or your mate, lower that high-jump bar
of life. Once you quit trying to jump so high, you can
stop asking your mate to do so as well.

3. *Define roles carefully to avoid arguments over control.*
In other words, decide who does what. One spouse
can do the shopping while the other pays the bills and
balances the checking account. Help your spouse with
assigned tasks and try to be considerate and aware of
his or her responsibilities. For example, if one spouse
does the shopping, the other should not complain about
the high grocery bill. I counseled one couple where the
perfectionist, critical husband complained incessantly
about this until his wife told him, "Okay, *you* shop this
week." He did and came home in "sticker shock," never
to complain again!

4. *Get rid of the we've-got-to-do-it-my-way attitude.*
There's more than one way to do things (and your way
isn't necessarily best). One of the best sentences any firstborn perfectionist can learn to say to his or her firstborn
spouse is, "You may be right. Let's try it your way."

Firstborns Find Middleborns a Paradox

The firstborn who marries a
middleborn should first take comfort in the fact that middles have the
best track record for building a last-
ing marriage. At the same time, the
middle child can be a vexing paradox. Middle children grow up having to learn to negotiate, mediate,
and compromise, but they can also
be secretive and play it close to the
vest with their emotions. Middle
children typically will throw their

> **Tips for Firstborn + Middle-born Marriage**
>
> 1. Make it a point to have regular recaps and discuss feelings and what is happening.
> 2. Make your spouse feel special.
> 3. If you're the firstborn, work on drawing out your middle child spouse.

firstborn spouses a bone once in a while without letting them know how they really feel.

Some practical suggestions for firstborns married to middles include the following:

1. *Make it a point to have regular recaps and discuss feelings and what is happening.* Do not let your spouse toss you a bone by saying, "Everything's fine." Ask what your spouse means by "fine."

   Daily recaps—or a recap at least every few days—are valuable in any marriage but are particularly useful if one mate tends to be less inclined to share feelings.

2. *Make your spouse feel special.* Remember that the middle child husband or wife very likely did not grow up feeling special, so anything you do—small gifts, love notes, saying *sincere* little things he or she likes to hear—will touch the heart and strengthen your marriage. While the following applies to every birth order, it's especially good for the firstborn husband of the middle child wife to remember: every day a wife asks in one way or another, "Do you really love me?" Every day she needs your affirming answer.

3. *Work on drawing out your middle child spouse.* Keep in mind that as a firstborn, your natural inclination is to give the answer, solve the problem. Instead, back off and ask, "What do you think?" "Tell me how you really feel," or "Tell me more." Firstborn husbands of middleborn wives should always ask for their opinion, particularly on issues of people and feelings. Middleborns are not only more perceptive, but they also like the problem-solving role and smoothing a way for everyone.

Firstborn Plus Lastborn Equals Bliss (Usually)

According to a study of three thousand families, the odds for a happily-ever-after increase a great deal when the firstborn marries the lastborn.[2] At work here is the opposites-attract-and-are-good-for-each-other factor. The firstborn teaches the lastborn little things that may be lacking, such as being organized and having goals, while the lastborn helps the firstborn lighten up and not take an overly serious approach to life.

> *Every day a wife asks in one way or another, "Do you really love me?" Every day she needs your affirming answer.*

According to the researchers, the best possible match you can find is the firstborn or only female and the lastborn male. I took no part in this research, so I can't be accused of making this claim, because that happens to be the match Sande, my firstborn wife, and I have. I'm just *very* thankful it happened.

Firstborn females are often mothering types, and lastborn males often need mothering. I was fortunate to be the lastborn brother of my firstborn sister, Sally. Eight years older, she mothered me quite a bit and taught me a lot about women. For example, she taught me that girls don't like being approached by a bunch of boys who are show-offs—pushing each other, talking loudly, and doing stupid things that guys often do. Sally also told me that girls want a guy who is tender, understanding, and a listener, who realizes manners have not gone out of style.

Most marriage counselors agree that men do not understand women very well. So *any* extra learning a boy can get while growing up is going to help him later when he has a wife and family of his own. Of course, I certainly didn't come into my own marriage a finished product. I still needed some work, and Mama Bear was happy to oblige.

Tips for Firstborn + Lastborn Marriage

1. If you're the firstborn, don't let the lastborn spouse take advantage of you.
2. Firstborns prone to fault finding must back off.
3. If you're the lastborn, remember that others need the spotlight too.
4. If you're the lastborn, remember that you're not a one-man team.

> *Good marriages are made, not born. Two people must work together on being considerate, caring, and mutually supportive.*

It may be a good rule of thumb to say that any combination of firstborn and lastborn has a better chance for marital success than do other combinations, but success doesn't follow automatically. Good marriages are made, not born. Two people must work together on being considerate, caring, and mutually supportive.

When I married Sande, it was a classic matchup of the pleaser Mama Bear taking on the playful Cub. Naturally the Cub took advantage of his new caregiver. Sande had to put up with my fussy eating habits and picking up my clothes wherever I dropped them.

This went on through the early years of our marriage. One day, while I was working on my doctorate, Sande heard me expound on how to discipline children and hold them accountable for their actions. The light dawned. *If holding children accountable for their actions is good, then holding a husband accountable might be even better*, Sande thought. She went into action.

Soon I found my piles of clothing where I had left them. In no time the apartment became covered with my piles. Then came the day when I could not open the door because Sande had shoved a giant stack of my clothes against it to make room for whatever she was doing. *That* got my attention. Sande and I had a long overdue talk and shared our feelings.

She said, "Look, I want to be your wife, not your mother. You learn to pick up your own clothes and put them where they belong. Also, I'm going to fix different things for dinner. I expect you to at least try some new dishes. You owe that much to yourself and to our children if you want to be the good role model you keep talking about."

I said, "Okay, I'll try to do better, but you have to promise me that you'll serve only canned peas and corn—no frozen peas!"

Learning to pick up my clothes and eating different foods was just a start as Cubby Bear learned how to grow up and become Papa Bear.

Here are some tips for firstborn/lastborn couples:

1. *If you're the firstborn, don't let the lastborn spouse take advantage of you.* Sande was gentle spirited but firm. She started expecting me to be a leader in our home and to take an active role in meeting responsibilities. At times, she reminded me of my high school English teacher—the one in whose class I *never* goofed off because I knew better. I even learned that changing diapers is not off-limits for a psychologist with a doctor's degree, and when our children started to arrive, I did my share of diapers, baths, and other baby care. In short, Mama Bear taught Papa Bear that parenthood isn't women's work. And I'm so glad she did.

2. *Firstborns prone to fault finding must back off.* If you want to find your lastborn spouse's flaws, you certainly can, because they're all over the place. Accept all the flaws you can or make gentle suggestions on how to correct them. And if you're the lastborn, remember not to flaunt your flaws in your firstborn spouse's face.

3. *If you're the lastborn, remember that others need the spotlight too.* Lastborns are notorious carrot seekers, as in, "Look at me, I'm performing—toss me a carrot." Your firstborn spouse may act as if they don't need any attention or strokes, but they do, and you should provide some.

4. *If you're the lastborn, remember that you are not a one-man team.* Because you have that firstborn spouse who is probably keeping things organized and running smoothly, you as a lastborn may impetuously go off on your own now and then—to buy something, schedule something, or just do something without letting your spouse know.

One of the best bits of wisdom I ever received concerning marriage came from Dr. James Dobson, founder of Focus on the Family and author of such best-sellers as *Dare to Discipline*, *The Strong-Willed Child*, and *Hide or Seek*. An only child, Dr. Dobson is scholarly, organized, conscientious, and reliable. So one day while Sande and I were having lunch with him, I asked, "Jim, if there was one bit of advice you could give to me, what would it be?"

> **Before you do anything, whatever it is, run it by your spouse first.**

He glanced at Sande and then back at me. "Kevin," he said, "before you do anything, *whatever it is*, run it by Sande first."

Obviously Dr. Dobson's advice applies to *any* birth order marriage match, but it especially applied to the lastborn Cub and Mama Bear! I said to myself, *If an only child with Jim Dobson's credentials thinks that's a good idea, then I do too!* I've tried to follow his advice ever since, and it has *always* paid off.

Middle Plus Middle Can Equal a Muddle

As we have seen, two married middle children will probably not communicate well. They tend to feel it isn't worth the hassle to confront each other. They may also discount the value of their own opinions. These attitudes are typical of middle children.

> **Tips for Middle + Middle Marriage**
>
> 1. Build up each other's self-esteem.
> 2. Provide plenty of space for outside friendships.
> 3. Do special things for each other.
> 4. Above all, show each other mutual respect.

One simple little device I have used with great success when counseling a middle married to a middle is the suggestion bowl. Place a clear bowl or jar in a prominent place where both of you can see it and deposit your suggestions in it. Keep pads of paper and pencils or pens handy. The husband should use one color of paper, the wife another. When the husband wants to tell his wife something, he writes a suggestion on his pad and drops it into the bowl. And when the wife wants to give hubby a suggestion, she does the same. Some spouses—particularly men—think the suggestion bowl is too much of a crutch, but I talk them into trying it anyway because, the fact is, some of us simply can't look our mate in the eye and tell him or her what is on our mind.

Some other tips to keep the middle child marriage healthy include the following:

1. *Build up each other's self-esteem.* Middle children often have a poor to only fair self-image, so let your spouse know you appreciate his or her strengths and abilities. Be sure to make sincere comments, not obvious pat-on-the-head remarks designed to flatter or manipulate.

2. *Provide plenty of space for outside friendships.* Remember that as middle children, you both are probably big on having friends and social acquaintances. Encourage each other to make these kinds of contacts, but only with the same sex. Keep your marriage and your intimacy as a couple at the forefront of your activities.

3. *Do special things for each other.* I've already mentioned this, but it bears repeating: middle children usually don't grow up feeling very special because they are squeezed and ignored. You don't have to spend a lot of time and money to do something special. Love notes are always good. A single rose, a small bottle of cologne, a special dinner—it's definitely the thought, not the amount of money, that counts.

4. *Above all, show each other mutual respect.* You show respect when you telephone if you're running late; check with your spouse before making commitments; refrain from talking about your marriage in front of others; back each other up in front of the children, particularly

on discipline matters; and never bad-mouth each other in the presence of others.

Middle Child Plus Baby—a Pretty Good Match

According to birth order studies, middle children and last-borns rank right up there as potentially successful pairings for marriage. The middle child, typically strong in negotiating and compromising, pairs up well with a socially outgoing baby of the family.

And somewhat paradoxically, this kind of marriage has a high probability for good communication—sharing feelings and rolling with the punches. Yes, I know I said earlier that middle children tend to clam up and not share emotions, but the plus factor here is that middle children are not as threatened by babies of the family as they might be by meticulous, exacting first-borns. So the odds—and remember, all of these birth order pairing observations go by the odds—are good for decent communication.

> **Tips for Middle + Baby Marriage**
>
> 1. If you're the middle child, work things out but guard against being condescending to your lastborn spouse.
> 2. If you're the middle child, blend your social interests with your lastborn spouse's desire to have fun.
> 3. If you're the lastborn, realize you have a selfish streak and a desire to hold the spotlight. Work at backing off.
> 4. If you're the lastborn, don't have fun at your spouse's expense.

Here are some tips for making a fairly good blend even better:

1. *If you're the middle child, work things out but guard against being condescending to your lastborn spouse.* Lastborn mates will smell that in a moment, because people have been writing them off in a condescending way all their lives.
2. *If you're the middle child, blend your social interests with your lastborn spouse's desire to have fun.* If you're

a typical middle child, friends are important, and you enjoy having people over and having other social outreaches. If your lastborn mate is typical, he or she will always be ready

> **Always try to laugh with *your mate, not* at *him or her.***

for adventure and trying something new. When daily connections and pressures make it impossible to get away, the middle child spouse should grant in fantasy that which is impossible in reality by saying something such as, "Honey, I'd love to go with you to that bed and breakfast, and we will as soon as the kids settle down a little [or as soon as things settle down at work]."

3. *If you're the lastborn, realize that you have a selfish streak and a desire to hold the spotlight.* Work at backing off from your demands for service or attention. Do everything you can to make your middle child mate feel pampered and special.

4. *If you're the lastborn, don't have fun at your spouse's expense.* This is good advice for any birth order, but it applies particularly to lastborns who want to have fun, play practical jokes, and get in sarcastic little digs—all just to get a laugh. Keep in mind, however, that many middle children battle feelings of inferiority, and it's easy to press the wrong button or push too hard. Always try to laugh *with* your mate, not *at* him or her.

Lastborn Plus Lastborn Equals Chaos

I have already touched on how lastborns can get into financial trouble in a marriage. They have a big problem with answering the metaphorical question "Who is

> **Tips for Lastborn + Lastborn Marriage**
>
> 1. Beware of selective listening.
> 2. Learn to be active listeners.
> 3. Hold each other accountable.
> 4. Stay loose and laid-back.
> 5. Keep your sense of humor and never give up.

running the asylum?" And before long their home has turned into a real one.

Two lastborns must put their heads together and decide who pays the bills, who does the shopping, who cooks and cleans up, who takes charge of the social calendar, who cleans the house, and who is point guard on disciplining the kids. Notice I said *point guard* for discipline, which suggests that Mom and Dad are a team but that one of them may have to take the lead while the other one is backup.

If lastborns don't get a grip and make firm decisions on these practical matters, they can arrive in big-time trouble fast. Babies of the family have a tendency to forget, or to assume their spouse was going to do what needed doing. ("Was *I* supposed to gas up the car? I thought *you* were going to!")

Lastborns have a built-in tendency to pass the buck and blame to someone else, and who is handier than one's spouse? But if your spouse is a lastborn, guess who's catching the buck and throwing it right back in your face?

Here are some other tips for the lastborn/lastborn couple:

1. *Beware of selective listening.* Remember that you're both manipulators. You may wind up playing games with one another and selectively hearing only what you want to hear. Then when you're finally called to account, you'll come back with the old standby: "Oh, I didn't understand it that way at all. I never really agreed to do *that*. . . . Why didn't you *tell me*? I had no idea!"

2. *Learn to be active listeners.* The best cure for selective listening is active listening, which means you listen with more than your ears. Look directly at your partner when he or she talks. Sense his or her feelings, and try to understand the facts being communicated. Sit in chairs facing each other with your knees practically touching. Hold hands and talk about your problems. There are only two rules: while one person speaks, the other can-

not interrupt; and before replying, the listener has to "feed back," to the speaker's satisfaction, everything the speaker said. Yes, this is a ponderous way to have a discussion. But it does wonders for helping spouses learn how to hear each other and understand what the other is saying.

3. *Hold each other account-able.* I suggest trying a simple plan. Sit down once or twice a week and ask some pointed questions: "How are we doing on the budget?" "Is the checkbook under control?" "Are we both aware of our next important date or engagement?" "Do you think

> *Look directly at your partner when he or she talks. Sense his or her feelings, and try to understand the facts being communicated.*

I'm really trying to listen to you?" That last question might open up the door for practicing more active listening, as long as you avoid being defensive. And that brings us to the next tip.

4. *Stay loose and laid-back.* Those are your natural qualities anyway, so use them when things get a bit tense. Remember, as the baby of the family, you "earned a living" by looking up and learning how to get around all the older kids and other insurmountable problems. You can get around marriage problems too, if you work together with your spouse. And that suggests one more tip.

5. *Keep your sense of humor and never give up.* But remember what I said to the lastborn spouse of the middle child, which applies here as well: Don't make fun of each other. Laugh together, not at each other.

An Arrow, Not an Answer

Now that I've touched on the "best" and the statistically "not so hot" birth order combinations for marriage, have

I left you encouraged or discouraged? Maybe you're a bit puzzled because according to your birth orders, you're supposed to have a great marriage, but things aren't going that well. Maybe you're indignant because you aren't considered a good match and you get along just fine, thank you! So what does this Leman know about anything anyway?

All of these discussions of which birth order combinations make strong or weak marriages follow the same principle that I have been repeating and will continue to repeat throughout this book: when talking about birth order, all general statements are *indicators*, not rules. In other words, all these general guidelines are arrows pointing in a certain direction, but that hardly means the fate of your marriage has been decided by your birth orders. And they aren't an excuse for saying, "Well, it's hopeless. We're both firstborns, and that means we're doomed to divorce."

I know plenty of marriages where two firstborns get along very nicely. My own firstborn sister, Sally, is an example. She married firstborn Wes, a meticulous perfectionist who is a dentist. You would think that by now Sally and Wes would have picked each other to pieces, but not so. They have built a great marriage around a common faith, a sense of balance, and plenty of hard work, and they have three super kids to show for it.

So the good news remains the same. Birth order is never a final determinant of anything, only an indicator of problems and tensions that you may discover or create for yourselves. No matter what your birth order and that of your spouse, what counts is how you use your particular strengths and how you modify or deal with your particular weaknesses. Knowing your own birth order characteristics and

> *No matter what your birth order and that of your spouse, what counts is how you use your particular strengths and how you modify or deal with your particular weaknesses.*

those of your mate is just one step toward learning how to get along and have a happy life together.

Another important step is understanding each other's *lifestyle*. In the next chapter we'll talk about what happens when a man and a woman try to build a home and family by putting their individual (unique) lifestyles together.

Want to Build Up Your Marriage?

Take this quiz and see how you're doing.

1. Do I nitpick? Do I find fault with what my mate wears, says, or does? How often?
2. Do I take the time to encourage my mate?
3. Do we talk things out? Have we set aside time just for us?
4. When was the last time we took a weekend away from the children?
5. When was the last time I gave my mate a compliment?
6. When was the last time I gave my mate a special present for absolutely no particular reason except to say, "I love you"?
7. Speaking of "I love you," when was the last time I said those three little wonderful words to my mate?
8. What is the one thing I *know* my mate would love to have me do? Am I planning to do it this week?
9. Do we share our thoughts, feelings, dreams, and struggles with each other?
10. Do I take the time to find out what my mate is really interested in? Do I take the time to understand the ins and outs of his or her favorite pastime or activity?
11. When was the last time I "kidnapped" my mate from the office (or maybe from the laundry room) to take him or her away on an overnight?
12. When was the last time I came home early from work to take care of little Fletcher or Mary and let my mate go window shopping or run some errands?
13. When was the last time I said, "I'm sorry. I was wrong. Will you forgive me?"

How do your birth order characteristics influence your strengths and weaknesses? In what areas are you succeeding? In what areas are you struggling? What are some steps you can take today to begin viewing your marriage through your spouse's eyes?

12

I Count Only When . . .

What Are You Really *Telling Yourself?*

How would you complete this statement: "I count only when . . ."?

The way you finish the sentence says a lot about you—and your marriage. When couples are having problems and have decided to "try the psychologist," one of the first things I look for is the lifestyle and life theme (or lifeline) of each spouse.[1]

Everyone has a *personal lifestyle*—a unique way of looking at oneself, other people, and the world. Every person sees life differently. For each of us, reality is what we see from behind our own eyes.

Everyone also has a *personal life theme*, or lifeline, which is lived out every day—actually, every moment. We may seldom state our life theme in so many words, but it is there, directing our every move.

Lifestyle is a term coined by Alfred Adler, who founded the school of individual psychology in the early 1900s. Adler believed that from early infancy, all of us start forming an individual life plan that causes us to pursue certain life goals. According to Adler, we would not know what to do with ourselves if we were not oriented to some goal or objective. As he put it, "We cannot think, feel, will, or act without the perception of some goal."[2]

Adler believed that when a baby is born, he quickly sizes up what is going on around him (his environment) and starts forming his goals. Obviously he doesn't do this consciously, making notes in his Blackberry or sharing it with his friends on Facebook, but the information is all being registered in his little brain nonetheless. Adler wrote, "The goal of each human being is probably formed in the first months of his life. Even at this time, certain sensations play a role which evoke a response of joy or comfort in this child. Here the first traces of a philosophy of life come to the surface, although expressed in the most primitive fashion."[3]

You may be wondering where genetics comes in. Does a child learn *everything* from his or her environment? Good question. Psychologists have long argued whether heredity or environment influences a human being the most. According to Rudolph Dreikurs, one of Alfred Adler's leading disciples, a growing child experiences both heredity *and* environment and draws his own conclusions. As he experiences his environment (mainly his family), he discovers where he is skilled and strong and where he is weak and lacking in ability. As the child sorts out all of his experiences with their pluses and minuses, his personality takes shape.[4]

> *Every child is born with the need for attention, and one of his or her primary goals is to gain attention in one way or another.*

As an infant grows and pursues his primitive goals, he starts developing what Adler called a *style of life*, or *lifestyle*. Every child is born with the need for attention, and one of his or her primary goals is to gain attention in one way or another. When a child's attempt to gain attention, either positively or negatively, doesn't get the desired results, the child becomes discouraged and then turns his or her efforts toward another goal: gaining power. If those attempts to be powerful (to control the parents) fail, he or she becomes still more discouraged, and the goal may become revenge.

Getting attention, power, or revenge are three basic motivations for a child's behavior. Most children concentrate on gaining attention or power; they seldom reach the revenge stage. Those who do often end up in prison or other correctional institutions.

As a child develops his or her own unique lifestyle by pursuing his or her basic goal, the child also develops a *life theme*. The complete psychological definition of a life theme, or what some counselors call a *lifeline*, could get a bit too involved and time consuming to wade through. For simplicity's sake, just think of a life theme as personal mottos or slogans, ideas that you subconsciously repeat to yourself daily and believe with all your heart. If you doubt that you have a life theme, look back over your behavior for a week, a month, or a year, and you can see this life theme exhibited again and again in your behavior.

What Is Your Life Theme?

1. What personal motto, slogan, or idea do you subconsciously repeat to yourself daily and believe with all your heart?

2. How does this idea influence your behavior? Your relationships? Your future?

A life theme always has to do with your self-image and your sense of self-worth. I like to describe anyone's life theme in terms of "I count only when . . ." The way you finish that sentence will tell me about your lifestyle and will give me some definite clues about your birth order.

The problem, of course, is that your life theme is a lie, or at least a partial lie. You are not *completely* what your life theme tells you that you are, because you have the capacity to change, to compensate for or conquer your weaknesses and capitalize on your strengths.

Controllers and Pleasers

While everyone's lifestyle is different to some degree, there are broad categories into which most people fit. Because the two lifestyles I counsel the most are controllers and pleasers, we'll look at those first. Then we'll also consider other broad lifestyles such as martyr, victim, attention getter, and driver.

Controllers

Controllers are powerful people who operate out of one of two motivations: power or fear. Often they are firstborns who were expected to take care of their younger siblings. Their strong need for power motivates some to want to control everything and everyone. Nothing escapes their critical eye; no one they deal with is free from the strings they try to attach. Another kind of controller, however, operates out of fear. This person is on the defensive and is basically out to be sure no one takes control of him.

Controllers are more comfortable with people at arm's length. They avoid intimacy because they fear losing control. Not surprisingly, controllers tend to fear death because, after all, death is the ultimate loss of control.

> *Controllers are more comfortable with people at arm's length. They avoid intimacy because they fear losing control.*

Another characteristic of controllers (and remember, a controller doesn't necessarily have all the characteristics mentioned here) is a critical, perfectionistic approach. They're always trying to clear the high-jump bar of life and making those around them clear it as well. Naturally, controllers have a tremendous need to be right. They love to argue and seldom lose an argument.

While it may sound as if controllers are aggressive, assertive people, they can also be temperamental, insecure, and shy. They may manipulate others, particularly their families, with tears or temper tantrums—or both. Whatever their weapons, they are always operating from a position of power.

Some controllers pound the table, shout, even scream. Others work quietly and may seem gentle, even loving on the surface. Underneath, however, it's a different story. A controlling mom can dominate her family by worrying about everyone. A controlling dad may keep everyone under his thumb with his silence, refusing to say what's on his mind. Fearing the unknown, the rest of the family walks on eggshells around him.

> **Life Themes for Controllers**
>
> "I count only when I'm in control of the situation."
> "I count only when I'm in charge."
> "I count only when I'm running the show, when what I say goes."

Pleasers

One hundred and eighty degrees from the controller is the pleaser, often a compliant firstborn. As you might guess, controllers are often married to pleasers, and we'll look at that more closely in a moment.

A driving force behind the pleaser is the need to be liked by everyone. Pleasers try to keep the oceans of life smooth so they can gain everyone's approval—particularly in their families.

> *Pleasers try to keep the oceans of life smooth so they can gain everyone's approval.*

Pleasers typically have a poor self-image. That's why they're always trying to do everything they can to keep everyone else happy. They believe they're valued for what they do, not for who they are. They live behind masks, smiling and nodding agreement, but inside they may not agree at all. Often they hate themselves because they don't have the courage to speak up.

Speaking up is something pleasers seldom do because they know
that's the sure route to rejection.
Pleasers much prefer to go along
with the ideas of others. They become skilled socially, able to read
signals that others send and know
how to keep everyone happy.

> **Life Themes for Pleasers**
>
> "I count only when I keep everything smooth and on an even keel."
> "I count only when everyone likes me."
> "I count only when everyone approves of what I do."
> "I count only when I put others first."

Pleasers, by the way, can be perfectionists, but they work out their
perfectionism differently from controllers. They are constantly worried about measuring up, being good enough,
being perfect. You might say they are perfectionists out of
fear of being anything else.

Controllers and Pleasers Often Marry

The two lifestyles I counsel most are controllers and pleasers, and there is a simple reason for this. Controllers often
marry pleasers (the old "opposites attract" influence), and
then the controllers, more often than not, give the pleasers a
bad time. Typically, the husband is the controller and the wife
is the pleaser, but there are some cases where the reverse is
true. In fact, I know of nine pleaser males in the continental
United States. However, we're not releasing their names or
addresses!

It's hard to get a controlling husband into my office for
counseling because he's sure that his wife is the one with
the problem; there's nothing wrong with *him*. But when the
controller finally agrees to come in and talk to me, he lets
his true colors show in a hurry. I hear statements that add up
to life themes like these: "I count only when I'm in charge,
when what I say goes, when I'm running things."

Are you married to a controller or a pleaser? Take the
quizzes on pages 238–40 to find out.

Are You in a Relationship with a Controller?

Take this quick quiz to find out. (Note: Because most controllers are male, I've used a masculine pronoun.)

Read each statement and score 4 for always, 3 for often, 2 for sometimes, and 1 for seldom.

_____ 1. He tends to be critical—a fault-finding perfectionist with a high standard of excellence for himself and others.

_____ 2. He finds it difficult to laugh at himself, particularly when he may have done or said something awkward or wrong.

_____ 3. He puts down or degrades others with subtle or not-so-subtle humor.

_____ 4. He has a weak (or even poor) relationship with his mother (or other women who have been or still are part of his life, such as a sister or a supervisor).

_____ 5. He complains about authority figures who "don't know what they're doing" (employers, teachers, pastors, or the president).

_____ 6. He is a real competitor who always has to win at sports or table games.

_____ 7. He gets his way, subtly or not so subtly, about where the two of you will go or what you will do.

_____ 8. He prefers to run the show rather than be a team player—on the job, in committees, or in situations involving family or friends.

_____ 9. He has a hard time saying, "I was wrong," or he makes excuses that will make him look good in the face of adversity.

_____ 10. He loses his temper (raises his voice, screams, curses).

_____ 11. He can get physical—shoving or hitting you or smashing things.

_____ 12. He makes you account for every penny you spend, but he spends rather freely.

_____ 13. Sex is something the two of you engage in for his pleasure and at his convenience.

_____ 14. When he drinks alcohol, even in modest quantities, he starts to become a different person.

_____ 15. He makes excuses for excessive drinking.

No quiz like this can be absolute proof of anything, but it can give you some clues that may help you analyze your relationship to your spouse or fiancé.

If the ratings you gave this person add up to between 50 and 60, he is a super controller whose only hope is a professional counselor—if he'll listen. If you're engaged and your fiancé scored between 50 and 60, my advice is to give back the ring and run.

If you scored your husband or fiancé between 40 and 49, he is a typical controller who is probably open to being confronted and asked to change his behavior.

If you scored your husband or fiancé between 30 and 39, he should be a fairly balanced person who can be in control at times but flexible at others.

If you scored your husband or fiancé at 29 or less, first recheck your figures. If you haven't made a scoring error, you may have one of the few pleaser males in captivity. But take a second look to see if he scored higher than a 2 on questions 10–14. All of these suggest a high degree of need to control, even dominate, with violence and abuse.

Are You in a Relationship with a Pleaser?

Take this quick quiz to find out. (Note: Because most pleasers are female, I've used a feminine pronoun.)

Read each statement and score 4 for always, 3 for often, 2 for sometimes, and 1 for seldom.

_____ 1. She walks on eggshells to keep everyone happy.

_____ 2. She wonders why she can't do things right.

_____ 3. She feels insecure and lacks confidence.

_____ 4. Her father was or is authoritarian.

_____ 5. She avoids confronting others because it "just isn't worth it."

_____ 6. She's often heard saying, "I should have . . ." or "I ought to . . ."

_____ 7. She feels overpowered by her spouse and even her children.

_____ 8. She gets little affection from others.

_____ 9. She feels like hiding or running away from life's hassles.

_____ 10. Others (especially loved ones) know which buttons to push to make her feel guilty.

_____ 11. She feigns agreement or approval when she feels just the opposite on the inside.

_____ 12. She is easily persuaded by others and will go along with whoever talked to her last.

_____ 13. She is afraid to try new things or take new risks.

_____ 14. It embarrasses her to stand up for her rights or take the initiative.

_____ 15. She gets little respect from her spouse/fiancé or her children.

No quiz like this can be absolute proof of anything, but it can give you some clues that may help you analyze your relationship to your spouse or fiancée.

If the ratings you gave this person add up to between 50 and 60, she would be considered a super-suffering pleaser who is easily manipulated and controlled. So the question is, who is doing the manipulating and controlling in her life? Could it be you?

Anyone scoring 40 to 49 is a discouraged or depressed pleaser for whom there is hope—*if* she is willing to take action and confront the person(s) doing the manipulating and controlling.

Anyone scoring 30 to 39 is a mildly discouraged pleaser. Her positives in life outweigh her negatives, but she still would like a little more respect, particularly from her loved ones.

Anyone scoring 29 or below falls into the "positive pleaser" category. She's able to balance her very giving nature with being able to receive the love, support, and respect she wants and needs.

Counsel for the Controller/Pleaser Couple

If you and your marriage are suffering as a result of controller/pleaser problems, here are my suggestions:

1. *If you are married to a controller, realize you are not going to change your spouse.* I tell husbands and wives, "Don't try to use a Brillo pad on the leopard's spots. You'll only make the leopard angry." In other words, you can only change *your own* behavior and way of interacting. Your spouse must decide to change on his or her own.

2. *If you are married to a controller, try being positive, but refuse to play your spouse's controlling games.* Pleasantly but firmly refuse to be controlled. If you can force the

controller's hand, he must act differently, because the payoff is no longer there. The key is to let the controller know that if he wants to control himself, he is welcome. But when he tries to control everyone else in the family, something has to give.

> *You can only change your own behavior and way of interacting.*

3. *If you are a particularly loud and blustery controller, try getting alone and ventilating feelings to yourself aloud.* People who have a hard time talking to others can really do much better by talking to themselves and learning to articulate their feelings in an acceptable way. Later they can try to communicate with their spouse in the same way. (Note: If your "controllerism" has reached any level of verbal or physical abusiveness, run—don't walk—to the nearest competent professional therapist and get some help. Your loved ones don't deserve such treatment from you. Nor will you respect yourself if this behavior continues.)

> *Let the controller know that if he wants to control himself, he is welcome. But when he tries to control everyone else in the family, something has to give.*

4. *If perfection is your goal, you'll always feel a void in your life.* You'll never get to that goal. It is a hopeless, fruitless quest. You must have the courage to accept yourself and your spouse as you both are—imperfect people, still learning, growing, and changing.

> *You must have the courage to accept yourself and your spouse as you both are—imperfect people, still learning, growing, and changing.*

5. *Don't try to control everyone and everything.* It simply doesn't work. For a marriage to be healthy and satisfying, and for two people to truly be one, *both* must be in control. And *both* must be free to do their own thing.

Martyrs and More

Each individual has his or her own unique lifestyle, but we can identify certain broad categories into which most men and women fit. Besides controllers and pleasers, there are many other broad descriptive labels for people, and many people can have more than one label. For example, a pleaser may also have a touch of the martyr or victim, both natural offshoots of wanting to please and always have the approval of others.

> **Martyrs have an uncanny ability to find losers who will walk on them, use them, or abuse them in some way.**

Martyrs are people who almost always have a poor self-image. They seek out others who will reinforce that poor self-image, primarily the people they marry.

Martyrs have an uncanny ability to find losers who will walk on them, use them, or abuse them in some way. Martyrs often wind up married to alcoholics, and they tend to enable their alcoholic mates by making excuses for them out of "love."

Martyrs learn to be doormats while growing up, usually from fathers who were very strict, possessive, and controlling. Martyr wives often have husbands who wander, who have left them, or who are planning to leave them for other women. The reason is simple: a martyr isn't worth pursuing. A doormat finally gets tiresome and worn out.

Martyrs suffer for a cause. Often the cause is a husband who has failed her in some way. The martyr wife makes excuses for her husband, vowing to "stand by her man" to the bitter end—and the end usually is bitter. Sad to say, many of the martyr wives I deal with have been taught to be "submissive" to their husband. At best, their interpretation of this teaching enables their controlling (and often chauvinistic) spouse to take advantage of them. At worst, they become victims of disrespect, neglect, and abuse.

Close cousin to the martyr is the *victim*. The victim's life themes are very similar to the martyr's. Victims or martyrs could be called super pleasers or pleasers who have

> **Life Themes for Martyrs**
>
> "I count only when I suffer."
>
> "I count only when I'm taken advantage of."
>
> "I count only when I'm hurt by others."

gone to seed. Victims, martyrs, and pleasers all have the same problem—low self-esteem. For victims and martyrs, the problem is simply much worse.

Many victims frequently use words like *me, my,* and *I* as they seek sympathy or pity while complaining about their misfortunes, aches, and pains. They often feel taken advantage of, but through all their complaining, victims get what they really want—to be the center of attention.

Other martyrs or victims aren't primarily after attention, but they keep their lifestyle because it's "comfortable." Perhaps the best illustration of sticking with something because it's comfortable, though less than desirable, is the way I cling to my old pair of crummy, ragged, worn-out slippers. Sande is always tossing them

> *Through all their complaining, victims get what they really want—to be the center of attention.*

out because they're "gross." She expects me to wear a new pair she gave me or one of the pairs the kids have bought me for Christmas or Father's Day.

Of course, I immediately rescue my old slippers from the trash can, and once more she finds me wearing them, as crummy and ugly as ever.

"Why," she wonders aloud, "do you insist on wearing those old, cruddy slippers when you have so many nice new pairs to choose from?"

All I can say in return is, "I wear them because they're comfortable."

The way I return to my crummy, old slippers is similar to the way martyrs and victims return to the same abusive relationship or continue to take the same guff they've been getting for years from family, friends, or co-workers. The abuse, lack of respect, being made fun of—whatever—is "comfortable." This type of victim is sometimes called a disaster waiting to happen.

> **Life Themes for Victims**
>
> "I count only when I'm put down."
> "I count only when I'm mistreated."

Another broad lifestyle category is the *attention getter*, which has some similarities to the controller. Whenever you're gaining attention, you are trying to take control to some extent. Lastborns of the family often have this lifestyle. They are the powerful little buzzards in the family who are desperately seeking lots of attention, mainly because they see all those bigger buzzards (their siblings) circling above them in a rather intimidating way.

> **Life Themes for Attention Getters**
>
> "I count only when I gain attention by being entertaining."
> "I count only when I'm in the spotlight."
> "I count only when I'm the star."
> "I count only when I make people laugh."

My own lifestyle is primarily attention getter because when I was very young, I perceived that I could never outdo my super-capable firstborn sister or my big brother. Obviously I had to take a different route. Because it was easy and fun, I chose to become the family clown.

My lifestyle was pretty well set by the time I was 5 or 6. (I'm not exactly sure because no psychologist dropped by to check on me.) After that, it was all downhill, so to speak, and whatever happened only confirmed my belief that I had to be funny and cute or a mischief maker. My life theme became "I count only when I gain attention by being entertaining."

Meshing Lifestyles in Marriage

Lifestyles and lifelines don't always have to cause tension in a marriage. Sometimes they can mesh nicely and be enjoyable, even when you put a manipulative lastborn husband together with a pleasing, gullible firstborn wife.

Just before we were to be married, I told Sande that there was a tradition in the Leman family that said the wife had to buy the marriage license. As we've seen, one of the strong traits in many firstborns is a willingness to please other people, and the pleasing firstborn is not as likely as a laterborn child to be worldly-wise and alert to the wiles of those trying to take advantage of them. In other words, my lovable wife is an easy mark.

So it was not surprising that she thought it was wonderful when I asked her to fork over five dollars for a wedding license. I took the five-dollar bill from her, laid it on the marriage license clerk's desk, and said, "You've just started a tradition."

She just laughed. I laughed too. We both knew I was trying to get through graduate school and was flat broke. She had the job, owned the car, and was our sole means of support. The whole thing was good for a laugh then, and we still chuckle about it today. At the time we both got a harmless payoff for the lifestyles we followed. I got noticed and had some fun; Sande got to play the pleasing role she enjoys so much.

What's Your Lifestyle?

I've discussed in this chapter only a few of the possible life-styles people choose. There are many others. A *driver* is a goal-oriented person who must reach his objective at any cost. His life theme says, "I count only when I achieve" or "I count only when I get everything done."

Another lifestyle I see quite often is the *rationalizer*, the person who tries to avoid or deny responsibility by throwing up a smoke screen of theory, facts, and opinions. The rationalizer's life theme says, "I count only when I can find a good excuse or explanation" or "I count only when I can put on a front that makes me look good."

A *goody-goody*, first cousin to the pleaser, is another common lifestyle. The goody-goody's life theme may be "I count only when I follow the rules" or "I count only when I live a righteous life."

Now that you have some basic information regarding lifestyles and life themes (or lifelines), take the "Which Are You?" quiz on page 247 to assess what your lifestyle and lifelines are. Even better, have your spouse take the quiz at the same time and then exchange papers. It'll make for intriguing dinner or coffee conversation for the two of you as you compare your individual perceptions of each other's lifestyles and life themes.

Lying Lifelines Shorten Marriages

Today's statistics tell us that the average marriage lasts seven years. No marriage will get very far if you and/or your spouse live out a lifeline that is so extreme and unhealthy that it becomes destructive to both of you. So why not abandon the lifelines that begin with "I count only when . . ." and begin to use ones that start with "I count because . . ." In marriage, you count because you are helping your spouse grow and mature.

If you continue to live out a lifeline that says you count only when you are in control, are perfect, please everyone, get attention, or do something else, you are lying to yourself. You count because you are created in the image of the almighty God himself, not because of what you do or don't do. So be aware of the lies you are always telling yourself at a subconscious level, and keep those lies under control with cognitive discipline. The next time you are in a stressful situation of any kind—at work, at a party, in your own living room, wherever—stop and use cognitive discipline by asking yourself, *What did the old me usually do?* After identifying your usual lifeline and course of action, ask yourself, *What is the new me going to do differently?*

Which Are You?

Take this quiz to find out.

1. What words below would best describe your lifestyle? If you feel you have characteristics that fit more than one description, check them both off, but put an "X" by the one that is predominant. Then write down your lifestyle, putting the dominant description first.

   _____ Controller

   _____ Perfectionist

   _____ Driver

   _____ Pleaser

   _____ Victim

   _____ Martyr

   _____ Goody-goody

   _____ Attention getter

   _____ Rationalizer

2. My life theme: "I count only when _____."

3. Using the lifestyles listed above, give your own estimate of which ones apply to your spouse. (Remember, you can use more than one style, but write the predominant one first.) _____.

4. From the descriptions that you've given of your spouse above, state what you believe is your spouse's life theme: "I count only when _____."

This isn't some kind of magic formula that causes instant change. But as you keep using this simple old me/new me approach, you will be able to change your lifeline and be able to say more often, "I count because I'm me!"

Lifelines

Do any of these sound like you?

"I count only when I perform."

This could be a lifeline for a perfectionist or someone who needs attention. It would depend on what you mean by "perform." Perfectionists have to realize they can never do it all and that their true worth lies in who they are as people, not in what they do as performers. As for people needing attention, they perform to be noticed, applauded, or given another carrot. This is selfish behavior and very frustrating because they can never get enough carrots! It's like the lab rat that's on a perennial moving treadmill and can never get off.

"I count only when I win."

This is a variation of "I count only when I'm in control." Another way to describe this lifestyle is "win-lose." There's no in-between. We hear a lot of talk today about succeeding and winning, but living by the win-lose code is a constant burden and hassle. I like to say that winning isn't everything—but helping others win *is* everything.

"I count only when I'm cared for."

This is a hybrid that relates back to "I count only when I'm noticed" or "I count only when people pay attention to me." It is a typical lifeline of a lastborn, especially a baby princess who is used to being spoiled, being cared for, and having her older brothers protect her.

"I count only when I give of myself."

This is a variation of the pleaser's line, a favorite of the compliant firstborn perfectionist who grows up never failing to obey Mommy and Daddy. But in a marriage, a pleaser must always be wary of overdoing it, especially if he or she is married to a controller or a critical perfectionist. Marriage is a give-and-take proposition. When one person has to do all the giving, it takes its toll on the relationship.

13

Flaunt Your Imperfections

Parenting Firstborns and Only Children

The scene is a preschool class, and the teacher has just handed little Emily a pair of scissors (rounded tips, of course) and a sheet of bright red construction paper. Emily's assignment is to cut out a nice big circle. She labors away and is doing a fairly nice job when all of a sudden she crumples up the paper and throws her half-completed circle on the floor.

The teacher comes over and asks, "Emily, what's wrong?"

"I can't do this!"

"I'll help you. Here, let me—"

"No! I'm not going to do it. It's dumb!"

And the teacher sighs and wonders, *What's gotten into Emily?*

It's really no mystery. Emily is a firstborn child, and her parents are both very capable, confident people. Already at the tender age of 5, Emily is exhibiting a major characteristic she shares with almost all other firstborns and only children, a burden she will carry throughout life: perfectionism.

Perfectionism

I know you may disagree with my assertion that almost all firstborns and only children are perfectionists. Parents tell me about their firstborn Harlan, who is 17 and has yet to make a conscientious move. In fact, he hasn't moved to make his bed for the last six months.

Or perhaps they'll mention firstborn daughter Amanda, who is so laid-back they have to put a mirror in front of her nose to be sure she's alive. She's getting a C- in history and math and an A+ in MTV and Facebook.

But even though Harlan and Amanda seem to act like anything but perfectionistic firstborns, I stick to my guns for two very good reasons, the same two reasons that have made Emily into a little discouraged perfectionist while still in preschool—Mom and Dad.

> *When you are little— very little—and try to imitate someone much older and bigger, you soon get the idea you have to be "perfect."*

When you are little—very little—and try to imitate someone much older and bigger, you soon get the idea you have to be "perfect." To show you what I mean, let's observe Emily at home with Mom. Emily has made her own bed, and for a 5-year-old she's done a very good job of it. Mom comes in to check and says, "Oh, Emily, honey, what a beautiful job you did on your bed!" Emily beams—until Mom proceeds to "straighten out a few wrinkles."

The message for Emily? "Your bed doesn't measure up. Your bed isn't perfect." No wonder Emily goes a little ballistic when she cuts a less-than-perfect circle at preschool. If she can't be perfect, she won't be anything at all. Emily is a budding discouraged perfectionist, and unless Mom stops nitpicking her to death in a very "positive" way, she will be in full bloom by the time she's a teenager.

I counsel many young children who are budding discouraged perfectionists. They are not hard to spot:

> They don't hand in a school assignment even though it's completed. Their problem is they're not sure it's done *exactly* right.
>
> They start lots of projects or activities but don't finish them.
>
> They fear the enormity of a task and therefore don't even start.
>
> They are described by their teachers as "having *so much* potential."
>
> They have controlling, critical, or pushy parents.

Two Cases: Frank and John

Two vivid examples of discouraged perfectionists that stand out in my mind are young men I'll call Frank and John. Frank was 12 when his only-child father (a surgeon) and his firstborn mother (a registered nurse) brought him to me because of his extreme "temper problem." It seems Frank would blow his cool when his "plans for the day" didn't go right. While most 12-year-olds can't plan the next fifteen minutes, Frank knew exactly what he wanted to do from morning until night, something he picked up from his highly exacting, tightly scheduled, surgeon father.

Frank, by the way, was a "functional firstborn" in that he was the second of two children, born seven years after his older brother. With that much of a gap and with such high-powered professionals for parents, Frank couldn't help but have a lot of firstborn traits.

In fact, Frank could have easily passed for an only child because he had a very difficult time getting along with children his own age, which is typical of only children. But it seems

Frank wasn't getting along with anyone. His friends could care less about his to-do list, and when Frank's day didn't go well (which was often), he would blow his top and get in fights. At home, if someone messed up his plans, Frank started kicking things, throwing things, and putting holes in the walls (once he tried to put holes in the family dog).

A very conscientious boy, Frank felt terrible about his behavior but was trapped in his prison of perfectionism. I was finally able to help Frank by pointing out that everyone makes mistakes and fails—even Babe Ruth, who hit 714 home runs but also struck out 1,330 times. But the real key was Frank's dad, who had the courage and the sense to start admitting his own faults and imperfections, which he had kept carefully hidden.

Frank remained a perfectionist in many ways, but at least he got control of his temper by learning that he couldn't control everything and, above all, that he didn't have to be perfect to win his father's approval and love.

Oh yes, John? I didn't counsel John; in fact, I never got to meet him when I was assistant dean of students at the University of Arizona. But I had access to his records. Throughout his academic career, John never got less than an A and was about to graduate summa cum laude from U of A. His suicide note said, *I just couldn't measure up to the standards of this world. Perhaps in the next world I can do better.*

Wanting to Be Just Like Mom and Dad

Perfectionism can get serious, even deadly, as in the case with John. So many people struggle with perfectionism because, in one way or another, they just can't measure up to Mom and Dad, who may or may not have been perfectionists themselves. Keep in mind that it doesn't take a surgeon and a nurse to turn out a discouraged perfectionist. It simply takes an adult who is just trying to be a capable, loving parent. Consider Harlan and Amanda again for a moment.

It's doubtful that their parents sat down just after the children were born and discussed how they could produce discouraged perfectionists. But they each produced one anyway simply by trying to be capable, loving parents. How? It's very simple.

> *Slobs and poor students are usually discouraged perfectionists who have given up trying because it hurts too much to fail.*

Very early during the first year of life, the firstborn starts to pick up on his or her adult role models—Mommy and Daddy—and starts setting his or her sights on being "just like them." That includes being just as capable as they are, which is obviously impossible for a tiny child. So when firstborns like Harlan and Amanda get older, they may not look like perfectionists or act like perfectionists, but they are discouraged perfectionists. Slobs and poor students are usually discouraged perfectionists who have given up trying because it hurts too much to fail.

The firstborn's desire to follow in Mommy's and Daddy's footsteps usually increases as the parents give the firstborn a lot of extra attention, or overparenting. They tend to be overprotective, and they unconsciously push the child to accomplish everything he or she can (and some things he or she can't). It's no wonder firstborns walk and talk earlier than any other birth order and that they have a larger vocabulary. Firstborns, along with their perfectionist cousins—the only children—grow up being little adults.

> *Firstborns, along with their perfectionist cousins—the only children—grow up being little adults.*

I often apply the adjective *precocious* to firstborns and especially to only children. According to the dictionary, *precocious* means "characterized by unusually early development or maturity, especially in mental aptitude." And that often describes firstborns and only children. They become very adult in a hurry because of all this imitating of Mom and Dad that they're trying to do. Part of their adult behavior is that they become very obedient to authority, another holdover from trying to please the two key authority figures in life—Mother and Father.

The Sting of Dethronement

Not only do all firstborns struggle with perfectionism, they also all undergo dethronement with the arrival of the secondborn in the family. Firstborns are the center of attention for a relatively long time (as time is measured in a young child's life). In chapter 12 I mentioned the lifestyle every child develops by age 5 or so. If Mommy and Daddy don't have a second child until the firstborn is 3 years old, three-fifths—60 percent—of the firstborn's lifestyle has already been formed before the intruder comes home from the hospital. A great part of that lifestyle has taught the firstborn that he or she is kingpin. One of the most challenging tasks of parenting is preparing the firstborn child for the intrusion of the second.

> *One of the most challenging tasks of parenting is preparing the firstborn child for the intrusion of the second.*

My advice to parents awaiting the arrival of #2 is to have their firstborn put away some of his or her special toys in a safe place so "the baby can't get them." At the same time, let #1 child choose some toys he or she is willing to give to the new little brother or sister. And finally, be sure to reassure your firstborn that when his or her little brother or sister arrives, there will be plenty of kisses from Mommy and Daddy for both of them.

When the secondborn child comes home from the hospital, it will soon dawn on the firstborn that the "thing" is not temporary, that it is going to stay. At this point it's an excellent strategy to get the firstborn involved in caring for the new baby. If the firstborn is big enough, he or she can help feed the baby, even diaper the baby if possible. Yes, the diaper may look a bit askew, but bite your tongue and fight off that urge to redo it "perfectly."

The second strategy is to talk with your firstborn about what the newborn *can't* do. "[Baby's name] can't catch a ball, can't walk, can't talk, can't do anything."

> Dethronement is a profound intrusion for your firstborn. He can't help wondering, Why? Wasn't I good enough?

And then there is bedtime. Tell your 3-year-old that he or she won't have to go to bed so early; he or she gets to stay up later with Mommy and Daddy.

Not a Minor Problem

No matter how much you try to help the firstborn with the adjustment, keep in mind that dethronement is a *profound* intrusion for your firstborn. He or she can't help wondering, *Why? Wasn't I good enough?* There is a natural rivalry that starts between the firstborn and the secondborn. It may not be overt and in plain sight at first, but it is always there, and it always comes out sooner or later.

Sande and I are still amazed when we watch some old super 8 movies my mother took of the two of us plus Holly and newborn Krissy. When we took the movie, no one— not even my mother—saw 18-month-old Holly slip into the picture and smile broadly as she dug her elbow into Krissy's midsection.

When we got the film back, our reaction was ambivalent. Yes, Holly's little elbow toss was cute, but it also graphically demonstrated how firstborns feel dethroned and how they make perfectly natural (selfish) moves to regain their "fair share" of attention from their parents.

This natural inclination toward selfishness (really a matter of self-preservation and survival as far as the child is concerned) is why you have to be careful about giving your firstborn "special treatment to balance things" when the new little intruder arrives. Guard against having your firstborn manipulate you to get special advantages or spoiling. Never give in to a temper tantrum or outburst of tears. If necessary, isolate the firstborn briefly and then go in and talk about it.

If you must discipline your firstborn, always follow up with lots of hugging, touching, and talking when you emphasize the firstborn's "superiority" over the new baby because he or she can do so many more things. Always enumerate the things the firstborn can do that the baby can't. This way you will lay groundwork for a cooperative firstborn child who will get through the dethronement crisis more easily, knowing that he or she is more capable, bigger, stronger, etc.

But while you assure your firstborn that he or she is bigger, stronger, and smarter, don't confuse that with being perfect. For probably two to three years, your firstborn has been learning to be a perfectionist by watching you. But when you tell your firstborn that he or she is bigger or stronger, be sure to let him or her know that everyone makes mistakes; no one does everything absolutely perfectly.

> *Everyone makes mistakes; no one does everything absolutely perfectly.*

Keep in mind also that when your firstborn does get dethroned by your secondborn, issues like power and authority become very important. No, he doesn't come to breakfast and say, "More power to the firstborns, pass the Cocoa Puffs." But inside his little head he understands plenty about power and authority and how precious it is. Dr. Alfred Adler emphasized the importance of the power struggle that goes on when a firstborn loses the exclusive small kingdom that had belonged to him or her before the secondborn brother or sister arrived. Consequently, as the firstborn continues to grow up into adulthood, he or she may exaggerate the importance of rules and laws. In other words, firstborns go by the book and don't want any deviations.

What better example of this than the prodigal son, who undoubtedly was a baby of the family. He split with his share of the inheritance and promptly lost it all. The elder son—the firstborn—stayed home and worked hard in the fields. When the prodigal finally wised up and came back, his father threw a big bash, complete with fatted calf and gold ring (today, he would probably buy the boy a nice Mustang convertible).

> *Firstborns go by the book and don't want any deviations.*

The elder son—who was out in the fields, naturally—heard all the commotion and came looking. When he saw what was going on, he got irate. Here his father was throwing a big bash for his ne'er-do-well younger brother, and what had he ever gotten? Not even one little party! Where was the fairness in *that*?

But as we see, the father was being fair by treating his children differently. He pointed out to the older boy that he had always been with him, and everything he had was his. But the younger boy, who needed love and understanding, had been lost and was now found, so why not celebrate?[1]

Also be aware that it's typical—almost inevitable—for new parents to be more strict and lay down more rules and regulations for their firstborn than they do with laterborn children. After all, they must "do it right" with this first child, so part of that is keeping a tight rein on him or her. Wherever I speak and teach, I emphasize the need to be an authoritative parent who is loving and fair but also consistent and firm. The authoritative parent is the happy medium between the permissive parent and the authoritarian, who overdoes it on rules and limits and simply cracks down too hard.

If I Had It to Do All Over Again . . .

Even psychologists with doctorates know there is a big difference between correct theory and right practice. People sometimes ask me, "As you look back on rearing your children, do you have any regrets or things you'd do differently?"

Good question. If there is anything I would have done differently, it would be in the way I handled Holly, our aggressive, go-by-the-book, perfectionistic firstborn.

In an earlier chapter I mentioned how a parent will tend to overidentify with a child of the same birth order. I tended to overidentify in an indulging way with laterborns in our family, particularly our son, Kevin. But when the only children we had were Holly and Krissy, I overidentified with Krissy, who was younger, because she was constantly getting teased and pressured by her older sister, who was still smarting from dethronement and wanted to compete with her little sister in every way she could. I became protective of Krissy and cracked down too hard on Holly.

Of course, I had good reason to crack down, or so I told myself as a young father with two daughters who were in constant competition. Actually, much of the competitiveness came from Holly's side (we're back to dethronement again, of course). When Holly threw that elbow at Krissy during the movie, it was just for starters. She proceeded to make a career out of running Krissy's life.

We have on tape an occasion when Holly snatched a certain toy from Krissy and said, "You don't want that. Here, play with this." Of course, "this" was an old, beat-up rubber frog.

And when it came to money, Holly would constantly try to tell Krissy, "Those big nickels are worth more than these little dimes."

To give Krissy her due, as she got a little older, she didn't take big sister's manipulation and direction lying down. There were many times when I would arrive on the scene after hearing a squall of protest from Krissy and would reprimand Holly because she was older and "should know better." Now I'm sure that in many of those instances, Krissy had set up her big sister with the skill that only younger children possess.

But I confess that Krissy usually faked me out (after all, she was laterborn, so how could *she* be guilty?). So I would correct Holly rather severely: "Holly, that's Krissy's. You have your own! Now stop it."

Occasionally, however, when Holly was being really unfair (in my opinion), I would send her to her room. Did I do this out of authoritarian perfectionism? Hardly. I did it out of lastborn frustration with an older child taking advantage of a younger one, something that had happened to me on numerous occasions while I was growing up, when my big brother, Jack (and even at rare times my loving big sister, Sally), would give me a bad time.

> *Fighting and arguing are acts of cooperation, and it takes two to cooperate.*

In retrospect, I realize that I should have followed my own reality discipline advice and disciplined both of them when I found them fighting and arguing. Fighting and arguing, after all, are acts of cooperation, and it takes two to cooperate.

Authoritarians Grow Discouraged Perfectionists

People often ask me which style of parenting is more harmful—the authoritarian or the permissive. I really can't give the nod to one or the other, since both are harmful, but I will say that authoritarian parenting is more likely to produce a discouraged perfectionist who can't measure up to the demands the parents place on him or her.

Nicole, 14 when her parents brought her in for counseling, is a good example. She had been suspended from school for cutting class and smoking pot. Her parents asked what I could do to cure her "rebellion."

I talked with Nicole alone and quickly learned she had little freedom and made very few choices of her own, even at 14. Her parents controlled everything—clothes, going out, coming in, bedtime. To hear Nicole tell it, she lived in a home with about as much freedom as juvenile hall. To find opportunities to slip away with her peer group, she would lie and sneak around, and that's how she'd begun using drugs and alcohol and being promiscuous with boys at school. Nicole had a plan—turn 18, get out of the house, buy a car, and split.

Nicole was the firstborn child and had a younger sister, 11, and a younger brother, 8. She also had an ultraperfectionist mother who kept the home impeccably neat. Interestingly enough, Nicole kept her room immaculate at all times, but it was actually a cover—part of her "I'll tell them what they want to hear" strategy.

> Nicole had a plan—turn 18, get out of the house, buy a car, and split.

I didn't make much progress with Nicole until I got her parents to see how they were being too authoritarian and why Nicole was afraid to tell them what was really going on—she feared retribution big time, and she feared maybe even being kicked out of the house completely.

Fortunately Nicole's parents listened and learned, and we did make some progress. At the end of six weeks Nicole wrote a summary of the positive things that had come out of counseling. Among the things Nicole said: "Mom and Dad are giving me more leeway, and I'm not lying to them. I am being honest with them, and it makes me feel good."

Nicole is a classic example of a firstborn child who grew up watching Mom and Dad and wanting to imitate them. But this lasts only to a certain age. As she became a teenager, the authoritarian treatment proved to be too much. She became a discouraged perfectionist and turned to wild behavior as a way of crying for help.

Nicole is convincing evidence for why I believe no parent should ever think a firstborn child is not a perfectionist simply because the child isn't toeing the mark and obeying all the rules. The child may be breaking a lot of rules because he or she is a perfectionist who can't handle the cards life has dealt.

Super Parents and the Critical Eye

Let's face it. There is a lot of concern about how to raise children. For any parent who wants to take advantage of them, there are literally tons of books, articles, pamphlets, CDs, films, and DVDs available to teach you how to be a super parent. And I'm well aware that at times I can sound just like the rest of the experts:

Be sure you don't do this; be sure you do that.

Be faster than a speeding bullet as you use actions, not words.

Be more powerful than a locomotive as you enforce the rules of reality discipline.

Leap tall problems with a single bound to be loving, caring, and aware of your child's feelings.[2]

If I have given that impression, I apologize. Actually, I believe that we don't need super parents, and that goes double or maybe triple when parenting all those little firstborns and only children. They have enough problems trying to be perfect and fail-safe as they imitate moms or dads who, in their minds at least, are giants and never make mistakes. I don't believe there is a parent alive who has never made a mistake. There are, however, a lot of them who refuse to *admit* their mistakes!

> I don't believe there is a parent alive who has never made a mistake. There are, however, a lot of them who refuse to admit *their mistakes!*

The Deception of Perfection

There's no doubt we have become a society of flaw pickers. Just listen to the newscasts or pick up your newspapers. A child brings home a report card with four As and a B. Dad gives it the critical eye and says, "Not bad. Too bad about the

B, though." The bottom line is that it's so easy to be critical, even while trying to be positive. Remember Emily's mother? She didn't shout at her child. She just nicely remade Emily's bed after Emily had done the best she could at the job.

But let me ask you: Are you perfect? Do you do everything perfectly all the time? Well, then why would you expect your child to be perfect? Don't you sometimes do stupid things that you wish you wouldn't have done? Don't you sometimes fail at something you've worked really hard on?

Instead of trying to be a perfect parent who has a perfect child, why not strive for excellence, doing the job to the best of your ability? (Remember the difference between excellence and perfectionism that we talked about in chapter 6?) Allow your child to do her job to the best of her ability, but without the pressure.

Also, what about forgiveness? Do you find it easy to forgive your children when they do something wrong (or stupid)? When Jesus told Peter that he should forgive seventy times seven, he was basically saying, "Forgive indefinitely." And no one needs to learn about forgiveness more than the critical-eyed parent who pursues perfection. You may do it politely and sweetly, but as you enforce your perfectionistic will on your children, are you showing them forgiveness for their mistakes, or are you judging them (all in the name of trying to help them, of course)?

> No one needs to learn about forgiveness more than the critical-eyed parent who pursues perfection.

The best way to learn to forgive is to ask for forgiveness yourself. Has your 3-year-old firstborn or only child ever heard you say, "I blew it. I was wrong. I forgot. I'm sorry"? Has your 13-year-old ever heard you say any of those things freely and openly? A lot of parents choke on those words, particularly the ones who are firstborn or only-child perfectionists themselves.

If you realize that you have a critical eye, to any degree, what should you do? It won't work to confess that you're guilty and tell yourself you'll never do it again . . . because you will. Again and again. It's because that critical eye is ingrained into your personality and lifestyle. What will work? When you find yourself slipping into perfectionistic overdrive, stop and shift gears. Ask your child to forgive you, and forgive yourself

> *All children need encouragement more than prodding.*

(perhaps the hardest of all). If you're a person of faith, ask God almighty for his help in changing your personality from a pursuer of perfection to a pursuer of excellence.

It also helps to remember that all children need encouragement more than prodding. Learn to simply hold your child when he or she is having problems. Just say, "Everything's going to be okay. What's the problem? Is something not working out right for you? Would you like me to help?"

Remember little Emily—the 5-year-old discouraged perfectionist who went ballistic when she couldn't cut out the perfect circle? Emily, by the way, grew up to be a perfectionistic career woman who went ballistic when her husband didn't do his share of the housework. She had to do it all herself after a long day of working. Emily and her husband wound up in my office, and I tried to explain what had happened to her and how much better it would have been if her mom or dad could have helped her learn to cut less-than-perfect circles. They could have said, "It's hard; I don't always cut perfect ones myself. I remember how hard it was when I was small."

The point is that teaching kids to seek excellence instead of perfectionism can start when they're very young.

Picture this classic scene: Mom is tired of the 4-year-old's messy toy box and messy room and sends him in there to clean it all up. But there's a problem. The task looks gigantic to the 4-year-old. Toys and books and crayons and puzzles are scattered from one end of the room to the other. How can he possibly do this?

He never will do it unless you, the parent, follow him into the room, sit down, and say something such as, "There's a lot to do here, isn't there? While you pick up your toys, I'll talk to you about what we're going to do tonight after dinner." Chances are, the kid will get on with the job and at least get part of the room cleaned up. If getting certain items in good order is extremely difficult, you can give limited help. But the last thing you should do is clean up most of it yourself.

> *If getting certain items in good order is extremely difficult, you can give limited help. But the last thing you should do is clean up most of it yourself.*

The idea is to get the child to do the job as you encourage him and show him how to organize the crayons, puzzles, and toy pieces. If he doesn't get everything just right, don't berate him or come along behind him and straighten everything up for him. The key is: *be satisfied with a less-than-perfect job.* (The room is going to look less than perfect soon anyway.)

> *The great temptation for the perfectionist, critical-eyed parent is to send messages to the child that say,* You have to measure up, kid. You have to do an absolutely flawless job, or I won't approve.

The great temptation for the perfectionist, critical-eyed parent is to send messages to the child that say, *You have to measure up, kid. You have to do an absolutely flawless job, or I won't approve.*

Please be assured that I am *not* saying you should let a child get away with goofing off or not doing the job at all. With true reality discipline in mind, hold him accountable for his responsibilities. But that doesn't mean you have to demand that he be perfect. Relax your perfectionistic rules a bit. Maybe part of cleaning up the room is making the bed. Since 4 is a bit young to make beds, you may have the child help you, but be sure he does as much as he can, and if it's wrinkled in spots, congratulate him but *don't do it over for him.* So what if some of it looks like a toy truck got left under the covers? You can shut the door, and no one needs to see it.

As you learn to be flexible, steer away from giving orders, and move toward helping your child do things. Remember, you are the child's role model, not his sergeant or supervisor. Few parents completely understand what I mean when I talk about being a role model. I'm not just suggesting that you set a good example for the child. You should, but there is much more to being a role model than that, especially for the firstborn or only child. He or she has no brother or sister to look to or pattern. *You* are what he or she has to pattern, and you are an awesome act to follow! So look for ways to show your child that you're human, that you understand, that you aren't perfect, and that mistakes are not the end of the world. In other words:

> *Steer away from giving orders, and move toward helping your child do things. Remember, you are the child's role model, not his sergeant or supervisor.*

Flaunt Your Imperfections!

Every time you do this, you help your firstborn or only child become less of a perfectionist who grows up to whip and drive himself with expectations that are far beyond human capacity.

One way to show your child you're not perfect is to ask him or her for help now and then. I don't mean simply helping with the baby or doing simple chores, as good as those things are. I'm talking about a deeper level where you ask your young child questions such as:

"Will you help me decide what to have for dinner tonight?"

"Where do you think is the best place to put these flowers so we can all enjoy them?"

"Do you think your little sister is old enough to play this game?"

In deciding about dinner, it might be wise to give the child a choice and ask if he would prefer chicken or hamburger; otherwise you may wind up with a request for peanut butter sandwiches, Oreo cookies, and lots of ice cream. You can give him some choices for dessert, but again, they should be choices that you know everyone will like.

Keep in mind that you are new at all this, and all children make mistakes—just as their parents do. So go easy on trying to turn out the world's first perfectly behaved child. I can assure you it isn't going to happen anyway—none of mine even made it. And *my* parents would have assured you that I didn't either!

Here are some great tips to keep in mind.

8 Tips for Parenting Firstborns and Only Children

1. *When disciplining the firstborn child, beware of reinforcing his ingrained perfectionism by "shoulding" him all the time.* Actually, it's not wise to "should" anyone in your family, but when the firstborn hears "should," it's like waving a red flag in front of a bull. The firstborn is already "shoulding" himself, and when you chime in, it's a double whammy. First, he resents it, and second, he is all the harder on himself in private, which will keep lowering his self-esteem and probably make him harder to deal with.

2. *Don't be an "improver" on everything your firstborn or only child says or does.* It's just one more deadly way to reinforce his or her already ingrained perfectionism. Accept the slightly wrinkled bed, the not-quite-cleaned-up room, or whatever your child has done. When you do it over, you only send a message that your child is not measuring up.

3. *Realize the firstborn has a particular need to know exactly what the rules are.* Be patient and take time to lay things out for your firstborn from A to Z.

4. *Recognize the firstborn's first place in the family.* As the oldest, the firstborn should get some special privileges to go along with the additional responsibilities that always seem to come his or her way.

5. *Take two-on-one time—both parents out with the oldest child alone.* A firstborn responds better to adult company than children of any other birth order. A firstborn often feels that her parents don't pay much attention to her because they're always concentrating on the younger ones in the family. Make a special effort to have the firstborn join you and your spouse in going out alone for a treat, or to run some kind of special errand.

6. *Stay away from making your firstborn your instant babysitter.* At least try to check with your firstborn to see if his or her schedule would allow for some babysitting later in the day or that evening.

7. *As your firstborn grows older, be sure you don't pile on more responsibilities.* Give some of the responsibilities to the younger children as soon as they are capable of taking on these jobs. One firstborn told me at a seminar, "I'm the garbage person." By that he meant that he had to do everything at home while his brother and sister got off much easier.

8. *When your firstborn is reading to you and has trouble with a word, don't be so quick to jump in with a correction.* A firstborn is extremely sensitive to criticism and being corrected. Give the child time to sound out the word. Give help only when she asks for it.

14

Two May Be Company . . .
or a Crowd

Parenting the Two-Child Family

Sande and I had decided to take Holly, our then 25-year-old daughter, out to dinner. Just her and us for a change, without the rest of the Leman clan. After ordering, we all settled back in our chairs, and Holly said with a big smile, "This is how it was supposed to be!"

Sande and I laughed as hard as Holly because we both knew what she meant. At age 25 she was still good-naturedly acknowledging that having siblings—particularly her arch-rival, secondborn sister Krissy—had not been all sweetness, light, and roses. She bore a few scars from dethronement, but here—for one night at least—she would enjoy a moment of triumph and have Mom and Dad all to herself!

And the Rivalry Begins

If parenting firstborns means preventing discouraged perfectionists, parenting secondborns means watching out for rivalries.

It all begins when that firstborn is dethroned and suddenly has to share the summit of the mountain with little secondborn. These days, more and more families get only that far—a first and a second—so it's well worth our time to devote a chapter to parenting the two-child family.

It's a lot like the car rental companies Hertz and Avis. While the analogy isn't perfect, in a way Avis came along and tried to dethrone Hertz. And how did they do it? By trying harder, of course, which is exactly what the secondborn may do when he or she looks up and sees the firstborn at the top of the family. In fact, I wouldn't be surprised if the copywriter who thought up that famous tagline that Avis used for years—"When you're number two, you have to try harder"—was a secondborn child!

> *I wouldn't be surprised if the copywriter who thought up that famous tag line that Avis used for years—"When you're number two, you have to try harder"—was a secondborn child!*

Whenever a secondborn child arrives, some key principles are always at work, such as secondborn children develop their own lifestyle, according to the perceptions they have about themselves and the key persons in their lives.

Needless to say, that older sibling is a key person in the secondborn's life. We've already touched on the fact that for every child in the family, it's always the next one up on the "ladder" who influences him or her the most—the secondborn by the firstborn, the thirdborn by the secondborn, and so on.

Secondborns may compete with an older brother or sister in various ways. Some do it quite openly, others are a bit more clever—even a bit sneaky—in trying to reach their goal.

One of the classic examples of a sneaky secondborn who put it over on his big brother is the ages-old story of Jacob and Esau. I sometimes wonder if parents Isaac and Rebekah didn't make some kind of self-fulfilling prophecy when they named their twin boys. They called their firstborn Esau (meaning "hairy," which he was), and they called their secondborn Jacob (meaning "supplanter"—someone who usurps the position of another, which he did).

Esau, the powerful older brother, was a rough macho type who spent a lot of time outdoors. Jacob was smoother—in a lot of ways. He hung around the house, was something of a "gentleman of the manor," and was a gourmet of sorts. He was also his mother's favorite. When Esau came home famished from one of his hunting trips, Jacob saw his chance. Esau asked for some stew that Jacob had just prepared. With the savory smells filling the room, Jacob decided to put a rather high price on Esau's snack time: "How about the birthright in exchange for the stew?" he suggested.

Down through history, the firstborn son of the family would be given privileges above those of his younger brothers. This practice is called *primogeniture* and still goes on today. For example, in countries with monarchies, the oldest succeeds to the throne. In Esau and Jacob's time, the birthright meant the firstborn son received a double portion of the inheritance, so when Jacob suggested to Esau that he trade his birthright for a helping of stew, he was obviously offering his brother an outrageously unfair deal.

For a firstborn, ol' Esau wasn't exactly strong on thinking things through. To be blunt, he was a bit dense. All he could think of at the moment was his very empty stomach, so he said, "Why not? What good is a birthright if I starve to death?"

Esau was "starving" only in the sense that he had been outdoors burning lots of calories chasing game, so he was *very* hungry. So Jacob ladled him out a bowl of stew and took the birthright in exchange. Later, he completed his role reversal with his not-too-bright big brother when he tricked his blind father, Isaac, into giving him the patriarchal blessing as well.[1]

In the typical American family, we don't have role reversal occurring with the secondborn cheating the firstborn out of a birthright. Instead, the younger child can "take over" from the older in areas such as achievement, prestige, assuming responsibility, and pleasing the parents.

Parenting Two Boys Can Mean Fireworks

Rivalry is the most intense when you have a two-child family with two boys. Something else to consider, however, is that while two brothers have no trouble learning how to interact with peers of their own sex, they tend to have little preparation for interaction with the opposite sex. The relationship between Mom and her two sons is critical. She is the one who has to do all of the teaching and modeling as to what women are really all about.

It's critical for the mother of two boys to use reality discipline firmly and consistently. She should never—and I mean *never*—take any garbage from them. She should never get into power struggles or put herself in a position where the boys can walk on her or be disrespectful to her. Why? Because not only is she representing parenthood and motherhood, but she's also representing all of womanhood to her two sons. If her two sons learn to walk on her, they'll learn to walk on their wives later. The recent increase in battered wives is really no surprise, and a lot of it can be traced to how the husband learned to relate to women when he was young.

But let's look at the two brothers and examine the older brother especially. Typically the older brother is going to identify very much with the establishment (Mom and Dad). He is going to be the standard-bearer, the one who picks up on family values and practices them faithfully. He will probably be the leader, and also the family "sheriff" or "policeman" as far as keeping the younger brother in line. Older brother often finds himself being the protector of baby brother.

Older brother usually gets a kick out of having younger brother follow him, and in this very basic way the older boy learns a lot of practical leadership skills. This is a very basic reason you find more firstborns in leadership positions in adult life.

> *The secondborn child will be the opposite of the firstborn, particularly if they are less than five years apart and of the same sex.*

At the other end of the family, the younger brother is eyeing older brother and deciding which way he will go. Another key principle that seems to apply in most cases is this: the secondborn child will be the opposite of the firstborn, particularly if they are less than five years apart and of the same sex.

The younger child looks the situation over and usually branches off in a different direction. That different direction may still put him in direct rivalry with his older brother. If he is determined to catch up with him and surpass him as far as leadership and achievement are concerned, this can get sticky. For the firstborn boy it can get downright devastating, if a true role reversal happens.

Rivalries are most likely to be heated if the boys are close in age. If there is a three- or four-year spread, the rivalry usually will be less intense, and there will be some good leadership on the part of the firstborn male. Put them eleven months apart, however, and Mom and Dad may really have their hands full.

When two brothers are born close together, there is less chance for the older brother to establish a clear superiority. This can be particularly true when physical size comes into play. Younger brother can pull a complete role reversal on older brother due to a sheer height and weight advantage.

Helping Little Jimmy Deal with Big Mike

One of the most graphic examples of role reversal I ever worked with was 15-year-old Jimmy and his younger brother,

Mike, who at age 14 was 6½ inches taller and 45 pounds heavier than his "big" brother. Mike had always been bigger, stronger, and even faster than Jimmy. All this left Jimmy feeling as if life had dealt him a very low blow. And it didn't help any when Jimmy's parents cracked down on him much harder than on Mike with all kinds of authoritarian rules. At 15 he had a bedtime of nine o'clock. He received no allowance because he "wasn't responsible." His parents claimed they couldn't trust him and gave him no freedom. Jimmy retaliated by becoming a liar, thief, and possessor of a volatile temper.

> *Telling the average youngster about to turn 16 that he can't drive for two more years is sort of like pulling the pin in a grenade and hoping it won't go off.*

When Jimmy was sent to see me, he had been putting holes in the wall, smashing windows, and "borrowing" the family car, even though he wasn't old enough to drive. When I got the whole story, my first suggestion to the parents was to loosen the tight reins on Jimmy. Bedtime was made more reasonable for a 15-year-old, and he was given an allowance. I also got the parents to modify their ironclad rule on "no driving until you're 18." Telling the average youngster about to turn 16 that he can't drive for two more years is sort of like pulling the pin in a grenade and hoping it won't go off. No wonder Jimmy had been having trouble with authority figures.

I also helped Jimmy make some progress in dealing with the role-reversal problem by suggesting he stop making so many comparisons between himself and his much larger brother. One thing that also helped was that Mike was a congenial kid who generally liked his older brother and wanted to be like him in some respects. He didn't try to reverse their roles; it simply happened.

Jimmy tried to take my advice on not making so many comparisons, and while he didn't completely rid himself of the sting of the role reversal, he made good progress. His bursts of temper subsided. The lying and cheating stopped, and his grades rose from Cs and Ds to As and Bs. The parents were so pleased that not long after he turned 16, he got his driver's license and particularly enjoyed giving rides to Mike, who was still too young to drive.

Parenting Two Girls Is No Cakewalk

What happens when both children in the two-child family are girls? The basic same-sex rivalry is there, but it probably isn't as intense.

In a two-girl family, I believe the father is a key figure. Realize, Dad, that the girls are vying for your individual attention. Try to give each daughter as much one-on-one time as you can. In recent years, a lot has been made out of "family time"—those times when everyone goes out together for ice cream or to see a movie. While family times are a great idea, they will never replace times when a daughter can have Mom or Dad to herself.

> While family times are a great idea, they will never replace times when a daughter can have Mom or Dad to herself.

Parents sometimes wonder if granting their children lots of one-on-one time actually caters to their selfishness. I say absolutely not. In most families, one-on-one time just isn't that plentiful, and when you do spend it, you build the child's self-esteem and sense of individual worth.

That's why Holly's remark while we were out to dinner ("This is how it was supposed to be!") was significant as well as amusing. While growing up, Holly always wanted more times when she could have Sande or me to herself, and so did Krissy, for that matter. I can clearly remember trying to work on a book through the evening and getting invitations from my first- and secondborn daughters:

From Holly: "Please come to my room to talk."
From Krissy: "Can I sleep on the floor in your bedroom tonight?"

Whenever these invites came, I did my best to honor them and spend one-on-one time with each child. Holly, in particular, often vied for my attention as she and Krissy grew up, trying her best to maintain her firstborn position of superiority, even when she really wasn't that superior.

While Holly has many talents and abilities, singing is not one of them. Monotone would not quite describe her voice. Nonetheless, when Holly was about 9, Krissy 7½ , and Kevin 4, they loved to put on shows for us. One of their favorites was their own Tucson production of *Annie*. Following Holly's explicit instructions, Krissy introduced Holly with great fanfare: "Here she is, our one and only Annie!"

And then Holly would dance onto the stage (the front of our living room) and sing "Tomorrow." Oh yes, Kevin's part? He crawled around on the floor playing Sandy, the dog.

My wife and I always marveled that while playing a dog, Kevin didn't howl a bit as Holly sang. Holly's rendition of "Tomorrow" always made you wish it was *yesterday*.

Krissy, of course, could sing like a bird and still does, but she never got to play the part of Annie. Her big sister saw to that because she didn't want that little intruder who dethroned her in the first place to get the starring role. It was hard enough having a little sister breathing down her neck and threatening her place as firstborn.

And so the competition went on all through the girls' childhood. They would play Marco Polo in our pool, and I would constantly catch Holly stretching the rules. In this game, one child yells, "Marco!" and the other child yells back, "Polo!" The rules are that both have to be in the water, and both have to have their eyes shut.

As Holly and Krissy would play, Krissy would dutifully keep her eyes shut while she hollered, "Marco!" When it was

Holly's turn, she'd yell "Marco!" then peek and easily find Krissy when she answered with "Polo!" Other times, Holly would stand up outside the pool with just a *toe* in the water (and therefore was technically in the water) so she could easily spot Krissy.

Now why would Holly—the firstborn stickler for rules—fudge on the rules? The answer's simple. Eighteen months behind her came these footsteps, and she always felt Krissy breathing down her neck, so she had to win. If that meant stretching the rules, then so be it.

> *Krissy was no pansy. She wasn't the "poor little girl" who constantly had to take abuse from her big sister. She could give as good as she got.*

Of course Krissy had not just fallen off the turnip truck. She often knew she'd been had. She'd retreat to the side of the pool and sit there with her little jaw jutting out, eyes narrowed, and arms akimbo—a pose well calculated to bring Daddy over and have him ask, "What's the matter?"

"Holly fudged!" she would say vehemently.

Back then I'd respond with sympathy for Krissy and admonitions for Holly. Now, in retrospect, I can see that Krissy was no pansy. She was as stubborn as a mule and as strong and quick as one of the little mustangs we have here in the Arizona desert. She wasn't the "poor little girl" who constantly had to take abuse from her big sister. She could give as good as she got. Now when I catch them arguing over something, I just smile and say, "You deserve each other."

A Boy for You, a Girl for Me

Rivalry between a boy and a girl is usually much less intense if it exists at all. Let's look, for example, at an older brother/younger sister combination. Three-year-old Bryan went through a mild dethronement crisis when little Megan came home from the hospital, but he soon realized Megan was a girl and not a serious threat to taking over his turf.

Little guys like Bryan seem to have a natural instinct about this. They are also very aware that they get different toys, different clothes, and so on. In most cases, the competition between a boy and his younger sister is not that strong. In fact, a firstborn boy and secondborn girl can often develop a close emotional bond.

> *Three-year-old Bryan went through a mild dethronement crisis when little Megan came home from the hospital, but he soon realized Megan was a girl and not a serious threat to taking over his turf.*

In this kind of combination, little sister usually grows up to be super feminine. She has Mommy and Daddy and also her big brother all waiting on her, interceding for her, caring for her. This can make for a fairly peaceful family while the two children are growing up, but it can cause trouble for younger sister later if she becomes too helpless and dependent on men. When this kind of woman gets married, she often winds up disillusioned and an excellent candidate for the classic seven-year marriage.

The helpless dependent woman runs the risk of marrying a controller. I haven't had many wives come to me for counseling over the years—in fact, the exact count is zero—who have said, "You know what I love about my husband the most? It's his controlling nature."

When the sister is the older child, the typical picture is that the little boy has a second mother. This can work out fine unless the little guy feels that two mothers are too much.

Shane, 15, ran away from home because his mother and older sister "ganged up on me to nitpick." In this case Mom was the chief culprit, but older sister didn't help when she told Shane, "You're *so* immature!"

Shane finally came home after spending a week or so at a friend's house across town. When the family came to me for counseling, I learned that Shane resented how his mom "wore the pants in the family" and dominated him as well as his quiet, passive father. Fortunately, the mother was wise enough to be willing to learn. After counseling sessions in which I encouraged the father to do the talking and leading for a change, we got it worked out. Shane didn't pull any more runaway capers and eventually wound up helping teach younger kids.

Granted, Shane's story is something of an extreme case. A more typical scenario finds the older sister and younger brother going in their own directions in a much less radical way. If given equal treatment and opportunity, they both take on firstborn traits as firstborn girl and firstborn boy.

That was exactly what happened with my older sister, Sally, and my secondborn brother, Jack. I have already extolled Sally's A+ qualities at great length. Jack wasn't quite in Sally's A+ league, but he held his own nicely with a B+ average in high school, making the dean's list in college and going on for a PhD. He also became an excellent football quarterback in high school and played on his college team. Jack always had lots of friends—especially among the young women!

> A basic parenting principle: accept their differences.

Jack never really competed with Sally that much, and she treated him with a lot of respect—even leading cheers for his football exploits. When they were small, Sally tried "mothering" her little brother (who was three years younger) on occasion, but he never bought into it much. She had a lot better luck when bear cub Kevin came along five years later.

Beware of Labels

Whatever combination you come up with, the two-child family is an excellent laboratory for practicing a basic parenting principle: accept their differences.

Of course, we should accept differences no matter how many children are in the family, but there is something about having only two that focuses the challenge more sharply. We soon see that we can accept some things more easily than others. For example, when one child is six inches taller than the other, we can accept that. But suppose one child tends to challenge the rules or has a completely different set of attitudes and emotions? One child is easy to handle, or what a lot of parents like to call "good." The other child is a handful, and naturally his behavior gets labeled "bad."

The challenge for parents in families like this is to remember they must love each child but relate to each child differently. They must maintain some kind of order and consistency in the family and yet always be aware of the individual differences.

I can recall Olivia, a 19-year-old secondborn, telling me in a counseling session, "I wish you'd tell my mother I'm not like my older sister."

I had a good hunch what Olivia meant, but I asked her to explain a bit more. Out tumbled her burden: her mother was always telling her she had to measure up to the standard-bearer in the family, big sister Rebekah. Because Olivia wasn't making it, she didn't feel accepted in life. I counseled the parents to realize that, even though Olivia was an adult, they needed to go out of their way to tell her what they appreciated about her and to look for the positive points in her life.

Also, they needed to do all they could to separate the girls at that point in life. Olivia had graduated from high school but had spent the past year working in menial part-time jobs while her sister, two years older, was about to start her junior year in a college the parents approved of a great deal. They had wanted Olivia to go to the same school, but I urged them to enroll Olivia somewhere else where she could make her own life and not be in the shadow of her older sister. If there is anything you can and must do as a parent, it's this: give your children unqualified love that is not determined by how good their grades are, how well they perform at home, or anything else.

The challenge is to love each child for who he or she is. If you can pull that off, the two-child family can really be a breeze. Think of all the advantages: The whole family fits better in the average car. When you all go out to a restaurant, you don't have to wait as long—most restaurant booths are made for four. And, if Mom and Dad are still up to it, they can ride with the kids on the roller coaster, two and two!

> *Give your children unqualified love that is not determined by how good their grades are, how well they perform at home, or anything else.*

The Night I Blew It Big Time

It's easy enough to hand out all this advice on reality discipline. I believe in it and have tried to practice it with all five of our children, but as I have already admitted, my firstborn daughter and I knocked heads as she grew up. Holly never stopped competing with her sister as she fought for her firstborn birthright as the oldest. She had the constitution of a salmon, which can leap tall rapids with a single bound. No matter how much I disciplined her for arguing and fighting with Krissy, she just kept coming. Whenever I thought I knew how to handle Holly, I discovered that I still had a lot to learn.

One of my most memorable lessons happened when Holly was 10 and I had just finished writing *Making Children Mind without Losing Yours*. Because I was leaving the next day for a sales conference at my publisher, I thought I'd better brush up on some of the tips I gave in the book about how to be a loving, responsible parent. So I asked Holly if she could spend some time with me that evening.

"Without *them*?" she asked incredulously.

"Just the two of us."

"*All right!*" she said, and we took off on what was, indeed, a great evening. At 10:30 p.m. we pulled into the driveway. It was well past Holly's bedtime on a school night, and I was eager to get to bed myself because I had to be up at 5 a.m. to catch a 7 a.m. flight to New Jersey.

"Daddy," Holly said, "for a special treat, can I pull my sleeping bag into your room and sleep on the floor next to your bed?"

As usual, my assertive little firstborn had really enjoyed her evening without *them*, and now she wanted a little icing on her cake. Faster than any expert on reality discipline should, I replied, "Holly, no. Listen, it's late; it's a school night. You need to get to bed and get a good night's sleep."

> *Don't always give an immediate response to a child's request. Think about it for a few seconds or a minute and then try to answer with understanding and reason.*

My snap answer contained excellent logic and adult wisdom, but in giving it I violated one of my own key principles: Don't always give an immediate response to a child's request. Think about it for a few seconds or a minute and then try to answer with understanding and reason.

But I was in a hurry. Five a.m. was going to come all too soon, and I was due in New Jersey, where I would extol the wisdom of making children mind without losing yours.

Holly was not impressed with my fatherly wisdom about a good night's sleep. I was being unreasonable, and the tears began to flow.

"But Daddy, I just want to sleep by your bed."

"Holly, no, the floor is hard; you won't sleep all that well. C'mon, we've had a great evening together. Don't spoil it!"

But for Holly everything was already spoiled. "You never let me do *anything!*" she wailed as our wonderful evening blew up in my face. As I got Holly into bed, she was still sobbing, "You never let me do anything" over and over.

Feeling frustrated, angry, and guilty, I tried to finish packing and be ready to go at dawn's early light. Sande had washed the slacks and shirt I wanted to wear on the plane, but my loving Mama Bear had forgotten to iron them and had gone on to bed. So there I stood at the ironing board. I could have probably worn something else, but I liked these clothes. Besides, when I spoke at the sales conference in the morning, I could use ironing my clothes as an illustration of what a loving and sacrificial husband I am!

As I ironed, I could still hear Holly. She hadn't stopped her wailing. In fact, it was getting louder. *She's being a powerful little buzzard, Leman,* I told myself. *Time to pull the rug!*

In this case pulling the rug meant firmly telling Holly to quiet down. But "firmly" turned into "loudly irate": "Listen up, Holly! I've had enough of this. Do you *understand* me? We had a wonderful evening—*wonderful.* Now it's time for you to be in bed and asleep. And do you know *why* I'm upset, Holly? I just found my clothes that your mother was supposed to have ready for me in a wrinkled mess, and I'm *not in a real good mood!*"

I capped my lecture by telling her she was going to *sleep,* and that was *final!*

Coming out of Holly's room, I slammed the door so hard it shook the whole house, waking everyone but Sande, who sort of rolled over. To calm down I turned on the late news, but then "the guilties" got to me. I knew I was wrong. In fact, I had lost it. Holly's cries had stopped, but I had to do something to make up. Maybe she was asleep by now, but I still wanted to give her a kiss.

Feeling terrible, I gently opened Holly's door. She wasn't in her bed! I tore through the house looking for what I thought was a disobedient child. What had I just written in *Making Children Mind* about using spanking sparingly? This time I had a few good swats to spare, all right.

I tried our bedroom where I thought Holly had carried out her original plan, but her sleeping bag wasn't there, and neither was she. I checked Kevey's room, but no Holly. Then Krissy's—still no Holly.

Had she run away—at 11:00 at night?

Now I was really anxious and did what any trained therapist does to pull himself together—I headed for the refrigerator. As I walked by the sewing room, there was Holly, ironing one of my shirts!

Her first words were sort of cute, coming from a firstborn perfectionist: "Daddy, I don't iron real good."

My 10-year-old was trying her best, using the old-fashioned method of sprinkling the shirt—with her tears. I just said, "Oh, Holly, will you forgive me?"

"I've ruined the whole evening!" Holly cried. "I've ruined the whole evening!"

"No, Holly, Daddy ruined the whole evening. I was wrong. Will you forgive me?"

One thing about Holly, she loves emphasis: "I've ruined the whole evening! I've ruined the whole evening!"

I tried again. "Holly, will you hush up and let me apologize?"

Holly put down the iron, then burrowed her head into my chest. She squeezed me, hugged me, held me, and told me she loved me. I did the same. Two minutes later, Holly was in her bed, fast asleep.

Somehow I got the ironing done and caught the plane the next morning with only a few hours' sleep. I presented my new book on parenting to the sales staff. I chose not to mention my bumbling and stumbling the night before, but the easiest part of my presentation were the following words, which are useful if you're parenting two children or

> *The time we really look big in a child's eyes is when we go to him or her to apologize for our mistakes, when we say, "I was wrong. Will you forgive me?"*

ten: I believe the time we really look big in a child's eyes is when we go to him or her to apologize for our mistakes, when we say, "I was wrong. Will you forgive me?"

Have your children heard that from you?

5 Tips for Parenting the Two-Child Family

It's important to emphasize consistency and fairness. For example:

1. *Give your firstborn a later bedtime.* Even if the difference is as little as half an hour, the difference must be enforced. Your firstborn is watching.

2. *Make responsibilities and allowances different.* The rule is this: the older child gets the most allowance and the most responsibility. But be sure the younger one does his or her share of the work.

3. *Avoid comparisons.* That's easy for a psychologist to advise but hard to do in day-to-day living. Be aware of the dangers of those famous words, "Why aren't you like your brother [or sister]?" Obviously one child is *not* like his or her brother or sister, and your remark is not only damaging, it is a foolish waste of breath.

4. *Don't feel compelled to do for one what you did for the other.* Treating each child differently may mean that sometimes one child gets a little more than the other. But it all evens out in the end.

5. *Do things with one child at a time.* Give both children plenty of one-on-one opportunities. How can you find time in your busy schedule to do this? You don't *find* it; you *make* it. Take one child alone on a shopping trip or even a business trip. If possible, leave half an hour early in the morning and stop for breakfast before dropping him or her off at school. Dozens of ways to spend one-on-one time will occur to you, if you really *want* to do it. Just remember the cardinal rule: if you do something with one child, be sure to do something with another, always gearing the activity to the need of each child.

15

Taking Off the Squeeze

Parenting the Middle Child

The only true middle child in the Leman family is Krissy, a very friendly, outgoing, together, 34-year-old who carved out a promising career in education both as a successful teacher and also as director of curriculum at her school. Then, when firstborn son Conner arrived, Krissy made the choice to stay home. Little Adeline came along a couple of years later. Presently Krissy has her hands plenty full, trying to keep up with the rigors of being a mom to two young, busy children.

Interestingly, Krissy has been very friendly and outgoing almost since the day she discovered her older sister, Holly, and the reality that she would never have Mom and Dad all to herself. Krissy is a graphic example of how the secondborn can play off the firstborn and take off in another direction.

Holly's always been on top of her game—a very competent English teacher and also in charge of the curriculum of the school for grades K–12. Kids like her. Other teachers and parents like her. She's a structured firstborn who can come off as very serious and sometimes Judge Judy–like, but she has a warm heart and compassion for others.

You would get the impression, from looking at Krissy's room as she grew up, that she is a very orderly person, but she is certainly not a perfectionist. She has always had a hang-loose, relaxed approach to life.

Her first day at kindergarten was a day my wife will never forget. With some trepidation, Sande put Krissy on a morning bus, said a "Thank you for taking care of her" prayer, and went back home to try to keep her mind on the morning's tasks.

> *She wasn't trying to be disrespectful; she was simply being her easygoing, sociable self.*

Meanwhile, Krissy went to kindergarten and apparently had a great day. At 11:45 a.m. the kindergarten bus stopped in front of the house, and two other little tykes who lived in the neighborhood got off. Krissy did not.

To her credit, Sande waited almost forty-five minutes before she hit the panic button. Surely, she thought, another bus would be along soon. When none appeared, she called the school. The principal informed her that Krissy had gotten on the bus, and he couldn't understand why she hadn't gotten off at her house.

At this point, Sande forgot all about keeping up appearances and looking as if she had child rearing under control. She went a little crazy. Failing to reach me at the office because I was out somewhere, she started calling everyone she could think of to ask if they had seen Krissy. Between calls, the phone rang.

"Hi, Mom, this is Krissy."

"Krissy! Where *are* you?"

"I'm at my best friend's house."

"Honey, *where are you*? *Whose* house are you at?"

Krissy put down the phone. "What's your name again?" Sande could hear her saying.

It turned out that "what's her name" was Jennifer—a little girl Krissy had met for the first time that first day in kindergarten. Jennifer's house was on the way home, and Krissy had decided to get off the bus and visit with her new friend. It had never occurred to her that Mom might be worried when she didn't get off the bus at our stop. She wasn't trying to be disrespectful; she was simply being her easygoing, sociable self.

Krissy Started Floating at 18 Months

Actually, Krissy was laid-back and easygoing even earlier than kindergarten. I can recall an 18-month-old Krissy swimming with the aid of floaties attached to her shoulders. Older kids were all over the pool, diving, splashing, making waves, and Krissy was out in the middle of it, just enjoying life. It seems Krissy has always gone along with whatever comes her way.

Holly, her older sister, has always taken the much more serious approach to things, which is typical of perfectionists. Holly *never* got off the kindergarten bus or any other bus before her stop. She always came straight home because rules are rules. Today, at age 36, Holly lives by the code or lifestyle she developed while growing up, which all conscientious people know instinctively—rules are rules. Holly is thoughtful and analytical; she was always an excellent student and voracious reader. Today she is a gifted teacher and still a voracious reader. Holly has lots of friends, but some of her closest friends are books.

Krissy is like her father. It always was an effort to read anything, and it still is. There's too much of life out there waiting to be tasted and enjoyed. Krissy would rather read people than books. She's a good example of hard work paying off. Schoolwork did not come as easily for Krissy as it did for her older sister, but she still did exceptionally well and graduated in four years flat from college, for which her father and his accountant give her heartfelt thanks!

So all this makes Krissy a typical middle child, right? Well, partly right. If you review the list of characteristics of middle children in chapter 8, you will see it is riddled with contradictions. One column tells us middle children are sociable, friendly, and outgoing. Krissy certainly fits all three of those. But another column says middle children are also characterized as loners, quiet, and shy.

> *The only child, the firstborn child, and the baby all stick out rather prominently, but the middle child sort of blends in like a quail in the desert.*

The chart also describes middle children as taking life in stride with a laid-back attitude. That's Krissy most of the time. Underneath that blithe countenance, however, is a sensitive woman who can be stubborn and very hard to deal with if you get her riled. (Just ask her younger brother, Kevin, who used to flee before Krissy's wrath before he grew up to be 6'3".)

So Krissy presents her share of paradoxes and contradictions and illustrates nicely the idea that it's harder to get a handle on the middle child than on anyone else in the family. The only child, the firstborn child, and the baby all stick out rather prominently, but the middle child sort of blends in like a quail in the desert.

> *Middle children follow their own version of Murphy's Law:* I'm going to live according to what I see just above me in the family. I'll size up the situation and then take the route that looks the best.

Keying on Big Sister or Brother

The same principles that apply to the secondborn are usually equally applicable to the middleborn. Like secondborns, middle children follow their own version of Murphy's Law: *I'm going to live according to what I see just above me in the family. I'll size up the situation and then take the route that looks the best.* The key to this middle child principle is "what I see just above me in the family." The second child

> *The same principles that apply to the secondborn are usually equally applicable to the middleborn.*

looks above to the firstborn, and in a family of four, the thirdborn looks above to the secondborn to get a clue on which route to take. For example, let's consider this family of four children:

Family K

Girl—16, firstborn female
Boy—14, firstborn male
Girl—12, middle child
Girl—10, baby

In this family, the 12-year-old is the true middle child, squeezed from above by an older brother (and an older sister, for that matter) and squeezed from below by her baby sister. For the most part, she will cue on her older brother to choose her lifestyle, but her firstborn sister will also have some influence.

Let's take one more example to see how spacing in the family may eliminate a true middle child altogether:

Family L

Boy—18, firstborn male
Girl—17, firstborn female
Girl—15, middle child?
Boy—8, baby

In this family, the thirdborn—a girl—appears to be the middle child, but is she really? She looks above to her firstborn brother and sister to get clues on which route to take to form her personal life goal and theme, but what about below? Her baby brother did not appear on the scene until she was 7 years old, and by then her personality and lifestyle were already determined. For the first seven life-forming years, she was baby of the family, and the odds are excellent that she will have many lastborn characteristics and few middle child traits because she never felt that squeeze when it really counted—during those all-important early years.

> If there is one generalization you can make about middle children, it's that they feel squeezed and/or dominated.

Feeling Squeezed

While Family L above doesn't have a true middle child, many other families do. And if there is one generalization you can make about middle children, it's that they feel squeezed and/or dominated. It's important for parents to be extra aware that the middle child often feels as if "everyone is running my life." Not only does the middle child have a set of parents in authority over him, but he or she has an older sibling right there also.

> It's important for parents to be extra aware that the middle child often feels as if "everyone is running my life."

If the older sibling is close in age (within two or three years), he or she is almost sure to tell the middle child what to do. And of course just below the middle child is the baby of the family, who seems to be getting away with murder. The middle child feels trapped. He or she is too young for the privileges received by the older sibling and too old to get away with the shenanigans of the baby in the family.

With these pressures from above and below, middle children wind up feeling like fifth wheels, misfits who have no say and no control. Everyone else seems to be making the decisions, while they are asked to sit, watch, and obey.

When only 8 years old, Krissy gave Sande and me a taste of how sensitive the middle child can be when parents make decisions for her. With her little lip jutting out and tears trickling down her cheeks, Krissy confronted her mother about a class in creative dramatics that Sande had enrolled her in a few days before. Our sensitive middle child let her mother know in no uncertain terms how unfair it was to be signed up for creative dramatics and to not even know about it! I happened to walk in on the conversation and asked, "But Krissy, don't you enjoy dramatics?"

"I love it!" (sob)

I laughed and said, "Then why are you getting on Mom's case?"

"You might think it's funny, but I don't think it's so funny. How would you like me to sign Mommy up for swimming lessons?"

Krissy's extremely perceptive remark stopped me short. We have a backyard pool, and Sande gets in it about twice a year to get wet. If Krissy or her dad tried to sign Sande up for swimming lessons, either one of us would wind up in the pool without the benefit of a bathing suit. I got Krissy's point and then some. She wanted to do her *own* enrolling in creative dramatics. She didn't need Mommy's help!

When telling seminar audiences this story, I hasten to point out that it's important to ask the opinions of *all* your children, not just the middleborns. Giving a child of any birth order a chance to choose and decide for himself or herself is a critical part of developing self-esteem and a sense of responsibility and accountability. But for parents of extra-sensitive middle children, the moral is clear: always ask middle children for their opinions and let them make their own decisions whenever possible.

Help the Middle Child Feel Special

So far this chapter sounds as if we should throw a big pity party for all middle children. What hope is there for poor little middleborn Mildred or Milford who wander off to find friends because they are fifth wheels at home? What can parents do for these kids who are such sensitive bundles of contradiction, who supposedly feel squeezed and dominated as adults ignore their opinions and make all their decisions for them?

> *Always ask middle children for their opinions and let them make their own decisions whenever possible.*

One of the ways I have always tried to make Krissy feel special is by taking her out to breakfast on her birthday. When she was growing up, May 16 on my calendar was completely cleared of appointments. The reason was simple: May 16 is Krissy's birthday, and we went out to breakfast together. If it was a school day, I'd take her to breakfast, then later I'd pick her up for lunch and take her to one of the classy places she enjoyed, like McDonald's.

Naturally there were two more inviolate dates on my calendar each year, November 14 and February 8. After all, Holly and Kevin also enjoyed choosing where they would eat, what kind of cake they would have, and so on. We have always been big especially on cakes at our house—rainbow cakes, space cakes, Charlie Brown cakes—*anything is possible on your birthday!* After Hannah and Lauren joined

> *We have always been big especially on cakes at our house—rainbow cakes, space cakes, Charlie Brown cakes—anything is possible on your birthday!*

the Leman band, two other dates became equally important—
June 30 and August 22. (You may observe that if the Lemans
had had more kids, there would have been very little time left
in the year to work.)

But I have to say that of all our children, Krissy was (and
still is, for that matter) the most sensitive about having Daddy
to herself on her birthday. In fact, on Krissy's ninth birthday when we were having breakfast together, a businessman walked by, recognized me, and said, "Aren't you Dr.
Leman?"

I said I was, and he went on, "I'm so glad I caught you.
Today is when I'm supposed to be writing you a note inviting
you to talk to our conference next year on May 16."

The moment he said "May 16," I knew we had a problem.
I was waiting for an opening to let him know that May 16
was my daughter's birthday and I simply wasn't available, but
he was going on in such grand style, describing the beautiful
resort where the conference would be held and how everyone
would love to have me come and share, that I found it hard
to interrupt.

Krissy, on the other hand, did not find it as difficult to
interrupt. As the businessman went on, she became more
and more agitated. Finally, she poked me in the ribs and said,
"My daddy can't come!"

This wasn't very good behavior for the daughter of someone supposedly skilled in reality discipline, so I said, "Now
wait a minute, Krissy. Daddy and this man are talking . . ."

The businessman went on with more of his glorious plans
for the conference on May 16 of next year as I kept hesitating
to tell him I simply wasn't available on that day.

Finally, Krissy could stand it no longer and said in an even
louder voice, *"He can't come!"*

While Krissy may have appeared to be a bit outspoken
(i.e., rude), I couldn't reprimand her too severely. The problem was mine because I hadn't wanted to interrupt the man
as he waxed eloquent about his conference a full year ahead

(undoubtedly, he was a firstborn). Finally I had to explain that May 16 was Krissy's birthday and that was, indeed, why we were there in the restaurant having breakfast. If May 16 was the day he needed me, I was not available.

The businessman then admitted he wasn't positive it was May 16; he would check. Later he called and told me he was wrong about the date. It turned out he needed me on May 18, so I was able to keep both dates *and* my integrity with Krissy. If May 16 had been the date, however, too bad! My daughter's birthday always comes first.

At our house, May 16 has always been off-limits to the outside world and always will be. Even today, with some of our kids living in other locations, we Lemans still make a big deal out of birthdays.

Give Middle Children Room to Share Feelings

In the birthday story, Krissy showed one of those contradictions that are typical of the middle child. She spoke up about her special birthday appointment, even when it was a year off. A lot of middle children would have been too shy, easygoing, or unwilling to confront and would not have spoken up. These middle children are the ones who neglect to tell you how they really feel. They are classic avoiders of conflict or confrontation.

But Krissy is sensitive, and in many middle children sensitivity bubbles over into anger. Krissy was so upset that she finally spoke up, and I'm glad she did, even though it looked as if she was being a disobedient child.

In my counseling, I find that people with anger or hostilities are usually firstborns or middleborns. It takes a while to flush some of them out because they are pleasers and they may be denying their anger. With Krissy, we always know when she's not happy with something. But with your middle child, you may have to dig and probe a bit.

Give your middle child plenty of opportunities to share feelings with you. If you have two middle children, for example, the second and third between a first and a last, keep a close watch on #3, who can really get lost in the shuffle. Don't just make an occasional "How's it going?" remark. Schedule time for a walk or take the child along on an errand and talk in the car. (Talking in a car is a good idea—it's easier for the child to look out the window than right at Mom or Dad when he or she is trying to share feelings.)

> *Don't just make an occasional "How's it going?" remark. Schedule time for a walk or take the child along on an errand and talk in the car.*

The Squeeze Builds Psychological Muscles

I've made a big point of how social and outgoing middle children may be. Feeling rejected, squeezed, or at least misunderstood at home, they are quicker to go outside the family to make friends.

Parents watch their middleborns come and go and wonder what it is that is so much more attractive about other people's houses. Meanwhile, without realizing it, the middle child is getting invaluable training for life. In making new friends, middle children get practice in committing to relationships and in working to keep them going. They sharpen and refine their social skills as they learn how to deal with their peer group

> *In making new friends, middle children get practice in committing to relationships and in working to keep them going.*

and other people outside the family. When the time to leave home really comes, they are far more ready to deal with the realities of marriage, making a living, and functioning in society than other children may be.

295

So don't despair over your middle child who always seems to be running off somewhere. In fact, you will be wise to let your middle child know that you understand friends are important. I realize that in some cases the peer group can be a problem, but don't automatically look on the friends as rivals who may lead your child astray. Try to invite your middle child's friends to your house for an overnight or even a weekend. It's another way to let your middle child know that you think he—and his friends—are very special.

And be aware of one other paradox at work in the middle child's search for friends. While the middle child may feel a little like a fifth wheel at home, his home should still remain a lot safer and more forgiving place than the outside world. While the middle child may feel good about all her friends, she can also foul things up with her peer group. When she does, her friends can melt faster than a fudgesicle on the Fourth of July in Tucson. That's when she can learn that a squeeze or hug from Mom and Dad isn't so bad after all.

The World Needs More Unspoiled Middleborns

Not all middle children are social lions, of course. Many factors may keep them from having a lot of friends: physical size and appearance, shyness, fears, the need or desire to work or study long hours. But even if the middle child stays home, so to speak, he or she still gets automatic training that helps make a better-adjusted person. That training comes in the form of negotiation and compromise.

Middle children can't have it all their own way. The oldest always seems to be getting more, staying up later, staying out later, and so on. The youngest is getting away with murder and receiving a lot more attention along with it. All this may seem very unfair at the time, but it's great discipline. Middle children are far less likely to be spoiled, and therefore they tend to be less frustrated and demanding of life. The typical hassles, irritations, and disappointments of being a middle child are often blessings in disguise.

On more than one occasion I have talked with mothers and fathers who are so very proud of their firstborn teenage sons or daughters because these kids don't give their parents any flak about anything. They are always willing to help, always obey the rules, and so on. I smile and wish these parents continued success, but I can't help wondering if their obedient firstborns may be headed for big trouble. Could they be bottling up their feelings?

> *Middle children are far less likely to be spoiled, and therefore they tend to be less frustrated and demanding of life.*

Could they be classic pleasers who would never think of crossing their parents? And what will happen in a few years when the family umbilical cord is cut and they're out on their own? Will they have the psychological muscles to deal with life?

Now I'm not saying that all obedient, ready-to-please teenagers are too weak to face life after they leave home. What I am saying is that I've counseled a lot of firstborns and only children who were obedient pleasers of Mom and Dad as they grew up, but as adults they wound up having trouble coping with life, spouses, or neighbors they couldn't handle. And that's why they came to see me. The more I counsel, the more I realize that being squeezed a little while you are growing up isn't necessarily all bad. It can be excellent basic training for the real campaign that starts when you leave home and strike out on your own.

So don't despair if you have a middle child who seems caught in the squeeze right now. Do your best to take off that squeeze or at least help him or her through it. Keep your middle child's candle lit, and in the end he or she may shine brighter than all the rest.

6 Tips for Parenting the Middle Child

1. *Recognize that your middle child may avoid sharing how he or she really feels about things.* If your middle child is an avoider, set aside times for just the two of you to talk. It's important to give this kind of time to every child, but a middle child is least likely to insist on his or her fair share. Be sure he or she gets it.

2. *Take extra care to make your middle child feel special.* Typically the middle child feels squeezed by the brothers or sisters above and below. The middle child needs those moments when you ask for his opinion or allow him to make choices. One night I took three of our kids bowling. As we sat down to start our score sheet, there was an intense discussion over who would bowl first. While Holly and Kevey clamored for the honor, I noticed Krissy was not saying a word. I said, "Krissy, you get to choose." So she put down her daddy's name first, then Holly, then Kevey, finally herself.

3. *Set up some regular privileges he or she can count on having or doing every day or every week.* Perhaps it is something as simple as watching a certain TV program with no interference from others in the family. Maybe it's going to a certain restaurant. The point is, this is the middle child's *exclusive* territory.

4. *Make a special effort to give your child a new item of clothing rather than a hand-me-down.* In some families, income is sufficient, so this is not a problem, but in other homes economics make hand-me-downs a regular part of growing up. An occasional hand-me-down is fine, but your middle child may be particularly appreciative of something new, especially a key item such as a coat or jacket.

5. *Listen carefully to your middle child's answers or explanations for what is going on or what he or she thinks of certain situations.* His or her desire to avoid conflict and not make waves may get in the way of the real facts. You may have to say, "C'mon now, let's have the whole story. You aren't going to get in trouble. I want to know how you really feel."

6. *Be sure the family photo album has its share of pictures and home movies of your middle child.* Don't let him or her fall victim to the stereotyped fate of seeing thousands of pictures of the older brother or sister and only a few of him or her! And be sure you take some of your middleborn alone, not always with big brother or little sister.

16

Helping the Family "Cub" Grow Up

Parenting the Lastborn

My first four words of advice for parents of the lastborn are: beware of being manipulated! When the lastborn arrives, the real enemy is not that cute little buzzard who marks the end of the family line. He can't help being so darling. She can't help it if she charms everyone with one toothless smile. The real culprit parents have to battle is well known to Pogo fans, who have met the enemy and realize "he is us."

Authoritarian parents say, "Do it my way, or else!"

Authoritative parents say, "I'd like to have you do it this way because . . ."

But permissive parents tell their little lastborn, "Ahh, you do it your way, you cute little guy."

Getting Away with Murder

Why is it that parents can run a pretty tight ship with their older kids, but the lastborn seems to have some mysterious power that lets him get away with murder? I'm not sure there is a definitive answer. Maybe the parents get tired, or maybe they get careless because now they think they "know the ropes" and can loosen up. Whatever it is, parents often look the other way when the lastborn skips chores and drives his older brothers and sisters crazy with pestering, or what I call "setups." (The setup is a particular skill of the lastborn and involves bugging an older sibling until he or she lashes out in anger, at which point the baby of the family runs screaming to Mommy for protection.)

> The real enemy is not that cute little buzzard who marks the end of the family line. The real culprit parents have to battle is well known to Pogo fans, who have met the enemy and realize "he is us."

I was an expert in setting up my big brother, Jack, whom I loved to call "God" because he was so big, strong, and superior to me, the little Cub of the family. When I heard him come home from school, I'd say within his hearing (but not necessarily my mother's), "God's home!"

Jack didn't appreciate being called "God," and he would often belt me one. Then I'd run to Mom, who always took my side, and Jack would wind up in trouble. If he belted me extra hard, he might wind up in trouble with my dad when he got home.

Recently Charles Swindoll, whose books have sold in the gazillions, shared with me on a radio show his own birth order adventures. As the baby of the family with an older brother and sister, he often felt put-upon and put down. "I usually called my older brother 'Hitler,'" he confided.

"Is that right?" I said. "Perhaps he knew my older brother, 'God.'"

For a second or two, one of America's great spiritual leaders looked at me in what seemed to be shock, and then we both burst into hearty laughter. Two babies of the family had found a common bond—memories of a big brother who made life a little miserable at times.

Calling my older brother by the unlikely name of "God" to set him up was just one way I got away with murder. There were many others. If lastborns aren't getting away with murder, they are at least trying to manipulate, clown, or entertain, and they're often likely to be found disturbing someone's peace.

> *If lastborns aren't getting away with murder, they are at least trying to manipulate, clown, or entertain, and they're often likely to be found disturbing someone's peace.*

Now I realize that not all parents fall for the lastborn's charms and antics. Not all lastborns get away with murder. Nonetheless, many of them still are able to manipulate parents with that famous line: "Mommy, I can't do it!" A plaintive cry for help is a great tool lastborns use to get parents (as well as older siblings) to snowplow the roads of life for them.

Babies are particularly adept at getting help with school-work. I have counseled several children whose seeming help-lessness turned their homes into a tutoring establishment right after dishes were done each evening. It's one thing to encour-age children with their homework and get them started; it's another to do it for them. A lot of parents get suckered into doing the child's work, all the while believing they are helping the child. Of course, they are only hindering the child because it prohibits him from learning to do his own thinking.

> *A plaintive cry for help is a great tool lastborns use to get parents (as well as older siblings) to snowplow the roads of life for them.*

For example, I worked with one seventh grader whose older brother was in his final year of high school. The parents sent this little redhead to me in the spring of his seventh-grade year because he was doing so poorly in school. The boy was the lastborn of two children.

At first we didn't make much progress. The boy was in all kinds of trouble at school, and the parents were going to more conferences than they really wanted to be bothered with. He managed to pass seventh grade, but not by much. I continued working with him throughout the summer, and in the fall big brother went away to college. This seemed to be the breakthrough that was needed. As the boy started into his eighth-grade year, he began responding to some reality discipline principles I had set up, and the parents finally saw some positive results.

The reality discipline I asked his parents to use was rather basic:

1. Make the boy stand on his own feet and do not help him with any more of his homework than absolutely necessary.
2. After dinner, no going out to play, no watching television, no doing anything of that nature until responsibilities are taken care of. Responsibilities include chores and certainly schoolwork.
3. No making Mom and Dad tutor for several hours each night. (This went back to making the boy stand on his own feet.)

The lastborn son made an excellent turnaround in the fall of his eighth-grade year. The misbehavior stopped at school, and his grades came up nicely without a lot of tutoring by Mom and Dad. The youngster had lived in the shadow of his older brother for so long that he had been completely cowed and discouraged. As I often put it, "His candle had been blown out." The

> *The youngster had lived in the shadow of his older brother for so long that he had been completely cowed and discouraged.*

older brother was so confident and competent and so much bigger and stronger that it just left the younger boy wiped out. Once elder brother physically left the house, the younger child began to bloom.

And Mom and Dad were relieved when they didn't have to spend three or four hours a night tutoring their lastborn to keep his grades barely above water. Once the son understood that he had the ability and could do it himself, everything changed.

I Just Didn't Like School

I have also counseled lastborn children who just don't care for school. I understand where they're coming from because I felt the same way when I was growing up. Sometimes a child has learning problems or disabilities, but in many cases the true issue is attitude.

I'm convinced my disastrous school record could have been greatly improved with one simple step on the part of my parents. My mother should have stopped running down to the school to talk to the counselors. She should have stopped trying to find the cause of little Kevin's problems. If she had simply said, "Hey, kid, no Little League unless you cut it in school," I probably would have turned around by the sixth or seventh grade.

But Mom and Dad never called my bluff. They never drew the line. In a word, they were permissive, and I played it for all I could. For example, I had a strange ailment called Monday and Friday stomachaches. I would wake up on Friday feeling terrible, and, of course, I couldn't go to school. But strangely enough, by mid-afternoon a miracle had happened. I was instantly healed when the clock struck three! I remained well throughout Saturday and Sunday, but then on Monday morning, back would come that stomachache.

There are other names for my illness. One might be "making the weekend longer by faking a stomachache on Fridays and Mondays." But somehow my mom never really caught on. I guess she just couldn't believe her little Cub could lie and be in such "pain" at the same time.

> Another trick I mastered was finding something "important" to do when there was work to be done.

Another trick I mastered was finding something "important" to do when there was work to be done. The dishes would be looming mountainously in the sink and the garbage cans and wastebaskets would be overflowing, but I let none of these mundane temptations keep me from what I felt I had to do—right at that very moment.

What or who spoils the lastborn? The obvious answer is, "Why, the parents do the spoiling, of course." And that's correct to a point, but sometimes parents can get a lot of help from the other children in the family. How spoiled a lastborn gets can depend on when and where he or she arrives in the family zoo. For example, let's diagram a family consisting of three girls and a lastborn boy:

Family M

Female—11
Female—9
Female—6
Male—3

In this family it looks as if the little guy is totally outnumbered by females. But what can usually occur here is a strong relationship between the mother and the son. After three girls, little Harold will be very precious, especially to Mom, and she is likely to give him the benefit of the doubt when older sisters come and complain about his pestering.

Actually, this family has two lastborns, a lastborn boy and a lastborn girl. This almost guarantees friction between the 6-year-old and the 3-year old. In this kind of family, it is very common for alliances to form. The way that will probably happen in this particular sequence is that the 11-year-old will form an alliance with the 6-year-old, and the 9-year-old with the 3-year-old.

In many cases the thirdborn child in this family could find herself in an unfavorable position. This would be especially true if both of the older girls decided to really mother the little boy and take his side in all of the various arguments and incidents that occur in a family of four. On the other hand, all three of the older girls may decide that the little guy is a pest and be particularly irritated if Mom asks them to do a lot of babysitting.

Let's take another look at a family where the lastborn becomes very special. In this case we have a firstborn girl followed by two boys, and finally along comes "baby princess." The diagram looks like this:

Family N

Female—13

Male—12

Male—10

Female—4

On the positive side, the lastborn girl is in good shape in that she has two older brothers who are likely to wind up becoming her champions, unless she is a total little brat. With two attentive older brothers, she can grow up learning that men are caring and loving. And with the older sister, she also gets the benefit of more mothering and cuddling, something that firstborn girls love to do.

The bad news is that the baby princess can get the idea that the world revolves around her. She may become the apple of

Daddy's eye and be able to wrap him around her little finger to get just about anything she wants. If this is carried too far, she can grow up believing she can do this with any man, and be a risky candidate for a happy marriage.

If parents are overly permissive, baby princess could be spoiled rotten. She could grow up to be an obnoxious adult who makes unreasonable demands on everyone.

How to Grow a Total Weakling

One of the most damaging effects of parental permissiveness is making things too easy for a child. Later, when the lastborn has grown to adulthood, he or she may not be prepared for real life. Adversities will just be too much.

I once worked with a family that consisted of a mother (a widow) and 7 children. There were 3 daughters, then 3 sons, and then the youngest daughter, who was 7 years behind the youngest son. The father had died when the youngest daughter was 13. At the time I counseled the family, the youngest daughter was 26 and totally dependent on the mother. For 13 years the mother and the youngest daughter had virtually lived alone together because the rest of the children had moved out of the house by the time the father had died.

The daughter had been totally protected and smothered by her mother to the point that when I saw her, she was uneducated and her confidence was at zero. The most challenging tasks she could attempt were housecleaning and babysitting.

I realize this is an extreme case of the parent needing the child so badly that she didn't allow the child to grow up. But the same thing happens to a lesser degree every time the parent acts permissively and does too much snowplowing of life's roads for a child. When a parent babies a child too much, the parent actually renders that child useless, or at least cripples him or her in one way or another.

The Other Side of the Lastborn Coin

One thing I've tried to emphasize throughout this book is that no birth order fits only one mold. The same characteristics are not always true in every lastborn child. Those ever-present variables can throw in a lot of curveballs for lastborns, as well as any other birth order. In fact, Sande and I have seen the variable of spacing working overtime in our "second family"—Hannah, born nine and a half years after Kevin II, and Lauren, born five and a half years after Hannah.

Hannah's official description is "firstborn in the second family," but I describe her as a compliant firstborn who acts more like a baby of the family than anything else. It's important to remember that for the first five years of her life— that period when her lifestyle was really formed—Hannah was the lastborn in the total Leman family. She was also the beneficiary of a lot of loving care from what amounted to five parents—Sande and myself, of course, and her older siblings, all of whom came across to her as very big, very capable, and very loving.

We doted on Hannah more than a little bit, and it took all of our determination and experience to apply reality discipline to balance things up and not let her become spoiled. When we'd go to University of Arizona basketball games or other public events, we would sometimes take Hannah along, and all our friends would hold her and cuddle her. Today Hannah is a very balanced, well-adjusted, fun-loving 22-year-old, who is extremely well liked, loves school, and loves her teachers. She has always wanted to be a teacher and has just graduated with a degree in special ed. Her heart is for Africa and the underprivileged. Our baby of the family in many ways, our little surprise child has a determination that is wonderful and will take her far.

As for Lauren, she definitely is the "caboose" of the Leman family(ies). But while she's the ordinal baby of them all, she really acts more like a firstborn or only child than anything else. Lauren is extremely thoughtful, analytical, and cautious—a sure sign of an only child or firstborn. I'm not sure why she's so cautious—maybe she just had too much adult influence with all those "big people" above her. Keep in mind that if Hannah has had five parents, Lauren has had *six*. She was born when Hannah's lifestyle had been thoroughly formed, and even at the age of 5, Hannah came across to her baby sister as very capable, strong, and all-knowing.

Earlier I mentioned that Lauren amazed her lastborn father at the age of 2 with the way she would line up her little cassette tapes on the floor in nice neat rows, and then play them one at a time. But perhaps the most significant incident of them all happened one day when I found Lauren down on the floor with one of 7-year-old Hannah's computer toys, which was designed to help her learn to spell, do math, and read. At the age of 2½, Lauren had figured out how to turn it on, and the computer toy said, "Hello! Please select a category now."

> *While youngest children are often coddled and cuddled, they can get more than their share of being cuffed and clobbered, especially by older brothers and sisters.*

The toy, appropriately named Whiz Kid Plus, was designed with a time delay. If no command was given, the voice would repeat the instruction. Lauren hadn't seen me come in, so I watched my little daughter as she sat there listening to the toy continuing to tell her, "Hello! Please select a category now."

What's she going to do? I wondered. Finally, after this was repeated several times, Lauren leaned down to the machine, cupped her hands, and said loudly, "Lady, I can't! I'm only 2 years old!"

At that moment I realized that my little girl was 2 going on 22, and we had a quasi–only child, or at least a functional firstborn, on our hands.

Lastborns Get Set Straight a Lot

These Leman second-family exploits are inserted here only to illustrate that lastborns can turn out in many different kinds of packages. You may be a lastborn who wasn't spoiled that much at all. Or maybe your youngest child is hardly what you would call a manipulator. If anything, your lastborn is the one being manipulated by the rest of the family. Ironically enough, while youngest children are often coddled and cuddled, they can get more than their share of being cuffed and clobbered, especially by older brothers and sisters.

Birth order specialists claim youngest children have difficulty with "information processing."[1] In other words, they seem to have trouble getting things straight. The older kids always seem to be so smart—so authoritative and knowing. No matter that the older kids are often totally incorrect in their dogmatic pronouncements to the baby of the family— the baby *perceives* they are right because they are so much bigger, stronger, and "smarter."

As a lastborn, I can remember feeling plenty stupid when Sally or Jack set me straight on anything from the facts of life to the time of day. My big brother, Jack, five years older, had a very direct approach for setting me straight: he'd belt me one.

Of course, I often had it coming. I was a pro at setting Jack up by goading and pestering him until he'd lose his cool and hit me. Then I'd scream bloody murder, and Mom or Dad would get on his case. It was great fun, but there was a high price tag. Sooner or later Jack would get me alone where I couldn't frame him or convince my parents that it was all his fault. Of course he never really killed me. It just felt like it as he pounded on me a little for the sake of general principles.

In one case, however, he had a different approach to setting me straight. He became an informer and turned me in for smoking cigarettes behind the chicken coop at age 8. That one really cost me. I had to go straight to bed with no dinner, pretty tough treatment for the baby Cub, who usually got away with everything.

As for Sally, I set her up much less often than Jack, but in all fairness to the memory of my checkered past, there were times when I could get to her just as easily as I got to him. I remember her screaming, "Mother, would you get him *out* of here?" And she also complained, "He gets away with murder—you never let me do that when I was his age."

But those were rare occasions, and most of the time big sister Sally set little Kevin straight in another way. As my second mother, she often became distressed when I was too coarse, too loud, or just plain smart-mouthed. But she had a way of making me want to do better. She wouldn't say, "Don't behave like that," or "What's the matter with you? Why don't you shape up?" Whenever anyone—parents, teachers—told me not to do something with that tone of voice, it was just like pouring gasoline on a fire. It only goaded me on to do more things to get attention by bucking the establishment.

> *When I acted up, Sally would often say things such as, "Do you really want to act like that?"*

But Sally's approach had a much different effect. Actually, she was something of a master amateur psychologist. When I acted up, Sally would often say things such as, "Do you really want to act like that?" I'd try to be cute and respond, "Sure I do—that's what makes it fun." But deep inside I knew differently. Sally was already planting seeds that were watered by my math teacher when I was in high school and then carefully cultivated by a beautiful nurse's aide I would meet while doing janitor duties in the Tucson Medical Center.

North Park: A Good Place to Get Smashed

I was a lucky lastborn in many ways. I was reminded of this vividly when I received a telephone call from North Park

University and was asked to come to their annual alumni banquet, where I was to receive their "Distinguished Alumnus Award" and be the featured speaker. To be honest, I was bowled over but didn't let the caller know it. I haven't done much research on this, but I doubt there are many students who get tossed out of a college for stealing the conscience-fund money, and then are asked to return more than thirty years later to be named "distinguished alumnus"!

I told North Park I believed I could work them into my schedule. I traveled back to my old alma mater, received my award, and spoke to all the alums who had made it and the assembled faculty. Some of the professors who still remembered me sat there amazed at how I had turned out, after leaving their midst being unofficially voted "most likely to do time" in some penal institution.

> *Some of the professors who still remembered me sat there amazed at how I had turned out, after leaving their midst being unofficially voted "most likely to do time" in some penal institution.*

As I looked out over the audience, I saw Carroll Peterson, who had been head resident of our dorm when I attended North Park. Very late one night and well past curfew, C.P., as we'd called him, had found me and my roommate, Beagle, lying on a landing between the first and second floors, slightly wasted because we had spent the evening discovering for the first (and definitely last) time what port wine tasted like.

We were fast asleep and would have spent the night on the landing, but C.P. awakened us and asked which room was ours. In our somewhat indisposed condition, we couldn't remember, so I got out my key and he got the number from that. Somehow he got both of us up to the third floor, to our room, and put us to bed.

The bottom line to this story is that Carroll Peterson did not report us for our lack of good judgment, which would have undoubtedly resulted in immediate expulsion. This good man had gone on to become dean of students, well liked by everyone on campus.

C.P. probably enjoyed my talk that day more than anyone else present. He laughed especially hard as I shared how lucky I had been as a young man to have a place like North Park to come to. Yes, I added, North Park was even a great place to get drunk at, particularly when the head resident was so forgiving! But I shared how glad I was that C.P. understood college students and knew the difference between a little bump in the road and a really big pothole.

Oh yes, one other minor detail: without the twenty-four units I earned at North Park, I could have never transferred to the University of Arizona and gone on to get bachelor's, master's, and doctorate degrees after I finally woke up in life.

Lastborns: Bed of Roses or Bed of Thorns?

With all of their legendary easy-street existence and their reputation for getting away with murder, lastborns face several bumps in life that belie the claim that they have it made. We've already looked at two major ones. I've summarized them below and added a third.

1. *Lastborns may become too dependent and stay babies if they are coddled and cuddled too much.* Of all the birth orders, lastborns are the least likely to learn to tie their shoes before kindergarten because an older sibling is always doing it for them. They end up doing the fewest chores too, either because they're not asked to do as much or because they charm another sibling into doing the tasks for them. But everyone in the family needs to pull their own weight. Small children can pick up a messy living room or empty the trash—even if they can't carry the bag out to the curb on trash day.

2. *Lastborns can get a lot of abuse, pressure, resentment, and teasing from older brothers and sisters.* Parents may sometimes think they need a crystal ball—or maybe a new piece of wonder software for the computer—to help them figure out when the baby of the family is really getting it in the neck or when he is just working his manipulative wiles. When counseling parents of lastborns, I usually tell them that if they must err, let it be on the side of helping the baby of the family stand on his own feet and cope, even it if means getting teased or intimidated on occasion.

> *Lastborns are well known for feeling that "nothing I do is important."*

3. *Because they are last, nothing they do is really original.* Their older brothers or sisters have already learned to talk, read, tie shoes, and ride a bike. And let's face it. It *is* hard for Mom or Dad to get excited about the third or fourth lopsided pencil holder or paperweight to be brought home from school art class in the last five or ten years.

Family specialist Edith Neisser catches the spirit of frustration lastborns often feel because nothing they do seems to be very big news. She quotes an eighth grader who had this to say about having older brothers and sisters:

> No matter what I ever do, it won't be important. When I graduate from high school, they'll be graduating from college or getting married; then if I ever do get through with college, Sis will probably be having a baby. Why, even when I die it won't be anything new to my family; nobody will even be here to pay any attention.[2]

If you have a junior high student in your home, you may have heard the same kind of exaggerated dramatics, but there is a kernel of real truth in what this girl said. The key phrase is, "Nobody will even be here to pay attention." That is something every parent can be aware of with the lastborn: *Am I paying enough attention to little Harold's "firsts" in life? Yes, it's my third or fourth paperweight, but it's only his first. I should make as big a deal out of his firsts as anyone else's.*

At least be assured that your lastborn is well aware of his special slot in the family. It's not likely he wants to trade. All of this was brought home to me in living color as I was driving alone with 7-year-old Kevey one day. Just for fun I asked him, "How about it? Would you mind if Mommy had another baby?"

There was a long pause as Kevey gave the question serious thought. Finally, he said, "I guess it's okay just as long as she's a girl!"

It was a purely hypothetical question, of course. When I asked it, Sande and I had no intentions of having any more babies, but as all of us know, the road to additional parenthood is paved with good intentions. . . .

7 Tips for Parenting the Lastborn Child

Because of the natural tendency of parents to ease up and slack off on lastborns, try these suggestions for encouraging accountability and responsibility.

1. *Be sure your lastborn has his or her fair share of responsibilities around the house.* Lastborns often wind up with very little to do for two reasons: (1) they are masters at ducking out of the work that needs to be done, and (2) they are so little and "helpless" that the rest of the family members decide it's easier to do it themselves.

2. *Be sure your lastborn does not get away with murder in regard to family rules and regulations.* Statistics show the lastborn is least likely to be disciplined and the least likely to have to toe the mark the way the older children did. It wouldn't hurt to make notes on how you held the older kids responsible and enforce the same bedtime and other rules on your lastborn.

3. *While you're making sure you don't coddle your youngest child, don't let him or her get clobbered or lost in the shuffle either.* Lastborns are well known for feeling that "nothing I do is important." Make a big deal out of your lastborn's accomplishments,

and be sure he or she gets a fair share of "marquee time" on the refrigerator door with school papers, drawings, and awards.

4. *Introduce your youngest child to reading very early.* Six months is not too young to start reading to your child with brightly colored illustrated books. When your child starts reading, don't do the work for him. Lastborns tend to like being read to and will let you do most of the work if they can get away with it. This may be one of the reasons lastborns are well known for being the poorest readers in their family.

5. *Whenever necessary, call the baby's bluff.* I have always felt my parents should have cracked down on me regarding school when I was young. But they never really put on the pressure. They never gave me choices such as, "Shape up at school or drop baseball," or "No homework, then no television programs tonight."

6. *Try to get your lastborn's baby book completed before he or she is 21.* Life seems to pile up on parents with the arrival of the third and fourth child. Check to see if you're neglecting the lastborn because you just don't seem to have as much time as you used to. Let other things go if necessary to be sure you provide time for each child.

7. *Oh yes—along the way, try to pick out a nice firstborn for your lastborn to marry.* The odds are high they'll make a great team!

Epilogue

There's Only One Thing You Can't Do Without

It isn't always *what* you know that's important. Everything doesn't ride on knowledge, skill, and technique. You could read all the books, use all the techniques, and say all the right words (you hope), and there is still only one thing that remains absolutely necessary. This one thing is every parent's secret weapon, and it works equally well with every birth order. I'm not talking about something you learn in so many lessons like operating a computer or driving a car. No, it's something you actually have at the start and then develop slowly and sometimes painfully. And just about the time you think you're getting the real hang of it, you are back to square one as you realize how basic life really is.

I Thought Our Family Was Complete, and Then . . .

That's really what happened to me, when we got our second family long after we thought our days of having children had ended. I'm not sure there are that many people who rear one family of three children and then, in their forties, have a couple more just to be sure they "got it right." So I'd like to share with you what it was like to learn—on two different occasions—that a new little ankle-biter was on the way, and all those late-night shows that we thought were over would go into reruns.

Just before Christmas in 1986, Sande called the office and surprised me by saying she wanted to take me out to dinner. As we were enjoying our meal, she pulled out a greeting card she had made for me. Because Sande is thoughtful and quite creative, I didn't suspect anything as I read the cover, which asked me:

"Are you ready to change your summer plans?"

"Are you ready to work late?"

"Are you ready to change your work schedule?"

Puzzled, I flipped it open and was greeted by a picture of Santa Claus saying, "Merry Christmas!" In his arms was a little baby with a toothless grin.

As the light began to dawn, I gave Sande a look, and she nodded yes. I couldn't help it. I let out a war whoop of joy that startled several nearby diners. The first member of our second family was on her way.

As I contemplated telling our three children the news, I was sure the girls would be thrilled, but I was concerned about Kevey, who was 8 years old and about to lose his privileged position as baby of the family. As it turned out, Holly, who had just turned 14, responded with shocked silence. Krissy, 12, just clapped her hands over her ears and wailed, "I don't want to hear this! I don't want to hear this!"

I'm still not quite sure why the girls reacted the way they did. Perhaps they were happy with the family the way it was and this was just too much of an unsettling idea. Maybe they were embarrassed because they thought their parents didn't do "that kind of stuff" anymore.

When we sat down with Kevey, I was really worried. I considered not telling him. Perhaps we could do it later—maybe when the baby was 3 years old!

As Sande and I faced Kevey, I said, "We have something to tell you."

"What is it, Dad?"

While I stuttered around trying to handle the situation as a professional psychologist should, Sande broke in and said, "I'm going to have a baby." (Firstborns always like the direct approach.)

I steeled myself for Kevey's explosion, but all he said was, "Hey . . . that's baaaaad!"

"Baaaaad?" I said, puzzled.

"Dad, you know . . . that means goooood."

"Oh . . . right, of course," I said, acting as if I were current on the latest "in" terms of Kevey's generation.

Giving his mother a hug, Kevey said, "This is great—hey, Dad!"

"Yeah?"

"Can we go to the store and buy some Pampers?"

Kevey was disappointed when he learned we wouldn't need Pampers for at least six months, but he was totally cool about no longer being the baby of the family. And in a matter of days, Holly and Krissy began talking to us again. When Hannah Elizabeth arrived, they couldn't wait to get her home from the hospital and start helping with her care.

And their interest wasn't just fired by momentary curiosity. They were always there and ready to help Sande with Hannah, and I really mean it when I say that this little girl had five parents who loved her very much. One of the really poignant proofs of that hangs on our wall in the family room—a framed copy of a poem that Holly wrote to Hannah when she was only 2 months old:

To Hannah Elizabeth Leman

Born June 30, 1987

A child with warm and tender skin, soft and smooth without a flaw,

The small body hasn't experienced life yet . . . just being born into it . . . but this is God's law.

The innocence of a child, something we should all have . . . something we should strive to be,

An innocent child, fresh in God's sight, as she ventures out to experience life.

—Holly Leman, age 14

But you'll notice that I keep saying Hannah was the first-born of our second family. This suggests that there would be still more children even though Sande was 42 and I was 44 when Hannah arrived. And, of course, there may be some readers (particularly wives) who are wondering, *Leman, you jerk, why didn't you get fixed?*

Well, let me explain. After Hannah was born, I went in to the doctor to inquire, and he said that it was a rather simple procedure, and he was sure I knew all about how it was done. Actually, I didn't, so I asked him for a very short course in Vasectomy 101.

"It's very simple. All we do is put a little metal clip here, and a little metal clip there . . ."

Metal clip? That was it for me. Surely we could try to rely on our usual methods of birth control and take whatever God gave us. I say to my shame that as a husband and father, I've left birth control matters to my wife, as many (most?) men do. I should have been brave enough to endure the metal clips, but as I look back, I'm glad I didn't because we have these two wonderful little girls who have brought such joy into our lives.

"Tell Me You're Not Pregnant!"

Five years went by, and it looked as if little Hannah would be a princess of the family with some firstborn—actually, quasi–only child—characteristics because of that large gap between her and her older brother. In actuality, she functions as a sweet, gentle-spirited baby—embracing many of her mom's best qualities—because we all doted on her. She was our "family mascot" for a good five and a half years until Lauren was born.

In February 1992, I drove the entire family over to California for a weekend at Disneyland. As we enjoyed the "happiest place on earth," I noticed that Sande, who is usually full of life and all smiles, was just a little distant.

We left Disneyland late Sunday afternoon, and being a typical male, I had visions of "driving straight through" and making Tucson by midnight. We dropped south to Interstate 8 and headed east. As we got to La Mesa, a suburb of San Diego, Sande announced, "We've got to stop. I need something to eat."

"Okay, we can grab something at a drive-through. I'd like to keep going."

"No, I don't feel so good. I need to stop at a restaurant."

As we pulled into a Coco's restaurant, I wasn't real happy because I hated the thought of having all those cars I'd worked so hard to pass go on by while I was eating! We placed our orders, and we were sitting at the table waiting to be served when Sande started to cry. Bewildered, I asked her, "What's wrong?"

All she would say was, "I don't feel so good."

Our son, who was now 14 and preferred to be called Kevin, observed perceptively, "She's pregnant!"

"Your mother is *not pregnant*," I said as I glanced at Sande with a look that said, *Tell me you're not pregnant.*

But Sande nodded in the affirmative, and more tears began to flow. My wife had announced that another baby was coming, but this time no whoop of joy escaped my lips. It was more like a gasp of dismay, and maybe a bit of angry frustration. It turned out she had been pregnant a couple of months, and here I was finding out about it at the very same moment as our children! And things didn't get much better when Sande said firmly, "I want you to call the doctor *now*!"

"Doctor who?" I wondered aloud, and she gave me the obstetrician's name and instructions on what to ask him. She was spotting and was afraid she was going to lose the baby. I went to find a pay phone and made the call. I was lucky enough to connect with the doctor, who was very concerned and very direct: "Get her off her feet immediately and to a motel. She needs to rest in bed tonight, and then get her here tomorrow just as soon as you can."

I came back to the table, and Sande was sitting there— alone. All the children were missing. This thought flashed across my mind: *Have they all run away?*

Later I learned that Kevin had taken Hannah for a walk, and the two older girls had retreated to the restroom, where Krissy spent some time crying and Holly thumbed through the pages of a greater San Diego phone book with no particular purpose in mind whatsoever.

Somehow we finished dinner and went off to find a motel. Even though it was a Sunday night, most of the motels were filled, but finally a Travelodge took us in with only one room and two double beds to spare. I can't say I slept much that night. I kept doing a numbers game in my mind and saying, *She can't be pregnant. She can't be pregnant. . . .*

I kept mulling over what the doctor had said—the possibility that she could lose the baby if she wasn't careful. And what about being parents at our age? Sande was 46, and I was 48. By the time the baby would arrive, she'd be 47 and I'd be 49! That meant I'd be almost 70 years old by the time our child graduated from high school!

The next morning it was a somber ride home, as each of us pondered how Sande's pregnancy was going to impact our individual lives. Our two younger ones, Hannah and Kevin, were taking the news in stride, particularly 4-year-old Hannah, who did not appear to fear dethronement at all. She was already looking forward to having a baby sister to mother.

But Holly and Krissy, 19 and 17 at the time, weren't taking this news any better than they'd taken the announcement about Hannah five years earlier. They just stared out the window, and I was sure they were probably thinking, *Hannah was bad enough, but Mom and Dad are* still *doing it even at their age!* I imagined Holly and Krissy getting together and collaborating on another poem, something like:

> Oh, Mom and Dad,
> We love you so,
> But don't you know
> How babies grow?

We got home in record time, and immediately I drove Sande to the doctor. After several days of bed rest, we went back in and talked to the obstetrician. By this time I was in a little better frame of mind. Because of Sande's age, this was a high-risk pregnancy. The doctor started going through all the statistics about the odds of bad things happening to the baby. In her classic firstborn style, Sande just looked at him and said, "Why are you telling us these things?"

The doctor looked at me in a helpless way as if to say, "Can you help me out here, buddy?"

> *"Can you think of a better family for that little baby to grow up in?"*

Then Sande quickly made the doctor understand that it didn't make any difference. Abortion would never be an option; she would go ahead and have this baby.

Only One Thing Remains Absolutely Necessary

Not long after we got back from Disneyland, I had to take a business trip east, and on the way home I stopped in Buffalo as I frequently do to check on our summer home at Chautauqua Lake, New York. While there I dropped in on my lifelong friend Moonhead and his wife, Wendy. Although the initial shock had worn off, I was still stewing and saying things such as, "Holy crow, I'm going to be 67 years old when the child's a senior in high school!" And then Wendy said it all—for me, for Sande, for everyone: "Can you think of a better family for that little baby to grow up in?"

That stopped me in my baby Cub tracks. I knew in a moment I had to stop holding my own little pity parties. Oh, sure, I had been joking, of course, but behind the jokes was a feeling of, "Why us? Why *me*?"

As for Wendy's question, I had to think about that for a few moments before answering. Surely there were parents who were younger, with more energy, and equipped with strong nervous systems that didn't need a 100,000-mile recall. But could any family love that little Cub more than Mama and Papa Bear Leman?

I said to Wendy, "You're right. You are so *very right*. Thanks—I needed that. I really did."

Wendy had referred to the irreplaceable secret weapon that no parent can do without: unconditional, go-for-broke, no-holds-barred, sacrificial love for your kids—and your mate. From that moment on I began telling myself, *I've got to suck it up. I'm Sande's partner, her helpmate. It's going to be tough on her. She didn't expect this either.*

> The irreplaceable secret weapon that no parent can do without: unconditional, go-for-broke, no-holds-barred, sacrificial love for your kids—and your mate.

On the flight home to Tucson, I kept trying to think of a way to tell Sande about my new attitude toward the pregnancy. When I left on the trip, I hadn't been that positive or supportive. In fact, I had been downright grumpy, and I wanted to make it right. When I got home, I found Sande still concerned about the well-being of the baby. I reminded her of the positive report from the doctor after we had gotten home from Disneyland, and then I said, "You know, I've been a jerk about this—feeling sorry for myself and not being there for you as much as I could have. But when I dropped by Moonhead's place, Wendy set me straight. She really got my attention when she asked me if I could think of a better family for that little baby to grow up in."

For a second I wasn't sure how Mama Bear would receive Wendy's wisdom. But then she smiled back at me with a twinkle in her eye, and I knew that I was forgiven for any self-pitying misgivings I'd had. And I also knew the joy we would experience together was among the greatest gifts we could ever receive.

I never thought I'd be glad I was such a chicken about metal clips, but in the end my lack of courage paid off. Lauren arrived whole and sound, and she's become the capstone of five incredible blessings.

No, I'm not going to claim that having Hannah and then Lauren was a piece of cake and that Sande and I were both so blessed that we wouldn't trade a moment of any of it for a little peace and quiet. There were plenty of times when we weren't sure we would make it through the night. But make it through the nights we did, and once Lauren was 6 and into school, Sande was once again at the place in life where she could see a little daylight and have a little freedom during the day.

As for me, I have that date with history. It will be 2010. I will be 67, and Lauren, 18, will be striding down the aisle to pick up her high school diploma. I confess I try not to think about it, but every now and then I get reminded in interesting ways. Like the time Lauren and I were walking up to the school door when she was in kindergarten, and a grandfatherly-looking fellow was leaning on the fender of his car, obviously waiting for someone. He smiled at us as we passed and said, "I've got a grandchild in this school too."

Thinking I would gently correct his error, I said, "Actually, sir, this is number five."

"Oh! *Five grandchildren!* Aren't you lucky!"

As I walked into the school with Lauren that day, I couldn't help but chuckle. Yes, I could have argued with him about "looking like a grandfather" (although I probably would have lost). But one thing was for sure. I *was* very lucky, and I still *am* very lucky.

The 6 Keys to Birth Order

1. As important as a child's order of birth may be, it is only an influence. It is not a final fact of life, forever set in cement and unchangeable, that determines how that child will turn out.
2. The way parents treat their children is as important as the children's birth orders, spacing, sex, and physical or mental characteristics. The key question is, was the environment provided by the parents loving, accepting, and warm, or was it critical, cold, and distant?
3. Every birth order has inherent strengths and weaknesses. Parents must accept both while helping their children develop positive traits and cope with negative ones.
4. No birth order is "better" or more desirable than another. Firstborns seem to have a corner on achievement and the headlines, but the door is wide open for laterborns to make their mark. It is up to them.
5. Birth order information does not give the total psychological picture for anyone. No system of personality development can do that. Birth order statistics and characteristics are indicators that combine with physical, mental, and emotional factors to give the bigger picture.
6. Understanding some basic principles of birth order is not a formula for automatically solving problems or changing your personality overnight. Changing oneself is the hardest task any human being can attempt; it takes lots of work and determination.

"Guess the Birth Order" Quiz Answers

Firstborn or only child, middle child, or lastborn/baby of the family? See if your answers from page 11 were right.

1. My sister was a charming show-off—make that a con artist who got away with everything—when we were growing up. Now she's the top salesperson in her company and highly successful.

Answer: baby of the family

2. I'd rather read people than books. I like solving problems and am comfortable being surrounded by people.

Answer: middle child

3. My brother Al was nicknamed "Albert Einstein" because he was so good in math and science. He's an engineer now and a conscientious perfectionist.

Answer: firstborn

4. I don't know how my husband does it. His workshop is an absolute mess, but whenever he wants to find something, he knows exactly which pile it's in.

Answer: firstborn

5. My friend is a bit of a maverick. She has a lot of friends but values her independence. She's a good mediator in arguments. She's about as opposite from her sister as you can get.

Answer: middle child

6. I get along better with older people than I do my peers. Some people think I'm stuck-up or self-centered. But in actuality, I'm not.

Answer: only child

US Presidents
and Their Birth Order

George Washington—fifth child of father, first of mother; ten-year gap before his birth

John Adams—oldest of three boys

Thomas Jefferson—third of ten; oldest son

James Madison—oldest of twelve

James Monroe—oldest of five

John Quincy Adams—second of five; oldest son

Andrew Jackson—youngest of three sons; two years between him and older brother

Martin Van Buren—third of five; three older half siblings; two years between him and older sibling

William Henry Harrison—youngest of seven; oldest son

John Tyler—sixth of eight; second son; two years between him and older brother

James K. Polk—oldest of ten

Zachary Taylor—third of nine; third son; two years between him and older brother

Millard Fillmore—second of nine; oldest son

Franklin Pierce—seventh child of father (sixth of eight in second marriage); one year between him and older brother

James Buchanan—second of eleven; oldest son

Abraham Lincoln—second child of three (in father's first marriage); oldest and only surviving son

Andrew Johnson—third of three; second son; four years between him and older brother

Ulysses S. Grant—oldest of six

Rutherford B. Hayes—youngest of five; seven years between him and older brother, with two sisters between them

James Garfield—youngest of five; five years between him and older brother

Chester Arthur—fifth of nine; oldest son

Grover Cleveland—fifth of nine; two years between him and older brother

Benjamin Harrison—fifth of thirteen (second of ten in second marriage); one year between him and older brother

William McKinley—seventh of nine; at least five years between him and older brother

Theodore Roosevelt—second of four; oldest son

William Howard Taft—seventh of ten (second of five in second marriage); two years between him and older brother

Woodrow Wilson—third of four; six years between him and older brother, with one sister between them

Warren G. Harding—oldest of eight

Calvin Coolidge—oldest of two (in father's first marriage)

Herbert Hoover—second of three; second son; three years between him and older brother

Franklin Roosevelt—second son (functional only child from father's second marriage); twenty-eight years between him and older half brother

Harry S. Truman—oldest of three

Dwight Eisenhower—third of seven sons; one year between him and older brother

John F. Kennedy—second of nine; second son; two years between him and older brother

Lyndon Johnson—oldest of five

Richard Nixon—second of five sons; four years between him and older brother

Gerald Ford—only child of parents' first marriage (three half siblings in father's second marriage; three half siblings in mother's second marriage)

Jimmy Carter—oldest of four (Billy was the baby)

Ronald Reagan—youngest of two; two years between him and older brother

George Bush—second of five; second son; two years between him and older brother

Bill Clinton—only child (in mother's first marriage); one younger half brother

George W. Bush—oldest of six

Barack Obama—functional only child (half sister nine years removed from him)

Notes

Chapter 1 Birth Order

1. See Richard W. Bradley, "Using Birth Order and Sibling Dynamics in Career Counseling," *The Personnel and Guidance Journal* (September 1982): 25. Bradley quotes from the article "Is First Best?" *Newsweek*, January 6, 1969, 37.

2. Deborah Skolnik, "Does Birth Order Matter?" October 12, 2007, http://www.parenting.com/article/Child/Development/Does-Birth-Order-Matter.

3. R. L. Adams and B. N. Phillips, "Motivation and Achievement Differences among Children of the Various Ordinal Birth Positions," *Child Development* (March 1972): 157.

4. Sally Leman Chall, *Making God Real to Your Children* (Grand Rapids: Revell, 1991); *Mommy Appleseed* (Eugene, OR: Harvest House, 1993).

5. Walter Toman, *Family Constellation* (New York: Springer, 1976), 33.

6. Ibid., 5.

7. James H. S. Bossard, *The Large Family System* (Philadelphia: University of Pennsylvania Press, 1966), 79.

Chapter 2 But Doc, I Don't Fit the Mold!

1. Herb Kelleher, quoted in Tom Peters, "'Personality' Has Southwest Flying above Its Competition," *Arizona Daily Star*, September 26, 1994.

2. Herb Kelleher, quoted in Kevin Leman, *Winning the Rat Race without Becoming a Rat* (Nashville: Thomas Nelson, 1996), 70.

3. "Former Arizona Governor Gets Two and a Half-Year Prison Term," *Los Angeles Times*, February 3, 1998.

4. Bradford Wilson and George Edington, *First Child, Second Child* (New York: McGraw-Hill, 1981), 259.

5. Ibid., 282.

Chapter 3 What's Parenting Got to Do with It?

1. Lee Iacocca with William Novak, *Iacocca* (New York: Bantam, 1986), 18.
2. Ibid.
3. Leman, *Winning the Rat Race*, 152–53.
4. Statistics provided by the Stepfamily Association of America, Inc., 215 Centennial Mall South, Suite 212, Lincoln, Nebraska 68508-1834.
5. Kevin Leman, *Living in a Stepfamily without Getting Stepped On* (Nashville: Thomas Nelson, 1994), 23.
6. Carmi Schooler, "Birth Order Effects: Not Here, Not Now!" *Psychological Bulletin* 78, no. 3 (September 1972): 171–72. Schooler concluded that "scores for different birth ranks show no significant difference" and that there is good reason to doubt "the importance of birth order as a determinant of behavior."
7. Cecile Ernst and Jules Angst, *Birth Order: Its Influence on Personality* (New York: Springer-Verlag, 1983), 242.
8. Joseph Rodgers, quoted in Geoffrey Cowley, "First Born, Later Born," *Newsweek*, October 7, 1996, 68.
9. Judith Blake, quoted in Kenneth L. Woodward with Lydia Denworth, "The Order of Innovation," *Newsweek*, May 21, 1990, 76.
10. Leman, *Winning the Rat Race*, 17.
11. Ibid., 118. The Dingman Company specializes in finding the right executive for the right company.
12. Ibid.
13. Frank J. Sulloway, in Robert S. Boynton, "The Birth of an Idea," *The New Yorker*, October 7, 1996, 72.
14. Frank J. Sulloway, *Born to Rebel: Birth Order Family Dynamics and Creative Lives* (New York: Pantheon, 1996).

Chapter 4 First Come, First Served

1. Only children are sometimes called "super firstborns" because they have many firstborn characteristics that are exaggerated to some degree. That and other differences between only children and firstborns will be discussed in chapter 7.
2. Kevin Leman, *Born to Win* (Grand Rapids: Revell, 2009).
3. We (the editors) affirm Dr. Leman's lack of editorial comprehension.
4. Harvey Mackay, *Beware the Naked Man Who Offers You His Shirt* (New York: Ivy Books, 1990), 24.
5. Leman, *Winning the Rat Race*, 64.
6. Ibid., 26.

Chapter 5 How Good Is "Good Enough"?

1. Jane Goodsell, *Not a Good Word about Anybody* (New York: Ballantine, 1988), 46, 50.
2. Fritz Ridenour, *Untying Your Knots* (Grand Rapids: Revell, 1988), 112. Used by permission.
3. Kevin Leman, *When Your Best Isn't Good Enough: The Secret of Measuring Up* (Grand Rapids: Revell, 2007). This book is being reissued by the publisher as *Why Your Best Is Good Enough* in March 2010.

4. Miriam Adderholdt-Elliott, *Perfectionism: What's Bad about Being Too Good?* (Minneapolis: Free Spirit, 1987), 18–20.

5. Kevin Leman, *When Your Best Isn't Good Enough* (Grand Rapids: Revell, 2007); and *Pleasers: Why Women Don't Have to Make Everyone Happy to Be Happy* (Grand Rapids: Revell, 2006).

Chapter 6 Perfect—or Excellent?

1. Leman, *Winning the Rat Race*, 125–27.

2. David Stoop, *Self-Talk: Key to Personal Growth* (Grand Rapids: Revell, 1982), 120.

3. Kevin Leman, *What Your Childhood Memories Say about You* (Wheaton, IL: Tyndale, 2008).

Chapter 7 The Lonely Only, Super Firstborn

1. Toni Falbo, "Does the Only Child Grow Up Miserable?" *Psychology Today*, May 1976, 60.

2. Alfred Adler, *Understanding Human Nature* (New York: Faucett World Library, 1927), 127.

3. Leman, *Winning the Rat Race*, 21–22.

4. My official title is "family psychologist and consultant to ABC's *Good Morning America*."

5. US Census Bureau, "America's Families and Living Arrangements: 2008," released March 2009, http://www.census.gov/population/www/socdemo/hh-fam/cps2008.html.

6. "Only Children: Cracking the Myth of the Pampered Only Misfit," *US News and World Report*, January 10, 1994, 50.

7. Peterson, "Kids without Siblings."

8. Lucille K. Forer with Henry Still, *The Birth Order Factor* (New York: David McKay, 1976), 255.

9. Leman, *Winning the Rat Race*, 146–51.

Chapter 8 I Never Did Get No Respect

1. Because Dr. Leman is a baby of the family, we (the editors) counted for him and learned that even in this new revised edition of *The Birth Order Book*, the middle children indeed still got the fewest pages. Sorry!

2. Wilson and Edington, *First Child, Second Child*, 92.

3. Forer, *The Birth Order Factor*, 77.

4. Eleanor Estes, *The Middle Moffat* (Orlando, FL: Harcourt, 2001), quoted in Edith G. Neisser, *Brothers and Sisters* (New York: Harper, 1951), 154.

5. Wilson and Edington, *First Child, Second Child*, 95.

6. Donald J. Trump with Tony Schwartz, *Trump: The Art of the Deal* (New York: Random House, 1987), 3, 43–44.

7. Wilson and Edington, *First Child, Second Child*, 99.

8. Ibid., 104.

9. Ibid., 103.

10. Alfred Adler, *The Individual Psychology of Alfred Adler*, ed. H. L. Ansbacher and R. R. Ansbacher (New York: Harper & Row, 1956), 379–80.

11. Alfred Adler, quoted in Irving D. Harris, *The Promised Seed* (Glencove: Free Press of Glencove, 1964), 75.

12. Pam Hait, "Birth Order and Relationships," *Sunday Woman*, September 12, 1982, 4.

Chapter 9 Born Last but Seldom Least

1. Wilson and Edington, *First Child, Second Child*, 108.

2. Mopsy Strange Kennedy, "A Lastborn Speaks Out—At Last," *Newsweek*, November 7, 1977, 22.

3. Wilson and Edington, *First Child, Second Child*, 109.

4. Ibid., 108.

5. Kevin Leman, *Parenthood without Hassles* (Eugene, OR: Harvest House, 1979), 11.

6. Ibid., 12.

7. Wilson and Edington, *First Child, Second Child*, 109–10.

Chapter 10 The Winning Edge in Business

1. For a complete discussion of using birth order knowledge in business, see Leman, *Winning the Rat Race*, from which this chapter was adapted. (See especially chapters 4, 5, and 6.)

2. Harvey Mackay, *Swim with the Sharks without Being Eaten Alive* (New York: Ivy Books, 1988), 23.

Chapter 11 Birth Order Marriages Aren't Made in Heaven

1. Toman, *Family Constellation*. Toman studied three thousand families before coming up with his conclusions. In a smaller study, Dr. Theodore D. Kempler, University of Wisconsin, researched 236 business executives and their wives and also discovered that certain birth order combinations made better marriages than others. The smaller study is documented in Lucille K. Forer, *The Birth Order Factor*, 187–88.

2. Toman, *Family Constellation*.

Chapter 12 I Count Only When . . .

1. Much of the material in this chapter on lifestyles and life themes is adapted from Leman, *Living in a Stepfamily*, chapters 6 and 7.

2. Alfred Adler, *The Practice and Theory of Individual Psychology* (London: Routledge & Kegan Paul, 1923), 3.

3. Adler, *Understanding Human Nature*, 31.

4. Rudolph Dreikurs, *Fundamentals of Adlerian Psychology* (Chicago: Alfred Adler Institute, 1953), 35.

Chapter 13 Flaunt Your Imperfections

1. See Luke 15:11–32.
2. Kevin Leman, *Making Children Mind without Losing Yours* (Grand Rapids: Revell, 2005), 88.

Chapter 14 Two May Be Company . . . or a Crowd

1. See Genesis 25:19–34; 27:1–40.

Chapter 16 Helping the Family "Cub" Grow Up

1. Wilson and Edington, *First Child, Second Child*, 110–11.
2. Neisser, *Brothers and Sisters*, 165–66.

About Dr. Kevin Leman

An internationally known psychologist, radio and television personality, and speaker, Dr. Kevin Leman has taught and entertained audiences worldwide with his wit and commonsense psychology.

The New York Times bestselling and award-winning author of *Have a New Kid by Friday* and *The Birth Order Book* has made hundreds of house calls for radio and television programs, including *Fox & Friends*, *The View*, Fox's *The Morning Show*, *Today*, *Oprah*, CBS's *The Early Show*, Janet Parshall's *America*, *Live with Regis Philbin*, CNN's *American Morning*, *Life Today* with James Robison, and *Focus on the Family*. Dr. Leman has served as a contributing family psychologist to *Good Morning America*.

Dr. Leman is also the founder and president of Couples of Promise, an organization designed and committed to helping couples remain happily married. He is a founding faculty member of iQuestions.com.

Dr. Leman's professional affiliations include the American Psychological Association, the American Federation of Television and Radio Artists, and the North American Society of Adlerian Psychology.

In 1993, he was the recipient of the Distinguished Alumnus Award of North Park University in Chicago. In 2003, he received from the University of Arizona the highest award that a university can extend to its own: the Alumni Achievement Award.

Dr. Leman attended North Park University. He received his bachelor's degree in psychology from the University of Arizona, where he later earned his master's and doctorate degrees. Originally from Williamsville, New York, he and his wife, Sande, live in Tucson, Arizona. They have five children and two grandchildren.

For information regarding speaking availability, business consultations, seminars, or our annual Couples of Promise cruise, please contact:

Dr. Kevin Leman
P.O. Box 35370
Tucson, Arizona 85740
Phone: (520) 797-3830
Fax: (520) 797-3809
www.drleman.com

Resources by Dr. Kevin Leman

Books for Adults

Have a New Kid by Friday
The Birth Order Book
Turn Up the Heat
Sheet Music
Making Children Mind without Losing Yours
Have a New Husband by Friday
Born to Win
Sex Begins in the Kitchen
7 Things He'll Never Tell You . . . But You Need to Know
What Your Childhood Memories Say about You
Running the Rapids
What a Difference a Daddy Makes
The Way of the Shepherd (written with William Pentak)
Home Court Advantage
Becoming the Parent God Wants You to Be
Becoming a Couple of Promise

A Chicken's Guide to Talking Turkey with Your Kids about Sex (written with Kathy Flores Bell)
First-Time Mom
Keeping Your Family Strong in a World Gone Wrong
Step-parenting 101
The Perfect Match
Be Your Own Shrink
Say Good-bye to Stress
Single Parenting That Works
*When Your Best Isn't Good Enough**
Pleasers

Books for Children, with Kevin Leman II

My Firstborn, There's No One Like You
My Middle Child, There's No One Like You
My Youngest, There's No One Like You
My Only Child, There's No One Like You
My Adopted Child, There's No One Like You
My Grandchild, There's No One Like You

DVD/Video Series

Have a New Kid by Friday
Making Children Mind without Losing Yours (Christian—parenting edition)
Making Children Mind without Losing Yours (Main-stream—public-school teacher edition)
Value-Packed Parenting

*This book is being reissued by the publisher as *Why Your Best Is Good Enough* in March 2010.

Making the Most of Marriage
Running the Rapids
Single Parenting That Works
Bringing Peace and Harmony to the Blended Family

Available at 1-800-770-3830, or www.drleman.com.

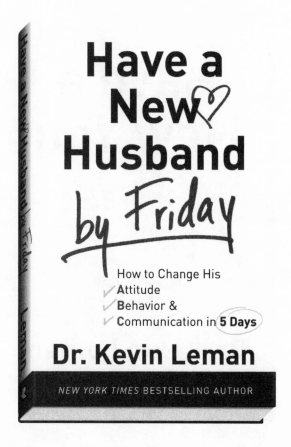

You can change your life—
in just **5 days**!

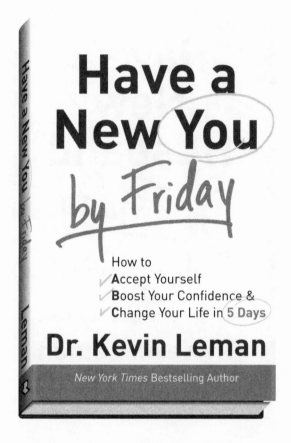

With his signature wit and commonsense psychology, Dr. Kevin Leman walks you through your own personal five-day action plan. You will come to accept the truth about yourself, build confidence, and change your life to be what you want it to be.

Take the
5-day challenge

Kid-tested,
parent-approved

If anyone understands why children behave the way they do, it's Dr. Kevin Leman. In this bestseller he equips parents with seven principles of reality discipline—a loving, no-nonsense parenting approach that really works.

Change your life with this great
resource from Dr. Kevin Leman

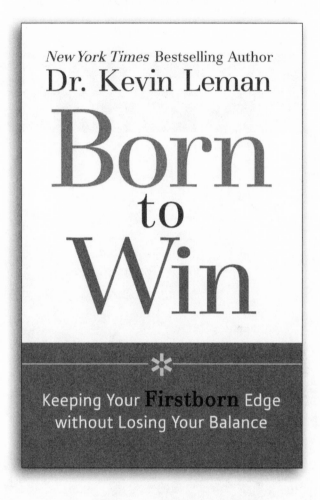

New York Times Bestselling Author
Dr. Kevin Leman
Born to Win
Keeping Your **Firstborn** Edge without Losing Your Balance

Dr. Kevin Leman helps firstborns understand their natural advantages for the highest level of personal success.

New York Times bestselling author answers all the questions you were afraid to ask about sex.

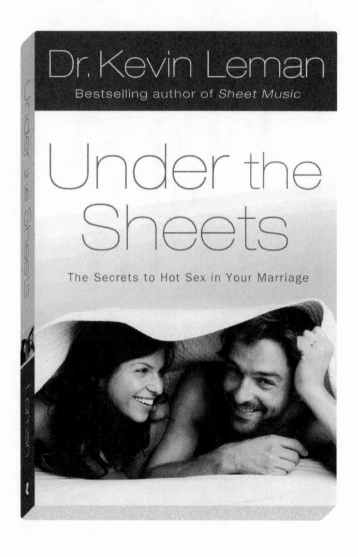

With insightful and often hilarious examples, Dr. Leman shows you how to make your marriage more satisfying, both emotionally and physically.

Creating Intimacy to Make Your Marriage Sizzle

Sex Begins *in the* Kitchen

Dr. Kevin Leman

AUTHOR OF **THE BIRTH ORDER BOOK**

Revell
a division of Baker Publishing Group
www.RevellBooks.com